PENGUIN BOOKS

CATHOLICS

Dennis Sewell is a current affairs journalist with BBC News and presents *Talking Politics* on BBC Radio 4. He lives in London.

Catholics

Britain's Largest Minority

DENNIS SEWELL

PENGUIN BOOKS

AMDG

and for Laura

PENGUIN BOOKS

Published by the Penguin Group
Penguin Books Ltd, 80 Strand, London WC2R ORL, England
Penguin Putnam Inc., 375 Hudson Street, New York, New York 10014, USA
Penguin Books Australia Ltd, 250 Camberwell Road,
Camberwell, Victoria 3124, Australia
Penguin Books Canada Ltd, 10 Alcorn Avenue, Toronto, Ontario, Canada M4V 3B2
Penguin Books India (P) Ltd, 11 Community Centre,
Panchsheel Park, New Delhi – 110 017, India
Penguin Books (NZ) Ltd, Cnr Rosedale and Airborne Roads,
Albany, Auckland, New Zealand
Penguin Books (South Africa) (Pty) Ltd, 24 Sturdee Avenue,
Rosebank 2196, South Africa

Penguin Books Ltd, Registered Offices: 80 Strand, London WC2R ORL, England

www.penguin.com

First published by Viking 2001
Published in Penguin Books 2002

1

Copyright © Dennis Sewell, 2001
All rights reserved

The moral right of the author has been asserted

Set in Monotype Bembo
Printed in England by Clays Ltd, St Ives plc

Contents

Acknowledgements

I must thank before all others my beloved Laura Cumming, who has done so much in so many ways to make this book possible. I could not be more grateful for her loving and tireless collaboration and for her infallible judgement. This is her book too.

I am also indebted to Hugo Young, Charles Moore, Mark Lawson, Richard Coles, John Wilkins, Libby Purves, Lord Rees-Mogg, Jimmy Burns, Paul Johnson, Damian Green MP, Fr. Andrew Greeley, Michael Hornsby-Smith, Scott Reid, John Haldane, Francesca Murphy and John Morrill. Monsignor Kieran Conry, Fr. Michael O'Halloran SJ and the late Auberon Waugh provided me with valuable information and advice.

Thanks to James MacMillan for his interest in the project and for permission to quote from his 1999 Edinburgh Festival lecture; to A. P. Watt Ltd on behalf of the Royal Literary Fund for permission to quote from the works of G. K. Chesterton; to Peters Fraser & Dunlop for permission to quote from the works of Hilaire Belloc; to Sheed & Ward Ltd for permission to quote from the works of Tom Burns and Maisie Ward; and to Burns & Oates for permission to quote from the work of Thomas Moloney. I thank the obituaries editors of *The Times*, the *Daily Telegraph*, the *Guardian* and the *Independent*. Extracts from Matthew D'Ancona's 1996 interview with Tony Blair MP appear by courtesy of the *Sunday Telegraph*. I am obliged to Simon Heffer for his recollections of the Gilbey coterie at the Travellers Club.

I acknowledge a special debt to the following writers, journalists and scholars upon whose works I have relied significantly in preparing this book: Joseph Pearce, Patrick Allitt, Henry Sire, Walter Arnstein, Sheridan Gilley, Frank Boyce, Aidan Nichols OP, Michael Walsh, Tam Dalyell MP, Peter Kilfoyle MP, Adrian

Hastings, Alan Watkins, A. N. Wilson, Mark Bence-Jones, Richard McBrien, Thomas Moloney, William F. Buckley Jr., Peter Stanford, Paul Vallely, Damian Thompson and Clifford Longley. I apologize to anyone I should have included in that list but have accidentally omitted. I am also grateful for the help and information I received in Scotland from Mr I. Pieri of Glasgow, David Ogston of Perth and Michael Tierney at the *Herald*.

My most sincere thanks are owed to my agent David Miller at Rogers, Coleridge & White; to my editor Andrew Kidd; to my copy-editor Anne Askwith and to all the staff at Penguin Books Ltd for their unfailing patience and professionalism. Thanks also to Gwyneth Williams at the BBC for her indulgence and support. Elizabeth Cumming put up with tremendous inconvenience on my account while this book was being written and was always ready with reassurance and encouragement when it was most needed. I am most grateful to her.

My father William Sewell took a close interest in the progress of this book but died before the manuscript was completed. He is now reunited with my late mother, Margaret Sewell (*née* Donovan), who first instructed me in the teachings of the Catholic faith. *Requiescant in pace*.

When I was sent away to the Jesuits at the age of eight, my paternal grandmother plotted to have me abducted. Family legend has it that her co-conspirator was Great Aunt Mary, a strict Presbyterian with a booming voice and a developed propensity to meddle. The plan was carefully laid. A car and driver were hired. Rooms were taken at a boarding house in Blackpool, where no one would think to look. Once the hue and cry had died down I would be transported to a farm outside Kilmarnock to undergo a process of 'deprogramming' – though that word was not yet in general circulation in 1965.

I have often asked myself what life might have been like had the scheme not unravelled in farce and had my father's family succeeded in having me raised in the Protestant tradition. Would I be more thrifty and hard-working? Given to fatalistic pessimism? Alternatively, glassy-eyed and evangelical? Or, would I, like so many of my generation, have come to regard religion with indifference, even hostility?

For sure, I would have been essentially *somebody else*, for Catholicism has always been to me an important ingredient of personal identity. It commands an allegiance that geography cannot. My childhood was spent constantly on the move, neither house nor town nor county supplying a cultural tether. I am the son of an Anglo-Scottish father and a London-Irish mother, and any feeling of Englishness has always stopped short at a hyphen. Consequently, I have had to interrogate my faith against the possibility that it may be little more than a psychological prop, a compensation for social rootlessness. This avenue of enquiry has led to a sometimes impertinent curiosity about how other Catholics perceive their religion, how it conditions their outlook, whether it is significant to their sense of themselves. It is to that personal quest to trace the lineaments of a common Catholic culture and a specifically Catholic identity that this book owes its genesis.

By the end of the twentieth century, baptized Catholics accounted for 1 in 8 of the population in England and Wales. Scotland's proportion was higher at 16 per cent, whilst in Northern Ireland Catholics were fast approaching parity. That represents 5 times the Muslim population and over 15 times the size of the Jewish community. In the UK as a whole there are at least twice as many Catholics as black people. Many find these raw figures startling, for during the past fifty years or so Catholics have re-engineered themselves as a stealth minority, undetectable by conventional social radar. It is nowadays possible to work in the same office as a Catholic or live next door to a Catholic family without ever discovering their religion. Many Catholics have struggled hard to achieve this degree of invisibility, regarding assimilation as a social good. Yet a feeling persists – shared by Catholics and non-Catholics alike – that in some ill-defined way Catholics are still not quite like 'ordinary people'.

The Tory politician, Ann Widdecombe, once described herself in her habitually emphatic manner as 'a Catholic, British, Conservative, woman from Kent . . . *in that order*'.[1] Her insistence that there must be some sort of ordered hierarchy to the constituents of selfhood is not surprising in a Conservative. But the fact that the Catholic faith should have flown right to the top of the tree only a short while after she had quit the Church of England is significant. The displacement of nationality by religion as a touchstone of identity has a long pedigree. One of the first acts of the Earl of Denbigh after his conversion to Catholicism in the nineteenth century was to re-inscribe the motto beneath his coat of arms to read: 'First a Catholic, then an Englishman.' The Catholic saints and martyrs during the Elizabethan and Jacobean Terror, when more than 200 died and countless numbers were imprisoned, tortured, expropriated or fined, stated their own priorities even more unequivocally than Miss Widdecombe. These days, it is common enough to hear Catholics – even those such as the Labour politician Clare Short who no longer practise their religion – styling themselves 'ethnic' or 'cultural' Catholics. Such epithets acknowledge a set of shared attitudes, habits of mind, terms of reference, tastes and inclinations that mark Catholics out in much the same way as those national or properly ethnic traits with which Catholicism overlaps. Catholics have, as Sebastian Flyte explains in Evelyn Waugh's *Brideshead Revisited*, 'an entirely different outlook on life – everything they think is important is different from other people'.[2] This specific perspective is the product of Catholic education and family life. It extends far beyond concerns of dogma and morality, expressing itself in attitudes to art, literature, politics, leisure and work. It is a mindset hard to shift, tending to survive not only the decline of religious observance, but in some cases the deliberate and determined renunciation of faith.

These cultural differences were once painted in vivid colours. Before the 1960s, the Catholic community lived in clearly delineated districts, married its own, huddled together in Catholic clubs and societies, and displayed outward marks of difference – such as eating fish on Fridays and parading banners through the streets on the feast of Corpus Christi. It was largely composed of immigrants or the descendants of immigrants, most of whom were poor and Irish. But its isolation did not betoken stasis. The Catholic community was already transforming itself from being almost wholly urban, working-class and northern to being more middle-class, suburban and southern. At the beginning of the twentieth century more than half of England's Catholics lived in Lancashire, Yorkshire or the north-east; in 1960, more than half lived in Greater London.

This upwardly thrusting immigrant community was leavened by a small number of extremely grand families – descendants of the recusants who had suffered for their faith in the centuries following the Reformation. These families exercised a peculiar hold over the popular imagination throughout the twentieth century, one which novelists and film-makers were hardly reluctant to exploit. Even those who refuse to be seduced by the spurious glamour that attaches to wealth and position have to admit the invaluable contribution the old families have made as guardians of the Catholic heritage. Simply by keeping up their houses and their priest's holes they have been

3

gatekeepers to the past, curators of an inspiring tradition that helps many Catholics sustain their faith even today. Behind the scenes, they have also proved accomplished negotiators and fixers. As discreet advisers to cardinals and archbishops they have headed off collisions with the temporal powers, and in the clubs and corridors where the Establishment's business was transacted for so many years, they have advanced the Catholic interest when public campaigning and democratic politics could not.

Indeed, the master narrative of Britain's Catholic community during the twentieth century became one of relentless social progress. It was written and rewritten at each significant milestone or anniversary. In 1950, marking the centenary of the restoration of the Catholic hierarchy in England and Wales, Cardinal Griffin rejoiced that Catholics had at last become 'a real force' and were now 'willing and able to make a valuable contribution to the life of their country'.[3] Throughout the subsequent decades, Catholic newspapers delighted in identifying one after another successful individual as Catholic. It did not much matter in what field of endeavour the person flourished – the professions, journalism, show business, arts and literature, sport and even, in the case of Giant Haystacks, professional wrestling; anything would do, though there was sometimes an implication that politics and public life counted most. Not even the *aggiornamento* – the bringing-up-to-date of the Catholic Church under the auspices of the Second Vatican Council (1962–5, also known as Vatican II), which introduced a more conciliatory and ecumenical note to exchanges with outsiders, did much to tone down the glee which greeted the advancement of any Catholic to head a major national institution. In the Catholic press, the cheer would go up as if another citadel had been successfully stormed.

By the end of the century Catholics had succeeded in capturing many of the top jobs in Britain and the secular media were beginning to mimic the self-congratulatory Catholic press, cheering on a procession of celebrity converts. Amazingly, the royal family, hitherto as viscerally anti-papist an institution as anyone could name, appointed the Catholic Lord Camoys to supervise its own *aggiornamento*. Princess Diana flirted with conversion; her mother Frances Shand-Kydd and the Duchess of Kent went ahead and did it. Suddenly, Catholicism was declared fashionable.

Official confirmation that the minority could finally punch its weight came with a radio news broadcast following the death of Cardinal Basil Hume in June 1999. The bulletin trumpeted the Cardinal's achievement in making Catholics 'socially acceptable'. Quite what the aristocratic Catholic families made of that I do not know. One pictures an H. M. Bateman cartoon in which the Duke of Norfolk, together with milords Petre, Mowbray and a brace of Tempests, stand by an old walnut wireless set looking as if someone has just shot a fox. But by then there were already plenty of middle-class Catholics who were sufficiently self-confident to find the phrasing startling. One of them was the journalist and broadcaster Mark Lawson. 'I nearly drove off the road when I heard it,' he told me. 'Imagine the fuss there'd be if they'd said Lord Jakobovits had helped end the pariah status of Jews.'[4]

Born in 1962, Lawson is perhaps among the first generation of British Catholics never to have experienced serious anti-Catholic prejudice. His *Guardian* colleague Hugo Young remembers being warned by the monks of Ampleforth, where he was at school in the 1950s, that he should not expect to enjoy a successful career. 'It was made very clear to me that there was little chance of reaching the top across a whole range of professions – the Civil Service, the Foreign Office and especially the Bar and politics. As a Catholic – however good you were – you would simply not get on.'[5] But Young's school and university years coincided with an upswing in Catholic fortunes. In 1960, Sir Hugh Fraser became the first Catholic to serve in a twentieth-century Conservative cabinet. By the time Young left Oxford for journalism, both the editor of *The Times* and the Director General of the BBC were Catholics.

Thereafter progress was evident but sporadic. In the general election of 1964, only 33 Catholics were returned to Parliament; in 1966, the number fell to 32. A marked under-representation of the Catholic population in the House of Commons persisted until the Labour landslide of 1997, when 64 Catholics were elected –

5

much closer to, but still short of a proportional figure. The numbers were higher in the Upper House. This meant that for most of the century the Catholic interest was mainly advanced in the Lords, with predictable consequences for the community's image in the media and the public mind.

Parliamentary representation is a notoriously poor indicator of a minority community's current standing. An MP can occupy a safe seat for more than thirty years, so that significant shifts in public attitudes may take place without even noticeably disturbing the make-up of the Commons. But the consistent under-representation of Catholics since the departure of the Irish members with Home Rule confirms that their attempts to make social progress encountered real resistance. Anti-Catholicism in one form or another remained endemic in British society throughout the century. The raw, demotic variety could involve the jagged end of a broken bottle thrust in your face on the streets of Glasgow or Liverpool, or a bullet in the back of the head in Belfast. Its more insidious, Establishment manifestation – the kind that might queer the pitch for an old-Amplefordian such as Hugo Young – was more a matter of arched eyebrows and clandestine interventions, usually prefaced by the bizarre enquiry: 'Does he dig with the left foot?'

The atavistic Protestant bigotry of the kind that impelled my grandmother to embark on her rash adventure to steal a small boy back from the clutches of the wily Jesuits began to evaporate in England and Wales during the early seventies. (Even so, as late as a few weeks before Pope John Paul's visit to Britain in 1982 an opinion poll showed that 12 per cent of the country – and 19 per cent of Londoners – were against allowing the Holy Father to come.) My grandmother did not live to witness the Papal visit, but her beef with Rome ended in happy reconciliation when she died in a Catholic hospice, comforted by nuns. For Great Aunt Mary there was no surrender. In the spring of 1969 she moved to Northern Ireland and for the rest of his days my father entertained the conceit that she had personally initiated the Troubles. As the Catholic composer James MacMillan observed in his lecture at the 1999 Edinburgh Festival, anti-Catholic prejudice remains 'Scotland's shame'. There, the death of Basil Hume was marked by a leader in the journal of the Free Presbyterian Church expressing the devout wish that 'the rapid progress of Romanism in the nation under Hume's leadership would not only be brought to a halt, but drastically reversed' and concluding that the Cardinal's soul now surely burns in the fires of hell.[6]

But Catholics are deluding themselves if they believe that the fact that this kind of pernicious nonsense is becoming increasingly rare outside Scotland and Northern Ireland owes very much to their own efforts at ecumenical dialogue in the spirit of Vatican II. They are also deluding themselves if they believe that their much-vaunted social progress can be ascribed to anything other than a general tide of economic and social modernization upon which the Catholic community has floated like so much driftwood. Popular anti-Catholicism has diminished in lockstep with the secularization of the national culture. As religion has withdrawn from the public into the private domain – or, in many cases, disappeared altogether – the particulars of Christian denomination have simply ceased to matter. Devout Catholics cannot take much comfort from that. Equally, the old ruling class's resistance to Catholics has declined only as that Establishment's power has itself been eclipsed. It remains in question whether much of what Catholics have mistaken for social progress is merely a belated access to shell institutions from which effective significance and influence have some time ago departed. Catholics may now be admitted to the Establishment's garden party, but only, it seems, to keep company with yesterday's men and a bevy of airheads.

In any case, social progress, as conceived in narrowly materialist terms, should be too worldly a concern to detain Catholic attention for long. Surely the important questions about Catholicism during the twentieth century ask what happened to the Catholic idea, the Catholic argument and the Catholic critique? And, to raise a sensitive issue, whatever happened to the Catholic 'project'? That there *is* some kind of Catholic project has widely been suspected by many non-Catholics for a long time and that apprehension has generated a good deal of paranoid rhetoric. But, in a sense, they are right to be concerned, for Catholics are nothing if not teleological. For centuries Catholics have prayed for 'the conversion of England' and vowed to deliver 'Mary's Ransom' back to the true faith. These have become somewhat more nuanced concepts of late, and the emphasis has shifted from prompting defections from the Church of England to a more ambitious plan of spiritual and cultural reclamation.

Even this is seen as too earthbound for some. The recusant tradition in England was one of quiet piety and reticent devotion. Religion was seen as an essentially private matter, which one did not discuss too freely in company. Salvation was negotiated between oneself, one's conscience and one's maker, and the clergy should be neither overbearing nor outspoken. Collective enterprises such as those implied in the notion of a Catholic project were seen as not only vulgar, but pointless. But for many years that tradition has been informed by another, which has taken many of its confident assumptions from Rome. In this tradition the Church has a divinely ordained mission not only to change the hearts of men, but to transform the world. It does not accept the compartmentalizing of religion; indeed it defines religion as something pervasive – an extra dimension within which ordinary life may be lived. Accordingly, Catholics – the laity as much as priests – find themselves exhorted to answer a vocation. They are called to exemplify and promote Catholic values, not only within the family, but in the public world of work and citizenship as well. Ultimately what is envisaged is a civilizing transformation of all spiritual, social, political, cultural and economic life. That is the true Catholic agenda, the real meaning of 'the conversion of England'.

For some Catholics this responsibility gives a welcome purpose and direction to their lives. For others it is a burden – one quite frequently refused, or borne, grudgingly, only part of the way. This book is about some of the many talented men and women who in many diverse ways have either advanced a distinctively Catholic argument in public debate in the twentieth century or whose careers have revealed some sign of their original Catholic formation. They include writers and poets, philosophers, economists, campaigners, entertainers, pundits, politicians, soldiers, historians and priests. In order to set them in their proper context, I also deal briefly with the period from 1850 to 1900.

The sheer size of the Catholic community means that many interesting people have been left out. The decision whom to include and exclude was entirely personal. Some of those I have written about are people I have encountered socially or professionally. I know others only through their writings or achievements. What they have in common is simply that they compelled me – someone living within the Catholic community within the period – to take notice of them. This is not, therefore, a definitive history of the Catholic minority or a chronicle of its social progress. Rather it is conceived as an opportunity to eavesdrop on the Catholic voice in the national conversation during the twentieth century and to sense the flavour of Catholic culture.

Even as I write, the word 'national' becomes increasingly problematic in these islands. A Scottish parliament has been established and there are new assemblies for Wales and Northern Ireland. However throughout most of the period in question Britain remained a highly centralized state run from London. Consequently, this book has an English and metropolitan bias. The situation is further complicated by the Church's own administrative structure, under which Scotland and Ireland are each governed independently of England and Wales. The extraordinary experience of the Catholic minority in the Six Counties is beyond the scope of this book and I touch upon it only briefly. Wherever possible I have tried to make national distinctions where they are significant and acknowledge the different historical experiences of individual parts of the United Kingdom, avoiding the easy and casual generalizations that Scots, in particular, find irksome. Sometimes, however, I have removed some qualifications for the sake of fluency. No disrespect is meant.

It may also be helpful to provide some gloss on the way the word 'Catholic' is used in this book. The more specific description 'Roman Catholic' once carried an implicit insult and helped sustain the myth that Catholicism was an alien creed, essentially out of place in this country. Nowadays, such a pejorative or provocative usage is rare and Catholics generally treat the label as neutral. It can sometimes be convenient for distinguishing between the Catholic Church and the Anglo-Catholic wing of the Church of England; but in my experience few Catholics outside the armed forces use the phrase, or its abbreviation 'RC', in everyday conversation. In recent years a failure to use the 'Roman' qualifier has sometimes been taken to be a mark of Catholic exclusivism, implying a refusal to accept the claims of Anglicans and others to be part of Christ's universal church. In this book its use or non-use is dictated largely by considerations of euphony and context and no other inferences should be drawn. More controversial still is the question of whether it is appropriate to describe someone as a Catholic if they have ceased to practise their religion. The Church draws no distinction between the observant and the lapsed, treating all the baptized – dutiful or prodigal – as children of one Catholic family. I have broadly followed the same approach, though I recognize there can be pitfalls. Some time ago I chanced upon an American website that boasted Voltaire among the 'great Catholic philosophers'. I have tried to avoid being quite so tendentious.

In 1852, John Henry Newman, poet, priest and a recent convert to the Catholic faith, preached a sermon so compelling that the robust Cardinal Wiseman cried much of the way through it and Lord Macaulay later learned it by heart. Nowadays it seems extraordinary that a homily should have possessed such affective power. But in Victorian Britain religion still mattered. It was often as central a public concern as politics. Consequently, God's ministry attracted men of ambition, brimful of talent and vigour. Their preaching could generate fervid passions, ignite controversy or scorch an indelible mark.

Newman was one of the greatest of them all. Yet, despite his intellectual rigour and pellucid style, his motives were sometimes misrepresented and his words misunderstood. In this sermon – later published as *The Second Spring* – Newman's intention had been to contrast the sunny optimism that had vivified the Catholic community since the restoration of its ecclesiastical hierarchy in 1850 with the bleak, 300-year winter of intolerance that had gone before. Unwittingly, he piqued those he least wished to offend: the old recusant families. Instead of portraying them as they liked to see themselves, as proud, unbeaten stoics who had worked tirelessly for emancipation, Newman described a tempest-tossed raft of ragged survivors, 'a mere handful of individuals who might be counted like the pebbles and detritus of the great deluge'.

What his critics mistook for condescension was the candid perspective of the outsider. Brought up in the Church of England, Newman had seen how marginal and contemptible England's Catholics seemed to the rest of society. Recalling his own boyhood impression of their community, he pictured 'an old-fashioned house of gloomy appearance, closed in with high walls, with an iron gate and yews, and the report attaching to it that "Roman

Catholics" lived there; but who they were or what they did, or what was meant by calling them Roman Catholics no one could tell – though it had an unpleasant sound'.[1]

It is understandable that English Catholics in the early 1800s were still leading a somewhat sequestered existence. Their forebears had suffered persecution since Tudor times. No other religious minority in these islands has been oppressed so bloodily, or for so long. Excluded from the universities, the professions and political office, Catholics had grown used to living apart from the mainstream of public life. Behind their high walls they had developed a distinctive sub-culture which kept the flame of their faith ardent. The stories that they passed on, generation to generation, would have been thought subversive, even seditious, by those brought up on the authorized version of the national past. The heroes of the Catholic minority were, according to the official record, traitors to their country who had been justly executed. The names of the most notorious, such as Guy Fawkes, became fixed in the national demonology even after their propaganda value was exhausted; but for the most part the honour roll of Catholics who suffered rack and rope under Elizabeth I and James I had been deleted from popular memory. Anniversaries of martyrdom and resistance were celebrated quietly at home or, until the Relief Acts of 1778 and 1791 finally made Catholic education in England lawful, at the special schools in France and the Low Countries to which Catholic children were smuggled, at the height of the persecution, by fishing smack on moonless nights.

These Continental academies developed a latitude of mind, an openness to intimations of a supernatural purpose in the development of European civilization, against which England had insulated itself behind channel fogs. Their pupils learned to discern how the Catholic Church was, by divine will, central to the unfolding story of the Continent from Roman times. They were taught that the Reformation was a disaster, and about the heavy responsibility their own country bore for that schism. Some even came to believe it might be quickly reversible and they worked and prayed earnestly for the conversion of England.

To their Protestant compatriots, the feeling that Catholics had some secret agenda was unsettling. Whether Catholics owed their primary allegiance to the Crown or to Rome had always been questionable. Their elaborate rituals smacked of idolatry. The Catholic cast of mind appeared alien and impenetrable, and the public pronouncements of popes sounded arrogant and presumptuous to English yeoman ears. These apprehensions were not at all dispelled when Catholics began to emerge from behind their iron gates with the Emancipation Act of 1829; indeed, they were exacerbated.

Emancipation coincided with one of those outbursts of 'no-popery' which punctuated the nineteenth century and during which the normally level-headed Englishman displayed himself at his most absurd. Partly this was because the campaign for Catholic rights had become bound up with the turbulent politics of Ireland, but its main impulse was not so narrowly political. A great resurgence of interest in religion swept Europe after the French Revolution in reaction to the rationalism of the Enlightenment. Amidst the rubble left by the revolutionary wars, Europeans yearned once more for the spiritual and the transcendent. This new quest to expand consciousness beyond the artificial constraints of reason found literary and artistic expression in the Romantic movement and lent a religious flavour to almost all intellectual and philosophical discussion. While Catholic ideas blossomed across the Continent, marked by the surging popularity of writers such as Chateaubriand and de Maistre, sobersided Albion witnessed an evangelical revival.

The success of John Wesley's Methodist movement had aroused other Nonconformist sects to missionary zeal. Itinerant preachers and colporteurs – many of them Ulstermen – tramped the country denouncing the Pope as the Antichrist and Rome as the Scarlet Woman of the Book of Revelation.

Before long, anti-Catholic feeling took on a political dimension. In many boroughs the local Conservative associations fell under the control of Protestant extremists. Politicians duly trimmed their opinions to the prevailing prejudice. Reporting on the general election campaign of 1847, *The Times* noted that the whole country has put on the appearance of a vast Protestant anti-papal league. The solicitors who manage the purchase of the borough seats are forced to cram their candidates with a sort of theological catechism . . . where they learn their attachment to religious truth as held pure and undefiled from any Romish adulteration. The newspapers teem with addresses to electors all breathing the same attachment to Protestant principles, all professing the most intense love for the reformed faith.[2]

But Catholics were determined not to be sidelined; they wanted to make their mark. The first manifestation of an ambition to transform their country was seen in the landscape. Before the Reformation, all Britain had been Catholic. Everywhere there were reminders of a Catholic past. A new generation of Catholic architects and designers revisited the monuments of the Middle Ages to reconnect with an unsullied Catholic tradition. Together with the rich 16th Earl of Shrewsbury, two dedicated medievalists, Ambrose Lisle Phillipps and Augustus Welby Pugin, helped spread the Gothic revival.

Phillipps was a Leicestershire landowner, the squire of Grace Dieu Manor on the edge of Charnwood Forest. He made his house the centre of missionary work carried out by Italian priests of the Rosminian order, founded a Trappist monastery at Mount Saint Bernard and commissioned several local chapels in the Gothic style. Phillipps had converted to Catholicism while still a schoolboy. As a student at Cambridge, together with a fellow convert, Kenelm Digby, he conceived an ambitious wheeze to revive not only the faith but also the architecture and ornament of the Middle Ages. Ambrose even Gothicized his own name, becoming Ambrose Phillipps de Lisle. The father of sixteen children, he was the founder of a Catholic dynasty that survives today.

Their project was not merely nostalgic and sentimental. Certainly, Kenelm Digby's political scheme for an England ruled by a wise and gentle Catholic aristocracy was a futile whimsy. But in the context of recent European history, their aesthetic ambitions did not seem so very far-fetched. Classical styles had, after all, been successfully revived. Surely the medieval could also be granted a second lease?

De Lisle's friend Pugin churned out a prodigious number of designs in the years following emancipation. His dreams were realized with cash dispensed by Lord Shrewsbury from his faeryland turret at Alton Towers (itself partly a Pugin creation). Dozens of Gothic churches sprang up around the country during the 1830s and '40s, more than fifty of them built by Pugin and many others by Joseph Aloysius Hansom, the designer of the Hansom cab. In 1848, a huge Pugin church (later to become St George's Cathedral) was built on the very spot in Lambeth where, in 1780, Lord George Gordon had incited a drunken mob to attack Catholics and burn their homes. In the Catholic mind, the distinction between an irony of fate and a small miracle need not always be a great one.

Pugin insisted that the Gothic was the *only* authentic Christian architecture. It was not simply a style but a principle, an expression of faith. In a book, *Contrasts*, he mischievously juxtaposed images of his sublime, 'pointed' architectural ideal with caricatures of 'pagan' buildings, causing offence to many of his professional colleagues.

When a fire devastated the Palace of Westminster in 1834, Pugin was among the spectators who watched it burn, cheering with gusto as the flames danced along the roofs. Subsequently he would collaborate with the architect Charles Barry in reconstructing the Houses of Parliament. Scholars are divided as to which was the dominant partner in the project. Generations of Catholics were taught that it was indubitably Pugin; even that his was the true hand that drafted the plans (submitted under Barry's name) that won the original commission. Certainly, every aspect of the interior right down to the wallpaper had to pass Pugin's stern test of coherence.

Pugin's intransigence in matters of style led to a squabble with his fellow Catholics – over, of all things, the cut of ecclesiastical vestments. He had revived the fuller, single-colour, pre-Reformation chasuble for the fancy ceremonial performed at Grace Dieu. He then demanded that all Catholic priests adopt it too. The Church authorities disagreed and Pugin was censured. Like many Catholics before and since, Pugin found the smack of firm episcopal authority hard to bear. He fell into a depression that developed, exacerbated by overwork, into a raving dementia. After a spell in Bedlam, Pugin died at the age of forty, a martyr to his own obsessions.

Catholic ideas and aesthetics were also taking hold in the wider culture. They can be detected in the work of some of the Romantic poets, in the Pre-Raphaelite movement in art and in the novels of Sir Walter Scott. It was, of course, possible to embrace the aesthetics but disdain the religion. John Ruskin and William Morris would prove that Catholics held no monopoly on medievalism. But culture was the ram that broke the gate. For generations, the enemies of Catholicism had succeeded in classifying it as a foreign incongruity – the religion of Spanish invaders, French kings and Italian popes. Now cultural archaeologists were excavating a Catholic past at home, many educated people were coming to the conclusion that it was not the Catholic minority but their own state and their own religion that were deviant.

At the end of the nineteenth century, the historian W. Gordon Gorman ventured a headcount of socially significant Catholic converts in the Victorian period. He identified:

29 peers
432 members of the nobility
470 writers and poets
306 army officers
64 naval officers
192 lawyers
92 doctors[3]

To these numbers must be added almost 600 Anglican clergymen who had succeeded in reconciling their difficulties with the Catholic doctrine of Transubstantiation or with the requirements of unity and authority laid down by Rome. Many were drawn from the leading Tractarians of the Oxford Movement, formed in 1833.

The Tractarians wanted to wrest the Church of England from

the Erastians, who thought it should be a 'national church' subordinated to the state, and to reconnect it with the Apostolic Tradition – the unbroken line of priestly ordination going back to St Peter. Some of them liked to revive old rituals and re-emphasize the sacramental in religious practice. In 1845, their opponents retaliated. William Ward, one of the leaders of the Movement, was condemned by the university authorities at Oxford and lost his degree. Within months he had been received into the Catholic Church, followed by Newman, Frederick Faber and many more, leaving behind Edward Pusey and John Keble to develop what became known as the 'Anglo-Catholic' wing of the Church of England.

The defection of Newman shocked the English Establishment. It was as if this man of great reputation and learning had negligently allowed himself to be suborned by agents of the Pope. As the century progressed, the shock would be repeated time and again. Everywhere they looked – in the arts, in society, in Parliament, even in the Established church itself – Protestant Englishmen detected Catholic militancy and subversion. If a man such as George Spencer, son of the cabinet minister Lord Althorp, could turn to Rome, might not the rest of the aristocracy soon follow? Indeed, half the great houses in England appeared to have a child or cousin prepared to bow down before a foreign priest. If one army officer, why not whole regiments? As the sixty-four naval officers showed, not even the fleet was safe from 'popish aggression'.

The fact that conversions continued throughout the Victorian period was proof that they represented something more than the emergence of closet Catholics after emancipation. The most spectacular instance was the reception into the Catholic Church in 1874 of the Marquess of Ripon, who was born in 10 Downing Street when his father was Prime Minister and who himself had served in the Liberal cabinet. Ripon went on to be Viceroy of India.

The Times was appalled by Ripon's defection. 'A statesman who becomes a convert to Roman Catholicism forfeits at once the confidence of the English people. Such a move . . . can only be regarded as betraying an irreparable weakness of character.'[4]

In 1868, Scottish society had been rocked by the conversion of

John Crichton-Stuart, 3rd Marquess of Bute. Crichton-Stuart was the richest man in Britain. The Glasgow *Herald* described his decision as a 'perversion'. The tenants and estate workers on the island propped a portrait of their young laird against a wall and pelted it with stones. The atmosphere became so toxic that the Marquess left the country for a while. But on his return, he continued to horrify his Presbyterian neighbours by stocking his park with wallabies and erecting an enormous marble chapel, complete with a replica of the tower of Saragossa Cathedral.

Protestants might have worried less about the relatively small numbers of toffs and intellectuals who were 'poping' and paid more heed to the arrival of a vast army of bedraggled Irishmen fleeing the potato famine. It was the Irish who brought the Catholic community in Britain up to critical mass. In 1770, native English Catholics numbered just 80,000; but by 1851, swelled mostly by immigration, the total Catholic population was three-quarters of a million strong.

At the mid-century circumstances portended a sectarian brawl. The occasion was duly supplied by the announcement of the re-establishment of the Catholic hierarchy. Between the Reformation and 1850, Rome classified the Catholic Church in England and Wales as a 'mission church'. That did not imply that successive popes regarded the population as savage heathens given to cannibalism and headhunting. Essentially, it meant that there were no local bishops. Church affairs were managed from Rome, which, once it was safe to do so, despatched Vicars Apostolic to undertake most of the pastoral and bureaucratic work that cardinals and bishops perform today.

Pope Pius IX decided that the man best fitted for the role of spearheading the new Catholic dispensation in England would be Cardinal Nicholas Wiseman, whom he appointed as the first Archbishop of Westminster in 1850. Wiseman was in Rome at the time of the announcement and promptly sent the good news to Catholics back home. He did not feel that an excess of discretion should spoil a moment of such significance. His pastoral letter, *From Out the Flaminian Gate*, read like a magnificent fanfare, culminating in a great crash of cymbals. It would result in an equally noisy collision of cultures.

'The greatest of blessings has been bestowed upon our country by the restoration of its true Catholic hierarchical government, in communion with the See of Peter,' Wiseman wrote. 'Catholic England . . . begins now anew its course of regularly adjusted action round the centre of unity.' The Catholic periodical, the *Tablet*, applauded the splendid contempt with which Wiseman had 'utterly ignored' the Church of England in his letter.

Clerical affronts alone cannot explain the enormous brouhaha that followed. The Cardinal's letter contained passages to irk the temporal powers too. 'We govern and shall continue to govern, the counties of Middlesex, Hertford and Essex . . . And those of Surrey, Sussex, Kent, Berkshire and Hampshire, with the islands annexed, as administrator with ordinary jurisdiction,' Wiseman trumpeted.[5] No wonder Queen Victoria, when the published text was shown to her, asked an attendant courtier 'Am *I* Queen of England or am I not?'[6]

The Prime Minister, Lord John Russell, hoping to gain political advantage through a confrontation with the Catholics, pretended to be furious at Wiseman's presumption. Lord Winchelsea, though, was in deadly earnest when he called for a declaration of war against the Papal States. A few days later, on Guy Fawkes Night, Wiseman was burned in effigy at Peckham.

The media response was just as inflammatory. *The Times* accused the Pope of plotting 'to restore a foreign usurpation over the consciences of men and to sow divisions in our political society'. *From Out the Flaminian Gate*, the paper concluded, was either 'a delusion of a fanatical brain or a treason to the constitution'.[7] *Punch* played upon the feeling that Catholicism was alien. 'The Hindoo government,' began its parody of Wiseman's bull, 'has sent over Hoki Poki to commence his functions as Brahmin of Battersea . . .'[8]

There was nothing for it but to write another letter. Wiseman's subsequent *Appeal to the Reason and Good Feeling of the English People*, issued on 20 November, was reproduced verbatim in six London daily newspapers. It was the most widely published Catholic communication since the Reformation and, significantly, was addressed directly to the people.

Wiseman gave an assurance that his vaunted *imperium* was spiritual, not temporal. The Crown was merely being asked to accept the same arrangements already in place in Ireland, and for that matter, in Canada and Australia as well.

For *The Times*, however, the *Appeal* was further evidence of Catholic duplicity. Its leader observed that

The Roman Catholic Church has two languages, an esoteric and an exoteric, the first couched in the very terms of that more than mortal arrogance and insolence in which Hildebrand and Innocent thundered their decrees against trembling Kings and prostrate Emperors; the second, artful, humble and cajoling, seizing on every popular topic, enlisting in its behalf every claptrap argument, and systematically employing reasoning the validity of which the Sophist himself would be the last to recognize.[9]

Moreover, Wiseman had once again insulted the Church of England bishops. He had sought to reassure them that he did not covet the wealth and pomp of Westminster Abbey, his chief concern being for the wretched of the Westminster slums. Unsurprisingly, the Archbishop of Canterbury and his colleagues found this moral one-upmanship more offensive than conciliatory.

But at the strategic level, the *Appeal* had done the trick. The restoration was secure. Any ruffled feathers could, as far as the Cardinal Archbishop was concerned, stay ruffled. He had explained himself clearly enough, both in print and in a series of public meetings and now intended to enjoy the revival of Catholic fortunes. He put on his red hat and had himself driven around London in a magnificent carriage.

Wiseman's promise of a preferential option for the poor would be realized in the work of his successor, Cardinal Manning. Far from being the vain, egotistical hypocrite depicted in Lytton Strachey's *Eminent Victorians*, Manning was the people's Cardinal, the workers' champion. He saw how the great engines of industrial capitalism crushed the human spirit and was unafraid to speak out against the greed of factory owners. He championed poorly paid agricultural workers and helped negotiate the settlement of the 1889 London dock strike. He even voiced the unfashionable view that no man who truly loves his country can desire that it should remain the centre of an Empire. To the Victorian bourgeoisie, Manning's radicalism made Catholics seem doubly sinister. They were not only peculiar, but quite possibly socialist.

Indeed, suspicion of Catholics in the second half of the nine-teenth century reached risible extremes. Newman's plans for the Birmingham Oratory were minutely scrutinized and vigorously opposed. The architects' drawings indicated several windowless store cupboards in the basement adjacent to the kitchens. Alert Protestants promptly intuited that their true purpose was to serve as dungeons and torture chambers, where the priests would perform unspeakable acts upon their hapless victims. The matter was raised in the Commons in a desperate attempt to stop planning permission being granted.

Meanwhile, newspapers despatched reporters to investigate the 'sorcery' inherent in Catholic liturgy. One, assigned to expose papist mummery in the City of London, attended a service of Benediction at the Catholic Chapel in King William Street. Note-book in hand, he positioned himself where he could have a clear view of the celebrant. Unfortunately, there was a pillar blocking his line of sight to the altar boy whose task was to ring the bell when the monstrance was held aloft. As the first plangent knell reverberated around the chapel, the reporter watched scornfully as the Catholics bowed down in awe. He assumed the poor saps took the sound to be some kind of tintinnabular miracle. Naturally the correspondent for the *British Protestant* was not so easily fooled. He reckoned he had spotted at once how the sleight of hand had been brought off. 'As Gordon raised the star . . .' he told his readers, 'he clearly showed the Popish deceit; for *in the candlestick there is a bell*, that rang three times of its own accord to deceive the blind fools more . . . and Gordon's finger at work underneath'.[10]

Protestant paranoia soon found a parliamentary champion in the

Warwickshire MP Charles Newdegate. The Newdegates had a long record of crimes against Catholicism. The family seat, Arbury Hall, had been confiscated from the Augustinian monks at the time of the dissolution of the monasteries and a later Newdegate had served Oliver Cromwell as Chief Justice.

Elected to Parliament in 1843, Newdegate was the cobbler's last upon which generations of Warwickshire MPs have been fashioned, right down to Enoch Powell and Nicholas Budgen. A foxhunting squire, he was a man of unbending principle who stood for the nation, the Conservative Party, the Glorious Revolution of 1688 and the Protestant faith, in interchangeable order, depending on the issue of the day.

Newdegate never married and was rumoured to be homosexual. There was no real evidence for this beyond an unwholesome dependence upon his domineering mother, something that in Victorian times was widely believed to be one of the principal causes of a homosexual inclination. Newdegate's relationship with his mother does, however, more persuasively explain his hostility to Catholics. The letters that passed between them when Newdegate was in London attending the House of Commons reveal his mother as a vehement religious bigot, and her son anxious to please her by demonstrating a competitive measure of prejudice.

The plight of nuns in Catholic convents became the issue that would occupy the greater part of Charles Newdegate's political career. He could not comprehend that a woman might, of her own volition, elect to become a bride of Christ. Only priestly coercion could account for it. He gave unquestioning credence to stories of nuns being imprisoned in cages and fed on nothing but bread and water. He was convinced that the lucky few who managed to escape were hunted down by a posse of bishops and returned to their confinement by sealed coach at dead of night. For thirty years Newdegate bored and irritated his parliamentary colleagues with ceaseless demands for public enquiries and select committee investigations into convent life. He did not bore alone. One of his closest collaborators was the Liberal MP George Whalley, whose own conspiracy theory was encapsulated in the title of his book *Popery in Ireland; or, Confessionals, Abductions, Nunneries, Fenians and Orangemen: A Narrative of Facts.*

There were a number of Catholic MPs ready to contest Newdegate at every pass, the most active being Lord Edward Howard. But in 1870, despite the entreaties of the Duke of Norfolk, Gladstone allowed Newdegate his select committee inquiry. Britain's grandest Catholic laymen met at a club in Piccadilly to draft a warning to the Prime Minister that his decision 'must and will be regarded as a declaration of war against the Catholics of the United Kingdom'.[11] Nevertheless, the investigation went ahead.

But when the committee eventually reported, Newdegate and his allies were trounced. No shackles, no instruments of torture, nothing sinister whatsoever had been discovered in the convents. Moreover, the sisters seemed adequately fed; some were even quite plump. To Newdegate's chagrin, the report led to the repeal of most of the discriminatory laws against Catholics still remaining on the statute book.

Meanwhile, on the streets of England's main industrial towns, a more vicious sectarian fracas was taking place. William Murphy, an evangelical Protestant from Dublin, mounted a crusade in the late 1860s to warn the English working class of the evils of Romanism. Relying on forged or deliberately mistranslated instructions for the priest in the confessional, Murphy played upon the sexual anxieties of husbands, alleging that priests were putting into the minds of their wives details of sexual practices and positions that left to themselves they would never have conceived possible. Murphy began his campaign by staging disruptive interventions of Catholic services, but was soon appearing on public platforms with George Whalley. The implicit endorsement of a Member of Parliament lent Murphy's crusade an appearance of respectability it did not deserve. The pair cynically set out to stir up anti-Catholic feeling, targeting their provocations on towns with large Irish immigrant communities.

The Irish responded by heckling Murphy's speeches and throwing stones at his audience. In Birmingham, Wolverhampton and across the north-east these rallies quickly degenerated into riots.

The Protestant mobs desecrated Catholic churches and torched houses in Irish districts. In some areas the authorities had to introduce emergency regulations equivalent to martial law.

Mayors dreaded Murphy's arrival in their towns and would entreat the Home Secretary to intervene. The government and the House of Commons struggled to reconcile the competing claims of free speech and public order. Newdegate, inevitably, became Murphy's parliamentary champion. But his eloquent defence of individual liberty was radically undermined when the substance of Murphy's lectures was read out to MPs. Murphy had declared that every Catholic priest was a cannibal and a pickpocket, and had made the baffling claim that the Virgin Mary was a Protestant. Catholic members thought this latter charge particularly outrageous.

Nor was Murphy's case helped when one of his associates shot a policeman in Rochdale or when a Catholic priest in the Midlands was forced to defend his chapel with a rifle. Yet the government chose neither to offer Murphy protection nor to impose any ban on his activities. They simply left the problem to the local authorities.

A solution was found one night in April 1871, when Murphy was due to speak at Whitehaven in Cumberland. A group of brawny Irishmen arrived at the Oddfellows Hall in advance of the lecture, manhandled Murphy outside and beat him unconscious. When he died, eleven months later, Newdegate claimed Murphy had been 'murdered by a Roman Catholic mob, aided by Papal emissaries'.[12] Of course, the mysterious foreigners clad in soutanes and birettas, slipping silently away from the scene of the crime, existed only in Newdegate's imagination.

Anti-Catholic polemics were not just the vice of maverick backbenchers such as Newdegate or rabble-rousers such as Murphy. The writer Charles Kingsley, whose *Westward Ho!* contained a spiteful portrayal of the Catholic martyr Edmund Campion, published a vicious attack on Newman in 1863, the same year as his altogether more appealing work *The Water Babies*. Kingsley accused Newman of licensing dishonesty and casuistry. Newman's reply –

his *Apologia pro Vita Sua* – became a best-seller and is still in print today.

Not long after the fuss occasioned by this spat died down, the papers were full of the amazing story of the Tichborne claimant. Roger Tichborne, scion of a rich Catholic family from Hampshire, had been lost at sea in 1854. His inconsolable mother persisted in believing he was still alive and placed advertisements in newspapers around the world. In 1867, she received a reply from Australia. Arthur Orton of Wagga Wagga was the obese and near illiterate son of a Wapping butcher. Nevertheless, so pervasive was anti-Catholic prejudice at the time that a large section of the press and public chose to champion the amiable oaf's claim to be the vanished Sir Roger, come home to collect his share of the family fortune.

The real Sir Roger would have spoken fluent French and, as a Catholic, been able to translate the Latin phrase *ad maiorem Dei gloriam*. But under examination, Orton could do neither. The case was complicated, however, by the fact that Lady Tichborne, by now almost completely batty, insisted the claimant was indeed her son.

The family's cause was not helped by the publication of a letter denouncing Orton as a fraud, signed by a group of prominent Catholics, including a Jesuit priest. This quickly turned the affair into a sectarian *cause célèbre*. The two subsequent trials became society spectacles, with members of the royal family turning up for the entertainment. After a total of 291 days in court, the bogus claimant was jailed for fourteen years.

By the mid-1870s, Gladstone, Disraeli and even Queen Victoria had joined the *Kulturkampf*. The Queen did not air her views publicly, but her private correspondence shows that she considered the Catholic Church a serious irritant. Disraeli's novel *Lothair* featured an attack on Manning and lampooned the Marquess of Bute. Gladstone, once out of office in 1874, issued a series of pamphlets – or 'expostulations', as he preferred to call them. These were prompted chiefly by the First Vatican Council's declaration of the doctrine of papal infallibility, which Gladstone believed would undermine the loyalty of Catholics to the Crown and to the nation state. Surely Catholics would surely side with a Pope whom they believed to be infallible against monarchs and politicians whom they knew were not?

Gladstone's intervention led to a permanent breach with Manning, who had previously been a friend. It also sharpened the divisions between two tendencies within English Catholicism: the Ultramontane, which emphasized the authority of the Pope and employed triumphalist rhetoric; and the Cisalpine or Gallican, which favoured a quieter style and greater local autonomy in Church affairs. The old recusant families formed the backbone of the Cisalpine faction. They wanted to avoid conflict with their fellow countrymen – especially with the state – and were eager to take what they saw as their deserved places in the higher reaches of society and in the apparatus of Empire. They disliked the noisy religious zeal of the converts and prayed for a quiet life. The Ultramontanes, led by Manning, regarded such attitudes as tantamount to appeasement. What he wanted, he said, were 'downright, masculine and decided Catholics – *more* Roman than Rome and more Ultramontane than the Pope himself '.[13]

In 1896 the Pope published a letter clarifying the status of the Anglican Church. Those members of the Church of England who saw themselves as part of the national branch of a single, universal Christian church were disappointed. *Apostolicae Curiae* declared Anglican orders to be 'utterly null and completely void'. The implication of this judgement was that all clergymen of the Established Church, from the Archbishop of Canterbury to the local curate, were deemed by what was overwhelmingly the greatest body of Christians in the world to be nothing but heretics and frauds. Pope Leo XIII held this judgement to be fixed, settled and irrevocable.

So what of the conversion of England, the recovery of Mary's Dowry? As the century drew to its close, it had become apparent that this was going to be a more long-term project than some optimists had expected in 1829. Emancipation had brought release from legal restrictions; it had allowed individual Catholics to play a fuller part in national life; it had prompted a number of significant conversions. But the institution of the Catholic Church was far from being accepted by society or state. It was tolerated, not welcomed. Most of those who had deserted the Established Church for atheism or agnosticism were at least as hostile to Catholicism as any mainstream Protestant. Newman may have been the first cuckoo, but his second spring was just a sunny spell. Catholic and non-Catholic remained separated by mutual distrust. How could two communities that spoke the same language and inhabited the same landscape possibly view the world so differently? Only by having a very different understanding of their history.

Some time ago an article appeared in the *Tablet* relating the grue-some story of Oliver Cromwell's head. When the Lord Protector died in 1658, he was given a state funeral and buried in Westminster Abbey. But two years later, his corpse was disinterred, along with those of other leading regicides, and ceremonially hanged at Tyburn. The head was removed and impaled on a spike on the roof of Westminster Hall, where it hung for the next thirty years. Eventually, blown down in a gale, it was picked up by a passer-by and sold. The *Tablet* charted its subsequent journey over 250 years through the hands of collectors, private museums and curiosity shops. At one point it was purchased by the proprietor of a peep show in London's West End, presumably as a penny-a-fright enter-tainment. In the 1950s, it became the property of a Church of England clergyman who used to bring it out, still on its spike, to liven up flagging dinner parties.[14]

What is interesting about the *Tablet*'s article – quite apart from the details of the story, which are not well known – is its ready assumption that Catholics will derive some grim satisfaction from the tale. The magazine knows its readers well. As recently as the 1970s, Catholic schoolchildren of eight or nine would be taught that Oliver Cromwell was a bogeyman and tyrant; a murderous beast whose facial warts expressed a foul inner corruption; and a Puritan who drank nothing but unsweetened lemon juice.

Of course, the secular curriculum of O-levels, GCSEs and A-levels provided a necessary corrective. But for many Catholics, however much the head might acknowledge Cromwell's part in securing the liberties of the English people, the heart would always ride with Rupert.

A similar ambivalence attaches to the Catholic attitude to the Gunpowder Plot. While genuinely relieved that the bomb never went off, Catholics often nurture a sneaking regard for both Guy Fawkes and the plotters' leader, the dashing Robert Catesby. In her book *The Gunpowder Plot – Terror and Faith in 1605*, Lady Antonia Fraser quotes these words from Nelson Mandela's speech from the dock at his trial:

I do not deny that I planned sabotage. I did not plan it in a spirit of recklessness or because I have any love of violence. I planned it as the result of a calm and sober assessment of the political situation that had arisen after many years of tyranny, exploitation and oppression of my people.

'These are not the words of Robert Catesby,' writes Fraser, 'but *mutatis mutandis* they could in fact have been uttered by him had he lived to defend his actions to the world.'[15]

Elizabeth I is another figure from history whose name evokes quite different responses among Catholics and non-Catholics. She may be Gloriana to some, but 'Good Queen Bess' was responsible for the deaths of 123 priests and 60 lay Catholics. Hundreds more were imprisoned, many suffering torture on the rack at the hands of the sadistic Richard Topcliffe. And Catholics are often puzzled that Henry VIII, despite his record of domestic violence, is sometimes portrayed along the UK heritage trail as a jolly, avuncular fellow playing 'Greensleeves' on a lute.

These two monarchs get their comeuppance in Catholic folklore much as Cromwell does in the *Tablet*'s tale. There is a somewhat Grand Guignol tradition of Catholic consolation stories in which something particularly nasty happens either at the moment of a wicked person's death or, failing that, to their corpse afterwards. There is no doctrinal basis for any of this. Sinners receive their deserts in the next world and it is their immortal souls rather than their putrefying remains that suffer. But these are essentially morality tales, and rather like their modern-day, secular equivalents – police procedurals – they exist to maintain the fiction that crime does not pay.

Henry VIII's most heinous offence was the murder of Margaret Pole. Previously a royal favourite, Margaret withdrew from the court in 1533 because she could not condone Henry's divorce from Catherine of Aragon and subsequent marriage to Anne Boleyn. Her son Reginald, Cardinal Pole, sent from Rome a strongly worded admonition of the King, insisting on a return to church unity. With the Cardinal beyond his grasp, Henry took revenge on his friends and family, executing the adults and imprisoning the children in the Tower of London. Margaret was beheaded in 1541 by an incompetent executioner who took half a dozen swings with his axe. And there we might choose to leave it, but for the requirements of the genre. The story, as told to generations of Catholic children, is not complete without its grisly coda. When Mary Tudor became Queen, Reginald Pole returned to England to serve as the last Catholic Archbishop of Canterbury. He had Henry's corpse removed from its tomb and burned.

The death of Elizabeth was the subject of a pamphlet written in the early years of the century by Monsignor R. H. Benson, the convert son of a former Archbishop of Canterbury and the younger brother of E. F. Benson, author of the Mapp and Lucia stories. Benson was much possessed by death. He had the walls of his home decorated with images of dancing skeletons, supposedly to terrify visiting Anglicans into converting to Rome. Contrasting the final hours on earth of Mary Tudor and Elizabeth, he pictured Mary, the scourge of Protestants, dying in a glow of spiritual tranquillity in a candlelit room as a priest celebrated Mass at her bedside. Her last words described the beauty of the angels who had arrived to escort her to heaven. Elizabeth, scourge of Catholics, died howling and squatting and scrabbling at her own flesh, her skull squeezed as if by an iron band, all the while suffering terrifying hallucinations.

Some traditionally minded Catholics found Benson's zeal hard to endure. Like Dr Catacomb in Ronald Knox's story *Barchester*

Pilgrimage, many English Catholics 'never thought of a convert but as a bird which had flown into the room by accident, to the embarrassment of the occupants'.[16] Benson's notoriously histrionic sermons certainly disturbed the austere tranquillity of the Catholic Mass. 'Sometimes he would suddenly lower his voice and simultaneously shrink down in the pulpit until only his head and face were visible,' reported one fascinated onlooker. 'Then he would raise his voice almost to a shriek and, like a figure in a Punch and Judy show, dart up diagonally and lean over the pulpit edge until one almost feared he would tumble out of it.'[17] The writer Shane Leslie recorded an even more dramatic performance when Benson preached in Cambridge. 'He gave the feeling he was preaching his last sermon on the eve of the Day of Judgement. He began to mop his brow, waved his arms and his eyes stared out of his face in agony. He seemed . . . to collapse in convulsions out of the pulpit, whence he was led to a hot bath.'[18]

Given his family background, it would have been a miracle if Hugh Benson had turned out a calm and well-adjusted character. His father, the Archbishop, chose his own bride when she was only eleven years old and spent years carefully coaching her for the role. But Hugh Benson did not become a Catholic in rebellion against his father's appetite for dominance and control. In his *Confessions of a Convert* he offers a cogent, and by now familiar, explanation for his decision: the Church of England's tendency to fudge awkward dogmatic questions.

Nevertheless he was a decidedly odd man with an even more peculiar friend in Frederick Rolfe, the self-styled Baron Corvo. Rolfe was another noisy convert. Turned down as a candidate for the priesthood, he wrote a masterpiece of wish-fulfilment, *Hadrian VII*, the story of an Englishman who becomes Pope and gives away all the Church's wealth to the poor. Bitter to the last that he had been cheated of his vocation, Rolfe died lonely and broke in Venice after an unhappy and guilt-ridden affair with a transvestite gondolier.

His friend and patron Benson, by contrast, enjoyed enormous popularity and critical acclaim among Catholics. In 1907, Hilaire

Belloc, who had read and enjoyed Benson's early work judged him 'just the man to write some day a book to give us some sort of idea what happened in England between 1520 and 1560. No book I have ever read has given me the slightest conception, and I have never had time to go into the original stuff myself.'[19] Belloc's remark expresses an unease, common among Catholics at the time, that there were serious shortcomings in English historiography.

It was not Benson but Belloc himself who would accept the challenge of reinterpreting the past from a Catholic perspective. The earlier Catholic historians John Lingard and Lord Acton were decidedly not propagandists – indeed Acton had been a pioneer of a rigorously 'scientific' school of history. But Belloc came to believe that much academic history was fundamentally anti-Catholic and needed a shamelessly Catholic rebuttal. In particular, he charged the historians of the eighteenth and nineteenth century with fabricating a national myth to justify and excuse the Protestant ascendancy. He was keen to refute the notion of 'progress' from the superstition and backwardness supposedly represented by the Middle Ages into the pure light of reason.

For Belloc the medieval period was an age where man was properly oriented towards God and the seasons, and where the Church – in the form of the monasteries – made generous provision for the poor. In a series of books written in the 1920s and '30s he went on to develop an alternative pageant of the past with quite a different cast of heroes and villains than are found in traditional history. Those deemed 'a Good Thing', in the taxonomy of Sellar and Yeatman's *1066 And All That*, would face a radical challenge in Belloc's counter-myths. For generations of Catholics who, directly or indirectly, absorbed Belloc's revisionist line, his ideas would have an important influence in shaping not only their view of their country's history, but often their social and political outlook too.

The key to understanding the Elizabethan Terror and the years of Catholic oppression, Belloc argued, lay in the dissolution of the monasteries. In particular, it was vital to ask *cui bono*? For the wealth seized from the Church did not end up in the hands of ordinary people and little of it swelled the treasury of the Crown. Something like 30 per cent of the economic capacity of England was transferred to a small group of families who already owned 20 per cent of it. A new class of supersquires grew not only in wealth but also in prestige and political influence. Meanwhile, without the monasteries, which had provided land at low rents as well as alms, education and healthcare, the conditions of the poor became immeasurably worse. Many people were uprooted from the land and began to tramp the countryside as beggars. Without the monasteries there was no social infrastructure to assist them.

By the time of Elizabeth I, Belloc calculated, the gangster squire-archy had under its control more than half the wealth of the country. It had also taken over the apparatus of the state. These very same families eventually came to dominate commerce and the professions. They tended to side with Oliver Cromwell during the Civil War (indeed, Cromwell himself was from just such a family) and loaded themselves with yet more booty once they had killed the King and exiled his supporters. Having contrived a Dutch coup in the late 1680s, they set down the conditions of a constitutional monarchy on terms very favourable to themselves, added to their ill-gotten fortunes substantial revenues from slave plantations in the West Indies, and acquired further lands and, in many cases, titles, before going on to dominate public affairs. 'That class,' Belloc wrote in 1936, 'remains to this day the chief enemy of the Catholic Church.'[20] Even now, the very same families Belloc was writing about constitute a potent social force in Britain. We still call them the 'upper classes' and their names are to be found on the letterheads of the leading merchant banks and stockbrokers of the City of London. They still own most of the agricultural land in private hands. Throughout the last century they held many of the senior positions in politics, the armed forces and the Civil Service and the judiciary. They even figure on lists of new dotcom millionaires.

But Belloc was not peddling any class analysis in which events are driven by abstract social and economic forces. He identified – and in his characteristically pugilistic fashion 'dealt with' – the corrupt and evil men he held personally responsible. Thomas Cromwell, instigator of the dissolution of the monasteries, is portrayed as a cynical careerist whose 'only motive was loot . . . perfectly indifferent to religion, an atheist concerned only with this world and therefore utterly without scruple'. William Cecil, Lord Burleigh, was 'one of the vilest men that ever lived', and his son Robert 'a dwarf and a hunchback with an enormous head'.[21] And the inheritance of these guilty men, Belloc believed, remained contaminated. That fusty smell in the air at White's and Pratt's and the other boltholes of the Establishment was the whiff of tainted money.

Belloc did not deny that he was writing a form of propaganda, acknowledging he was a publicist, not an historian. But he believed that the provocative counter-myth he was publicizing was essentially true. 'Though his facts were sometimes wrong, they were never lies,' writes the author of an appreciation of Belloc issued by the Catholic Truth Society; 'it is likely that the extremism of his historical revisionism was calculated for effect . . . his histories are valuable because they stimulated readers to reassess their assumptions'.[22] Belloc's biographer, A. N. Wilson, though a more detached observer, reaches a similar conclusion. 'It is not my purpose to criticize Belloc as a historian. His inaccuracies and defects are obvious. They should not be laughed at too smugly. For in his way he was a pioneer in exposing the fundamental absurdity of the "Whig view of history".' Wilson goes on to quote Hugh Ross Williamson, who confessed shortly after Belloc's death in 1953 that 'Twenty years ago I found it difficult to read him without anger. If my masters, Pollard and Gardiner, were right, Belloc was an inaccurate and tendentious crank . . . my mind was changed not by reading Belloc but by studying sources, which revealed not only the consistent and conscious dishonesty of Pollard and Gardiner but the general rightness of Belloc.'[23]

Belloc's histories are not found on the syllabuses of many Catholic schools today. Since the Second Vatican Council, Catholics have been discouraged from causing offence to other faith communities and Belloc's emphatic style is considered 'inappropriate'. And in a sense, he is no longer needed. Catholic historians have flourished. In the middle part of the century David Knowles, a Benedictine monk at Downside Abbey, produced a three-volume, definitive study of English monasticism and became Professor of Medieval History at Cambridge. In many schools nowadays the set text on Elizabethan England is by the Catholic scholar J. J. Scarisbrick. Eamon Duffy's *The Stripping of the Altars* has more or less rounded off the revisionist project, revealing the aesthetic and liturgical richness of the pre-Reformation church and demonstrating that it was much loved and nothing like so venal as it has been painted. And Felipe Fernandez-Armesto, a self-styled 'Roman Catholic of Tridentine inclinations', can now cheerfully collaborate with the Evangelical Christian Derek Wilson, in an ecumenical study of the Reformation.[24]

But there is more to Catholic history than highlighting facts that have been overlooked by non-Catholics, or exploding Protestant or secular myths. Indeed, though Catholic history will, by definition, be written by Catholics, it need not necessarily be *about* Catholics at all. John Morrill, Vice-Master of Selwyn College, Cambridge, defines a Catholic history as 'one informed by a Catholic understanding of the Incarnation, of a world suffused with the presence of its Creator and Redeemer; but it is a history open to honouring the witness and sanctity of those outside the Catholic tradition'.[25] For the theologian Francesca Murphy too it is a question of sensibility, a quality of imagination and interpretation, an acknowledgement of a presence that the non-Catholic might deny, ignore or simply lack the conceptual apparatus to discern. 'The mark of a Catholic history is a description of a lifting-up of natural human beings and human culture by and toward the Christian spirit. A Catholic historian captures the moment of moral transformation. He is one who can imagine historical events as being to some extent infused with a Christian charism.' Murphy stresses that she is not thinking of the spiritual 'as a gaseous substance, steam-powering the direction of history'. Rather, 'the spirit appears in history in people. The Catholic historian is writing biographies of the Spirit, showing how the moral energies of particular human beings were inventively deployed within projects which allowed history to move one stage upwards.'[26]

The supreme practitioner of this kind of history was Christopher Dawson. He was born in 1889 near Hay-on-Wye in a Tudor house built out of the ruins of a twelfth-century castle. His mother was the daughter of the local Church of England vicar and it was not until 1914, after Oxford, that Dawson became a Catholic, following the example of his best friend, the convert historian and epistemologist E. I. Watkin. But Dawson already had a clear idea of his vocation. In 1909, he had travelled to Rome, where he had fallen under the spell of the Catholic Baroque. Moreover, standing in precisely the same spot where Gibbon had conceived his scheme to record the decline and fall of the Roman Empire, Dawson felt a sudden intimation that God was calling him to be an historian of culture.

Culture, Dawson quickly discovered, was the product of religion; and not the other way about. Religion was the energizing force that built up civilizations, and without which they would swiftly and surely disintegrate. 'The society or culture which has lost its spiritual roots is a dying culture,' he wrote, 'however prosperous it may appear externally.'[27] This perception was one Dawson shared with T. S. Eliot, who invited him to contribute to *Criterion*.

Dawson set out to write his history of civilizations in five volumes. The first in the series, *The Age of the Gods*, was published by John Murray in 1928. A detailed study of the societies of the ancient world, it had taken him almost fifteen years to write. *Progress and Religion*, however, followed only a year later and he had completed *The Making of Europe* by 1932. Soon Eliot was describing Dawson as the most influential thinker in England.

Dawson began his career as a lecturer at Exeter University, but found that anti-Catholic prejudice was a barrier to academic advancement. He took himself out of the university system and supported himself through books, journalism and a small private income. In the late 1950s, he moved to the United States, where he was awarded a chair at Harvard.

Though he lived until 1970, Dawson never completed the five-part history that he planned. His creative attention was distracted in the 1930s by a crisis in Western civilization. Dawson saw that the divorce of religion from social life, a feature of both the totalitarian systems and also of secular liberalism, urgently needed to be addressed. Western man's experiment in living without religion was not working. Dawson set about examining and criticizing the intellectual and historical causes of this secularization. He did not rail impotently against the modern world; nor did he retreat into nostalgia. Dawson's was a message of hope. His early studies of the so-called Dark Ages had shown him that the Catholic faith was capable of transforming the hearts of men, of developing a new consciousness and a new society; and of establishing order and unity. Perhaps it could do the same again.

3

Before the Second Vatican Council (1962–5), Catholics were a much more distinct minority than they are today. The sociologist Michael Hornsby-Smith describes a high degree of social homogeneity among the Catholic community before the council, reinforced by exclusive rules like those discouraging mixed marriages. Bishops and priests commanded a quite extraordinary degree of deference and enforced strict discipline in the Catholic family. Turn out for Mass on Sunday, or Father O'Reilly will be on the doorstep to know the reason why. Catholics socialized within their own clubs and societies, educated their children at Catholic schools and only slowly began to penetrate institutions such as Oxford and Cambridge, the Civil Service and the City. There were two worlds: a Catholic world that was cosy, safe and culturally sequestered, its familial focus epitomized by the weekly magazine *The Catholic Fireside*. Beyond lay enemy territory: hostile, corrupt, a minefield of temptation. The term 'ghetto' has frequently been used to describe the position of Catholics in this period. And for the majority – the Irish immigrants and their offspring in the urban centres – the word is apt. But recent commentators have tended to swap 'fortress' for ghetto, acknowledging that the community's isolation was as much chosen as imposed.

The idea of a fortress suggests continuing hostilities; and though violent anti-Catholicism had abated somewhat by the turn of the twentieth century, there would still be running street fights in Liverpool and Glasgow for another sixty years and more. But new enemies had now emerged. The very idea of religion itself was under attack from atheists, freethinkers and militant apostles of the cult of science. Some Catholics regarded all these as manifestations of the same protean devil. Others, like Belloc, would characterize what he called 'the Modern Mind' as a set of 'mental states, policies, ignorances'; not so much an enemy as 'a series of obstacles, a difficulty of cultural terrain'.[1]

Beneath the turbulent religiosity of nineteenth-century Britain, a tectonic shift had taken place. For the first time in more than a millennium of English Christianity, atheism suddenly became socially and intellectually respectable. This change had come about in just a few decades in response to a series of important scientific discoveries.

In the 1830s, the geologist Sir Charles Lyell showed that the world was many millions of years older than had previously been thought and that it had already been the fate of many species to become extinct. To those who believed that God gave names to all the animals, this was chilling news indeed. Partly at Lyell's prompting, Charles Darwin later supplied his even more radical challenge to the story of creation set out in Genesis. Meanwhile, scholars were discovering that certain biblical texts had been written by more than one hand, sometimes over several generations. Others concluded that the sequence of historical events, or the statistics given for the consumption of quail in the desert, or the number of sons that such-and-such an Old Testament patriarch supposedly begat, simply did not add up. The bastion of belief began to crack. If the Bible were not literally true, Jesus might at best be the subject of an unreliable biography; perhaps merely a character in fiction.

For many, that would do well enough. The narrative of Christ's life, even if legendary or folkloric, was still a good yarn. It taught a system of ethics to keep men's appetites within bounds. It was beautiful, in its way. Around it a religion of a sort could be sustained: a religion of improving Sunday sermons, weddings, christenings, funerals and coronations, observances that marked out a community as civilized. These rituals would preserve social cohesion, and dissipate potentially dysfunctional emotions. It would be a sterile religion, but one conducive to the orderly transaction of commerce and tranquil enjoyment of wealth.

For many of the Victorian and Edwardian bourgeoisie, that was precisely what the Church of England had become. As Matthew Arnold's Sea of Faith continued its 'long, withdrawing roar', religion was increasingly regarded more as a diverting pastime than a substantive truth imposing a set of personal obligations. Simple piety – let alone zeal – became viewed as a mark of eccentricity and religious talk was deemed unfit for a gentleman's dinner table. Earnest discussion of the supernatural was strictly for the clergy, excitable women and Catholics.

For radicals the death of God was a heaven-sent opportunity. Man could be released from the social and moral constraints that prevented him from fulfilling his potential. Free, at last, from superstition and fear, Progress could lengthen its stride. Hegelians and Nietzscheans celebrated the downfall of Catholic 'obscurantism', apparently without irony. Among fashionable intellectuals, religious belief became by 1920 not merely perverse, but pernicious. The sign of the cross – the sure sign of the reactionary – was considered intolerable in a freethinking society. The Bloomsbury Group were among the most vehemently anti-religious of all. In some instances this can be ascribed to childhood trauma. A number of the group were, after all, the walking-wounded of a Clapham Sects upbringing. Maynard Keynes was perhaps affected by the unpleasant experience of being exorcized by the Anglo-Catholic John Capron at Cambridge. Some witnesses to the performance reported seeing a demon flying out of Keynes's mouth. None claimed to see it fly back in.

But all that would come later. The scientific novelties of the mid-nineteenth century did not at first spark militant atheism so much as a non-specific but pervasive doubt of the sort that often afflicts curates in Victorian novels. A faith built on a rock should have been able to sit out the intellectual earthquake. Its shocks do not seem to have registered too alarmingly on Newman's seismograph. He was able to accept the new geology, and was certainly not prepared to maintain – as some Protestant fundamentalists insist even today – that all fossils are part of some elaborate hoax. Instead, he declared himself prepared 'to go the whole hog' with Darwin on evolution.[2]

Newman was keen to head off the threatened polarization of culture that would see religion and science striking mutually antagonistic attitudes. He saw no need for conflict. Theology was a *deductive* science, basing its reasoning upon revelation; whereas physics, biology and so on were *inductive*, arriving at general laws from observed instances. Any contradictions, Newman thought, would be more apparent than real.

Sadly, some scientists were less open-minded. A key date in the mythology of scientism is June 30 1860. It was then that the scientist T. H. Huxley is said to have worsted 'Soapy Sam' Wilberforce, the Anglican Bishop of Oxford, in a debate on Darwin's *Origin of the Species*, exposing the clerical Establishment as dim-witted philistines. According to legend, Wilberforce turned to Huxley during the debate and asked acidly whether it was through his grandfather or grandmother that he claimed descent from a monkey. But even as he paused, no doubt anticipating appreciative applause, the preening prelate was knocked flat by Huxley's riposte: 'If I had to choose between having an ape for a grandfather or a man who would use his great powers of rhetoric to obscure the truth, I should unhesitatingly prefer the ape.'

Though this may not seem particularly funny today, in 1860 it is supposed to have brought the house down. More importantly, it marked a crucial shift in public attitudes. From that day on religion was increasingly seen as the enemy of science and bishops as ignorant boobies who had no place in scientific discussions, which were better left to men of reason.

The truth is that the story is largely an invention. No such exchange was recorded in contemporary accounts of the meeting. Moreover, Wilberforce was not a buffoon but an accomplished scientific commentator in his own right, and one whose arguments were taken particularly seriously by Darwin. Huxley, however, was hungry to develop a reputation and proved an adept self-publicist. He cast himself as the man who had humbled the *ancien régime* in the name of a scientific revolution. Together with a number of like-minded Darwinians he started a dining society known as the 'X-Club' and campaigned relentlessly against religion, and particularly against the Catholic Church, which he held to be an implacable enemy of progress.

Educated Catholics, however, shared the general excitement at the new discoveries and wanted to engage in the controversies they sparked. The polymath St George Mivart was a qualified barrister who became in turn lecturer in anatomy at St Mary's Hospital in Paddington, Professor of Biology at the Catholic University College in Kensington, and Professor of Philosophy at Louvain. On the way, he also qualified in medicine, picked up a pontifical doctorate from Pius IX and became an expert in the classification of primates. Mivart accepted that man had evolved from apes, but had reservations about some aspects of the theory of natural selection. He wrote a response to Darwin in which he raised the famous question of how birds' wings had evolved.

Mivart was trying to reconcile Darwinism with Christian orthodoxy. He proposed, for instance, that though the human body may have evolved, man's intellectual and moral faculties were part of a separately created soul. This was a hypothesis designed to please both the bishops and the scientists. It was not claimed as a truth, but ventured as a possibility. There was plenty more to learn and Mivart wanted to show that the future might supply answers that would satisfy both sides. But Huxley and the Darwinians turned on him, launching a series of vicious attacks on his character and reputation.

Nevertheless, St George Mivart still hoped to show how scientific enthusiasm could coexist with Catholic faith. As a Fellow of the Royal Society, he could command a respectful hearing when he condemned some of the decidedly unscientific extrapolations from evolutionary theory, such as the social Darwinism of Herbert Spencer. He also tried to help the Church understand and adapt to advances in the physical sciences so that it would not repeat the mistake it had made with Galileo.

Consequently, the harsh sanctions ultimately taken against Mivart by the Catholic Church came as a shock to his supporters. After all, the titles of two of his best-known published works, *The Common Frog* and *The Cat*, hardly suggested a candidate for excommunication. But, as has been the case with so many scientists since, Mivart strayed beyond his realm of competence and wrote a series of articles that brought him into direct conflict with the ecclesiastical hierarchy.

Cardinal Vaughan, who had succeeded Manning in 1892, disliked controversial journalism. In 1868, he had become so riled by the *Tablet*'s habit of opening up papal pronouncements to public debate that he bought out the journal's proprietors with his own money and installed himself as editor. He had come by his fortune as the eldest son of an old Herefordshire recusant family, the Vaughans of Courtfield. He was one of thirteen children; five of his siblings were priests and five nuns. As well as their faith and their money, Vaughan inherited from his squirearchical antecedents their Tory politics and a passion for field sports. As a priest, he tended to the ascetic, wearing a gruesome iron-toothed bracelet for the mortification of the flesh. Manning thought Vaughan humourless – and told him so, lending him humorous books to teach him how to laugh.

Grim though he was, Herbert Vaughan was not entirely colourless. In his thirties he had been something of an adventurer, sailing round the Caribbean to raise money for missionaries, helping out during a smallpox epidemic in Panama and spending two years exploring darkest South America. As Bishop of Salford, he bought the Manchester Aquarium, opening it to a paying public. Vaughan was also one of the founders of the League of Catholic Rescue, a charity established to recover Catholic children confined in Protestant orphanages. The Cardinal would appear from time to time trailed by a group of grateful urchins – muddied but winsome – clinging to the hem of his robe. The moppets' favourite outing was to the building site of Westminster Cathedral, where they could always be sure to find a sandpit.

But Vaughan extended no such avuncular indulgence towards Mivart. The trouble began with a theologically controversial article entitled 'Happiness in Hell' in the December 1892 edition of *Nineteenth Century*. Next came a piece criticizing Catholic complicity in the persecution of Dreyfus. Finally, he backed scientific methods against the judgement of bishops in determining questions of fact.

Cardinal Vaughan was not prepared to ignore these provocations. In 1900, he invited Mivart to sign a 'profession of faith' – a document repudiating past errors and agreeing to stick to the orthodox line in future. Mivart declined and was promptly excommunicated. When he died a few months later, Vaughan refused him a Catholic burial. Mivart's friends appealed to the Cardinal to reconsider, pleading that in his final years Mivart had been of unsound mind. Eventually, Vaughan's successor, Cardinal Bourne, accepted this face-saving formula. Three years after his death, St George Jackson Mivart was allowed to go to paradise by way of Kensal Green.

Behind the Church's quarrel with Mivart lay a much wider anxiety about the implications of biblical criticism and interpretation. The Catholic Church had rather less at stake here than Protestants. Catholics prefer a nuanced approach to scripture, resisting the more literal readings often preferred by Protestants. The questionable authorship of particular translations or texts does not necessarily pose insuperable problems. Catholics hold that revelation inheres not in scripture alone, but also in the Tradition – the teachings and example of the Apostles and the early Church, transmitted down the generations. Accordingly, Catholics like Mivart could display self-confidence and panache in their encounters with sceptics and debunkers, secure in the certainty that their Catholic faith was not simply a theory, liable at any time to be exploded by some newly discovered fact. Nevertheless, Rome became noticeably tense as the appetite for novelty began to infiltrate theology, threatening the ruin of dogma.

That tension erupted in the Modernist crisis. At first sight, Catholic Modernism of the late nineteenth and early twentieth centuries was one of those innocuous-seeming heresies that make one wonder why Rome got quite so agitated. It posed no immediate threat of schism; it called for no fundamental change in the style of Catholic worship; and represented a genuinely well-intentioned attempt to square religious observance with contemporary knowledge and philosophy. But it had its roots in a kind of pride, a petty intellectual vanity. So many intelligent people were turning away from the faith that many of those who still clung to it appeared, perhaps as much to themselves as to others, to be doing so against all reason. They craved a smarter argument, a more sophisticated rationale than they believed traditional teaching could at the time supply.

This sense of inadequacy was, not surprisingly, most acutely felt in France, the cradle of the Enlightenment and home to an acerbic atheist tradition. There, the Abbé Alfred Loisy and his colleagues raided earlier German scholarship to devise a new theory of religion, one designed to preserve their own intellectual self-respect while also protecting the Church from the faith-shattering effects of scientific progress. Among this circle, scripture, and indeed all the teachings of the Church were recast as myths, metaphors or symbols. Some connected these outward expressions to a corpus of mysterious, anterior truths to which the myths and symbols were said to correspond; for others the psychological potency of the symbols themselves was enough to make the religious life worth living. The intellectual justification for religion would lie in its consonance with a human craving, communicated in a whisper from deep inside the psyche. God was known not by reason or by external revelation, the Modernists argued, rather through personal religious encounters so intense they enabled individuals to conquer their scepticism.

Modernism was more of a tendency than a programme and it came in many varieties. To its critics, it gave too much emphasis to historical scholarship in determining the theological meaning of scripture, downplaying the interpretative function of the Church itself. It regarded doctrine as something that evolved over time, requiring constant adaptation to the *Zeitgeist*; and it reduced religion to a subjective experience, severing the crucial link with an external world of facts and objective truths. Catholicism is, above all, a *realist* faith.

In 1907, Pope Pius X issued the decree *Lamentabili Sane Exitu*, a list of condemned errors; and the encyclical *Pascendi Domenici Gregis*, a refutation of Modernist dicta. Taken together, these documents represented a ruthless crackdown on Modernism. 'It is not enough to hinder the sale and reading of bad books,' Pius wrote in *Pascendi*; 'it is also necessary to prevent them being published.'

Pope Pius X, born into a poor peasant family, was in the militant tradition of St Peter the Fisherman. St Peter, it may be remembered, was the disciple who took his knife to the ear of one of the soldiers who came to arrest Jesus in the garden of Gethsemane. True, Jesus healed the ear and chided Peter. But this was the same Jesus who legitimized wrathful indignation when, among the upturned tables and flapping doves, he gave the moneychangers a taste of his belt.

According to Pius X, the Modernists should be 'beaten with fists'.[3] He was determined to protect the Deposit of Faith from Modernist taint. Though he promised to keep up a conversation with science and discovery, his initiatives radically altered the intellectual climate within the Catholic community. After 1910, priests were required to take an oath against Modernism, an oath which remained compulsory right up until 1967. The denunciation of deviant colleagues was encouraged. Suspects were questioned by Vigilance Committees in an atmosphere that some found reminiscent of the Inquisition.

One of the leading British Modernists was the Jesuit priest Fr. George Tyrrell. At one time Tyrrell's job was to counsel Catholics experiencing intellectual difficulties with the faith. But increasingly he found himself sharing the anxieties of those who sought his advice. 'When a fairly intelligent priest happens to come into contact with modern doubt, the fabric of his seminary theology collapses like a card-house,' Tyrrell wrote to his Jesuit colleague Fr. John Gerard SJ in 1900.[4]

Tyrrell, though himself a convert, wanted a total re-evaluation of the whole of Catholic teaching. He even wanted the institution of the Catholic Church first to perish, then to rise again. Tyrrell developed an idea of a church which, instead of prescribing doctrines and rules, would simply guide, advise and steer the individual believer. In his own words, such a church would be 'an art-school of Divine Majesty'.[5]

One of Tyrrell's closest collaborators was Friedrich von Hügel.

Of Austro-Scottish extraction, von Hügel was a Baron of the Holy Roman Empire who had settled in Hampstead. Though his name and background suggest a Wilkie Collins villain, the Baron was a profoundly holy man who became – supported by a sizeable private income – one of Britain's foremost theologians. Thanks to an extensive network of Continental correspondents, von Hügel was always kept abreast of developments in his chosen speciality. If, as Pius X said, Modernism was like a venereal disease, then von Hügel was the probable agent of transmission into the English Catholic body.

There is no doubting the sincerity of von Hügel's devotion. He loved God so much that he frequently wept as he prayed. He was dutiful, even scrupulous, in his observance. He was inclined to mysticism. Yet in his social conversation the Baron could scandalize even fellow Modernists with his casual dismissals: of Jesus as nothing but an ignorant and excitable itinerant rabbi; of Mary as 'an unnatural mother' but 'certainly not a virgin'.[6]

Tyrrell's circle included another forthright Modernist, Maude Petre, who was somewhat in love with him. Many – perhaps most – intelligent and attractive Catholic priests form a close relationship with a woman, which, given the context, it would be inappropriate to term 'Platonic'. The French have a phrase for it: *une amitié religieuse*. Even solemn old Cardinal Vaughan had one – with Lady Herbert of Lea. Such friendships typically involve lengthy exchanges of correspondence about religious experience, spiced with clerical and social gossip. Petre had her own dream of a new church, one that would unite all the faiths of the world. Such notions had become increasingly fashionable ever since Swami Vivekenand addressed the World Parliament of Religions in Chicago in 1893. His talk of 'oneness and harmony', of art, science and religion all being different expressions of 'a single Truth . . . ascending to the Spiritual' would become the stock patter of godless New Agers as well as devout syncretists. But those who listened attentively to the Swami's words could even then discern that his message was, at heart, one of atheistic humanism. 'Who can guide you to the Infinite?' the Swami asked; and before the lips of the

Christians among his audience could form the word 'Jesus', the Swami had supplied his own answer: 'Even the hand that comes to you through the darkness will have to be *your own*.'[7]

Von Hügel managed to escape censure – largely because he had written vigorously against 'immanentism', another strain of Modernist heresy. But Tyrrell was not so lucky. After a long battle with the authorities, he was eventually excommunicated.

Tyrrell accused early medieval popes of inventing the powers and prerogatives of the papacy and of falsifying the documents of the early Church to justify their new privileges. He called for the whole ecclesiastical edifice to be demolished. To his friends and allies he was a tragic figure brought down by a singular passion for truth. To his opponents he was destroyed by the sin of pride, insisting upon the primacy of his own ideas over the legitimate authority of the Church. When he died, unreconciled, in 1909, Tyrrell was also denied a Catholic burial, provoking an unholy public row between Maude Petre and Dr Amigo, the Bishop of Southwark.

Maude Petre was excommunicated in her turn, but paid absolutely no attention to the ban, resolutely continuing to attend Mass. She came from an old, upper-class Catholic family – the Petres of Ingatestone Hall in Essex. In her tradition, the clergy were guests in the house and expected to behave accordingly.

It was partly because of the Modernist crisis that the Church retreated into its fortress, lowering the portcullis against subversive novelty. In the minds of non-Catholics, it was now seen as the enemy not just of theological Modernism, but of modernity in all its manifestations. Catholics stood for deference to tradition and authority, and for stubborn resistance to change.

To many, this made the institution all the more attractive: a rock of enduring principle amid the flux. And this obduracy did not deter converts. 'I came into the Church . . . in a white heat of orthodoxy', wrote one convert who became a Catholic priest in 1919, 'and when I took the anti-Modernist oath, it was something of a disappointment that the Vicar-General was not there to witness the fervour I put into it – he had gone out to order tea.'[8] Even as the clergy were keeping their heads down, lay converts emerged as the most vocal Catholic champions. During the first half of the twentieth century Britain's Catholic writers, artists and intellectuals would build what amounted to 'a Catholic party'. This was not a political party but a social *bloc* with a distinct and challenging voice in the national conversation. Catholicism would no longer be the private religion of a minority. It would become a cultural force: a powerful critique of the modern world and all its errant ways.

After William Shakespeare and Oscar Wilde, Gilbert Keith Chesterton is probably the most quoted writer in Britain, yet his books are hardly read. Behind his store of one-liners, adaptable to almost any rhetorical occasion, lies a substantial body of writing that remained largely ignored during the second half of the twentieth century.

This may soon change as Ignatius Press, a US-based publisher, issues his collected works in forty-eight volumes in anticipation of a worldwide revival. In 1974, a Canadian, Ian Boyd, launched an International Chesterton Society and today corresponding societies meet in cities across the United States and Canada as well as in France, Germany, Poland, Lithuania, Australia and even Japan – where a fifteen-volume translation of Chesterton's work had sold more than 50,000 copies. Since the mid-1990s Chesterton has become a cult figure on the Internet, with the online magazine *Gilbert!* and a dozen other websites devoted to Chesterton studies. Britain has its own G. K. Chesterton Library, founded by Aidan Mackey under the auspices of the Centre for Faith and Culture in Oxford.

The survival of Chesterton's literary reputation in spite of mainstream critical disregard owes a good deal to the great Argentinian writer Jorge Luis Borges. As a master of twentieth-century letters, Borges's acknowledgement of Chesterton as an important influence has proved the secular equivalent of an *imprimatur*. Rehabilitation, though, is proving a slow process. Some American universities have begun to take Chesterton's writing seriously once again, yet it is still neglected in most British syllabuses despite the author's revived celebrity overseas.

Chesterton has become so widely admired in Borges's homeland that in the early 1990s a group of Buenos Aires notables approached Cardinal Hume with a plan to have him beatified, the first step towards sainthood. This unexpected proposal cited Chesterton's contribution to 'rebuilding the Catholic imagination and sensitivity of England'.[9]

Whether or not he was a saint will take many years and the painstaking investigation of at least two miracles to determine. What is not in doubt is that Chesterton was, as Cardinal Carter of Toronto once declared, a 'true prophet'.[10] He accurately foresaw the disastrous consequences of many of the ideas and ideologies fashionable in the early part of the century. Racialism, eugenics, Fascism, socialism and unrestrained capitalism all developed much as Chesterton predicted they would before his death in 1936.

Chesterton would have been embarrassed to hear the Cardinal's tribute. He saw himself as a humble, jobbing journalist, even though he also wrote essays, novels, criticism, biography, history, apologetics, social philosophy and poetry. Though even his staunchest supporter, Hilaire Belloc, would later gloss over the verse when appraising Chesterton's contribution to literature, slyly excusing himself as 'fastidious' in such matters, the poems were compulsory reading for Catholics. One collection ran to fifteen editions. An epic tale of battle on the high seas, *Lepanto*, remained for many years a classroom favourite with boys. The Catholic writer, Paul Johnson, can still recite it as a party piece ('Don John of Austria has gone by Alcala . . .'), having first learned the poem by heart for an elocution competition at Stonyhurst.

Liberal opinion today might frown on this spirited celebration of biffing Johnny Turk and on Chesterton's sympathy with the Crusaders. And there is no denying that most of Chesterton's anthologized verse – *The Rolling English Road* and so forth – chiefly appeals to romantic conservatives in the English shires.

When the independent 'anti-sleaze' candidate Martin Bell read from *The Secret People* during his victory speech at Tatton on the night of the 1997 general election, it appeared for a moment that Chesterton was at last being rescued from the reactionary camp.

(Bell is a confirmed Chesterton buff and has delivered the annual Chesterton Society lecture.) But before long, reports began to surface that *The Secret People* was one of Margaret Thatcher's favourites too. The idea that 'the people of England have never spoken yet' was one that cried out to be appropriated by a populist politician who wanted to evoke the mute assent of some 'silent majority', particularly ahead of a referendum on a European single currency. But anyone reading the poem all the way through would discover that its theme is the historic taint in English society identified in Hilaire Belloc's indictment of the ruling class. Chesterton remarks how, at the dissolution of the monasteries, 'the gold of the King's servants rose higher every day' as they destroyed the social security system supplied by the religious orders:

> They burnt the homes of the shaven men, that had been quaint and
>   kind,
> Till there was no bed in a monk's house, nor food that man could
>   find.
> The inns of God where no man paid, that were the wall of the weak,
> The King's servants ate them all. And still we did not speak.

In subsequent stanzas the larcenous squirearchy get their comeuppance, finding themselves in hock to lawyers and moneylenders and haunted by revenant monks. Finally, the landed upper class yields to a bureaucracy whose 'loveless pity is worse than the ancient wrongs', and civil disorder marks 'God's scorn for all men governing'.[11] It is hard to believe that Margaret Thatcher would endorse a single one of the sentiments expressed in this poem if she properly understood them.

The idea that he was in any sense a 'conservative' was one that Chesterton always indignantly rebutted. It was the function of progressives, he observed, to make mistakes; that of conservatives to prevent those mistakes being corrected.

The first great campaign of Chesterton's public life was fought against British imperialism in South Africa. Chesterton was introduced to Hilaire Belloc in a Soho restaurant in 1900. The Mont

Blanc was a regular haunt of opponents of the Boer War. Many were pacifists, but Chesterton and Belloc (who were not) found themselves united in moral revulsion against a conflict they saw as chiefly serving the interests of financiers in the City. The public consensus favouring the war, amounting to a bloodthirsty bellicosity, was something both men found distasteful. 'What I hated about it,' Chesterton wrote in his *Autobiography*, 'was its confidence, its congratulatory anticipations, its optimism of the Stock Exchange. I hated its vile assurance of victory . . . The note struck from the beginning was the note of the inevitable; a thing abhorrent to Christians and lovers of liberty.'[12]

Chesterton was twenty-six and Belloc thirty when they met. Right from the outset of their friendship the older man exercised a profound influence on the younger's thinking, providing a solid grounding in historical analysis for Chesterton's airily romantic conception of the past, and guiding him subtly, but relentlessly towards Catholicism.

Chesterton canvassed for the Liberals in the general elections of 1902 and 1906. In the latter contest, Belloc was the Liberal candidate in South Salford, a predominantly Nonconformist Protestant district. The party agent was keen to keep his candidate's religion from surfacing as an issue in the campaign. His professional instinct was never to mention it; but Belloc chose to address the problem directly. 'I am a Catholic,' he announced one day on the hustings. 'As far as possible I go to Mass every day. This is a rosary. As far as possible I kneel down and tell these beads every day. If you reject me on account of my religion, I shall thank God that He has spared me the indignity of being your representative.'[13] He was elected.

Within a year, however, his ally Chesterton was attacking the Liberals over the sale of honours. Political corruption became another issue on which the two friends would make common cause. In Parliament, Belloc began to press for greater transparency in party donations. The Liberals' response was to deselect him as a candidate for the election of 1910; but Belloc fought and won Salford as an Independent. However he soon withdrew from parliamentary politics, after lecturing the members of the Commons on their own impotence. A parliamentary seat, he told them, was utterly worthless because an oligarchy of plutocrats controlled the leadership of both main parties, decided all senior appointments and, through the Whips, rigged the votes of the House.

As soon as he was out of Parliament Belloc unleashed a fusillade of books, articles and pamphlets arguing for an end to this scandalous carve-up through wholesale reform of the party system. But nowhere would he better encapsulate the shameless nepotism and squalid political fixing than in his cautionary tale for children *Lord Lundy*:

> We had intended you to be
> The next prime minister but three:
> The stocks were sold; the press was squared:
> The Middle Class was quite prepared . . .[14]

Belloc left the Commons to join Chesterton in Fleet Street. Together with his brother Cecil, Chesterton founded a newspaper, *The Eye Witness*, in June 1911. Belloc became its editor. After twelve months the backer went bankrupt and the paper had to be relaunched as *The New Witness*, with Cecil Chesterton at the helm. According to G. K. Chesterton's biographer, Maisie Ward, the paper's twin aims were 'To fight for the Liberty of Englishmen against an increasing enslavement to a plutocracy; and to expose and combat corruption in public life.'[15] Belloc's most recent biographer, A. N. Wilson, offers a more jaundiced interpretation of the group's motives. 'It was,' he says, 'trying to establish an alternative source of power to that of Westminster, to substitute government by a clique of well-born or wealthy families with government by a posse of journalists.'[16]

Not long after the paper was established, the Marconi scandal broke. Some of the most powerful men in Britain had become involved in insider dealing on the stock market. Marconi's managing director, Godfrey Isaacs, had signed a draft agreement with the Postmaster General, Herbert Samuel, to set up and operate radio stations throughout the Empire for a fat fee. Neither the public nor

Parliament had been told the terms of this contract when Isaacs began selling shares in Marconi's American affiliate to a group of politicians. The purchasers included the Chief Whip of the Liberal government; David Lloyd George, Chancellor of the Exchequer; and the Attorney General – Isaac's own brother, Rufus. The shares were sold at a preferential price before the general public was allowed to subscribe, and were sure to be traded at a considerable premium. The transaction smelled very like a bribe, a pay-off to the politicians who had awarded Marconi the contract in the first place. The press posse saddled up and followed the money trail.

Two court cases and one parliamentary inquiry later, the politicians had got clean away with it. Rufus Isaacs was made Lord Chancellor – much to the disgust of Rudyard Kipling, who wrote his poem 'Gehazi' to mark the occasion. Cecil Chesterton, who had made the mistake of widening his allegations to encompass some of Isaacs's previous business deals, was convicted of criminal libel. Disillusioned with the Liberal Party, Belloc and G. K. Chesterton turned away from Westminster to develop a more innocent politics of their own.

But their project would be interrupted by a series of personal tragedies. Belloc's wife Elodie died in 1914. As a young man he had walked all the way across the United States, from New York to California, to propose to her. He would remain in mourning every day of the forty years he outlived her. During the First World War Belloc also lost his son Louis. Chesterton lost his brother Cecil.

Already, in their critiques of capitalism and socialism, particularly in Belloc's *The Servile State*, they were beginning to develop the outline of a 'Third Way', which in the 1920s would become widely known as Distributism – a social philosophy which called for the widest possible sharing-out of capital among the people. A Distributist utopia would be one where every agricultural worker was a smallholder, every town-dweller a self-employed artisan, shopkeeper or professional. Where mass production could not be avoided, it would be organized on a co-operative basis with every worker having a stake in the business. Distributism was opposed to exploitative capitalism and statist socialism alike; its core values were human dignity and liberty, which Chesterton saw as essentially the same thing. 'Three acres and a cow' might have been the movement's proud slogan, had it not become the sneer of its detractors.

In the United States, an abortive attempt was made to put Distributist ideas into practice by Dorothy Day, Peter Maurin and their collaborators in the Catholic Worker Movement in the 1930s. Maurin 'translated' many of the works of Chesterton and Belloc into easily read synopses for America's urban poor and preached a specifically Catholic brand of social action. 'The only way to go to the roots is to bring religion into education, into politics, into business,' he insisted. 'To bring religion into the profane is the best way to take the profanity out of the profane.'[17] In the emergency conditions of the Depression, however, the Catholic radicals found themselves increasingly side-tracked into conventional charity work before being upstaged by Franklin Roosevelt's New Deal.

In Britain, Distributism became a home of lost causes. In the twenties, it championed the rights of allotment holders when the state compulsorily bought up their land for housing development. It was also on the side of the 'pirate' bus drivers in London (most of them were war veterans who had bought their vehicles with their demob money) when they tried to break the near-monopoly of the London Omnibus Company. Though it never really took off as a viable political project in its own right, a Distributist strand did develop in each of the main political parties. From council-house sales to industrial democracy, from popular share-holding to interventionist strategies for inner-city regeneration, one can trace the enduring influence of this early attempt to reconcile individual liberty with social justice.

Underpinning the idea of the Distributists was the social teaching of the Catholic Church as set out in Pope Leo XIII's encyclical *Rerum Novarum* of 1891. This document, although anathematizing class struggle and unambiguously affirming the inviolability of private property, was nevertheless condemned as 'socialist' by the more reactionary sections of the non-Catholic European bourgeoisie. It enumerated some basic workers' rights (coal miners and quarry hands were entitled to a shorter working week to compensate for the arduous nature of their work) and controversially endorsed the principle of 'combination' – whereby workers could organize themselves into collective bodies to bargain for better pay and conditions. *Rerum Novarum* reminded governments of their obligation to promote the interests of the poor, informed employers that 'It is shameful and inhuman to treat men like chattels to make money by' and instructed priests to strive for the good of the people. The Catholic Church was the only international organization of any size or consequence at this time. It could command the allegiance of large numbers of people in all the developed countries. In issuing such an encyclical the Pope was putting both capitalists and socialists on notice that the Church did not intend to confine itself to a set of narrowly ecclesiastical concerns.

Radical as all this may have been at the turn of the century, much of the language of the encyclical now seems quaint. *Rerum Novarum* was conceived when industrialization was a relatively novel phenomenon and its prose is saturated with a wistful yearning for a vanished, bucolic past. Anxious to divert Catholic workers from socialist trade unions, it holds up the medieval guild system as a somewhat implausible model of employer–employee co-operation for modern industrial society.

Some critics detect a similar difficulty with G. K. Chesterton's own medievalism. He ornamented even his topical journalism with images of elves from faeryland, Crusaders and castles, tabards, tourneys and so forth. None of this made much sense to modern men who, like H. G. Wells, preferred to find beauty in turbines. Yet Chesterton was no Kenelm Digby, no Ambrose Phillipps de Lisle. His fanciful imagery may have irritated as many readers as his sometimes over-clever paradoxes, but he was not engaged in aesthetic posturing, nor was it his aim to revive the tropes of the high point of Christendom in the same way as Pugin had revived its architectural styles.

What at first glance may appear anachronistic or just plain silly in Chesterton's writing usually repays patient consideration. For most of us, the language of imagination is constantly being revised. We grow out of one vocabulary as we grow out of school uniform. We discard another, and then another, as fashions change. Chesterton threw nothing out. He never lost childhood's innocence, or its clarity of perception. The performances in the toy theatre that had been his earliest plaything were still vivid to him at fifty. He had a rare integrity of mind where infancy and adulthood, yesterday and today, real life and imagination, this world and the next were fused in every moment. The flow of imagery, too, rolled on from childhood through to death with nothing discarded.

Though the Modern Mind was busy declaring a complete secession from the past, Chesterton allowed it to live on in him. Modernity denied tradition; Chesterton affirmed its legitimacy, calling it 'the democracy of the dead'.[18]

On the day of his marriage Chesterton stopped at a shop and drank a pint of milk as a ritual act to connect that special day to the countless others on which he had, as a boy, called at the same shop with his mother. He next visited a gun dealer and purchased a revolver to protect his new bride from the pirates he feared might infest their honeymoon destination – the Norfolk Broads. The Modern Mind may find such behaviour utterly risible, remaining oblivious to any poignancy, humour or symbolic significance in the gesture. But to the extent that one is prepared first to allow oneself to be charmed by such whimsies and then to learn to see a glimpse of a faery world in all creation, so one approaches that Catholic sensibility that it was Chesterton's vocation to revive and renew.

Chesterton's medievalism was not nostalgic; it was a metaphorical tool. He used the glories of long ago to mock the dreary deficiencies of the modern. His own declared fondness for the medieval guilds was not, like Pope Leo's, a doomed fancy to re-establish anachronistic institutions; rather a shorthand by which he could reassert the human values those societies had once represented. If H. G. Wells celebrated the mechanical, conjuring up a vista of exciting possibilities to be achieved through scientific progress, Chesterton saw the power of machines to grind down the human soul. Modernity might provide food and shelter, but it denied another essential sustenance. If the spiritually half-starved seemed to look backwards to the Middle Ages, it was not out of a sentimental attachment to the past but as 'thirst can remember water and hunger remember bread'.[19]

The new mechanistic, materialist philosophies, as rhythmically plangent as the factory production lines themselves, seemed to Chesterton both dangerous and dull. A jolly and flamboyant man, he loved to spend his evenings at public meetings jousting with Determinists – who denied free will to man – or Rationalists who would credit only what was as self-evident as an elaborated syllogism. Sometimes, for light relief, he would take on Spiritualists, Theosophists, food-faddists and Fabians. He found modern creeds either irritatingly solemn or charmingly batty. It was his particular gift to pinpoint clownish absurdities in the solemn ones, and discover malign tendencies in the batty.

Many evil projects were championed in the name of modernity during this period. H. G. Wells would quite cheerfully have slaughtered all disabled people – indeed all stupid people – for the sake of improving the quality of the gene pool. Catholics are still mocked for the Church's fuddy-duddy opposition to the introduction of IQ tests early in the twentieth century, but the reason for the objection – a perfectly understandable apprehension about the uses to which they might be put by the likes of Wells – tends to be overlooked.

In the early part of the century, people who styled themselves 'liberal' were in the vanguard of campaigns for the compulsory sterilization of the 'feebleminded' and it was the view of some 'progressives' that a man and woman should be forbidden to marry and have children if either had a history of serious physical illness. Chesterton parodied this latter enthusiasm in his story of the Good Eugenicist, who breaks off his engagement when his fiancée crashes her bicycle.

Racism, today regarded almost exclusively as a vice of the political right, was then – as 'scientific racialism' – another progressive cause. The Catholic intellectual Christopher Dawson was the first to argue that races were constructs of cultures rather than cultures expressions of races, and Chesterton sounded one of the earliest warnings of the perils of allowing pseudo-scientific notions of racial superiority to fuse with German nationalism.

It was against such pernicious doctrines, whose champions always sought to justify them with dispassionate logic and appeals to science, that Chesterton fought throughout his career. If he were alive today he would no doubt be in the vanguard of the campaigns against genetically modified food and human cloning. He himself embodied a generous and expansive humanity. He was plump and pink and convivial; his opponents – like their ideas – were gloomy, lean and ascetic. The fuller man would usually trounce them in debate.

The rented halls in which these tournaments took place were the television and radio studios of the time. They enabled the public to see the men behind the newspaper bylines as they matched their wits in mediated contest. A sell-out was guaranteed when Chesterton was pitted against the Fabian dramatist George Bernard Shaw. The two men appeared unable to agree about anything (Shaw was abstemious, vegetarian and atheist), yet they became close friends. Though he would pepper his conversation with anti-Catholic provocations, and signed his letters to Chesterton with teasing postscripts such as 'To hell with the Pope!' Shaw was always welcomed among Chesterton's largely Catholic circle of friends. Shaw was determined to make Chesterton a playwright. Though he met only limited success in this ambition – Chesterton's play *Magic* – the pair did find more fruitful ground for collaboration. Their polemical rivalry helped catalyse a new awareness of the desperate condition of the poor. Shaw and Chesterton – the Social-ist and the Distributist – conspired to bring about an earthquake that would vividly impress the realities of poverty upon the bour-geois mind. They disagreed, of course, on what to do about it. Bernard Shaw wanted to give the poor money; Chesterton wanted to give them power.

By the early 1920s, Chesterton was one of the most famous men in Britain. His books, his columns and his public appearances had made him what we would call a media celebrity today. Together with Belloc (who was enjoying a similar renown), Chesterton steadfastly resisted the pull of Establishment institutions and the drift of fashionable ideas. A new title, *G. K.'s Weekly*, became from 1925 the vehicle for their joint campaigns and the main organ of the Distributist movement. In lean times the paper was kept going by the profits earned by Chesterton's fictional detective Father Brown – a character based on Fr. John O'Connor, a priest from Bradford who was a regular guest of the Chestertons at their house in Beaconsfield. Fr. O'Connor's experience in the confessional had made him an expert not only in the psychology of sinners, but also in many of the stratagems of criminal enterprise. Chesterton was fascinated by this clerical worldliness. 'That the Catholic Church knew more about good than I did was easy to believe. That she knew more about evil than I did seemed incredible.'[20]

In 1922, Chesterton finally joined the Catholic Church himself. His brother Cecil had converted at the beginning of the Marconi affair; most of his friends and colleagues – Belloc, the novelist Maurice Baring, the Wilfred Wards – were Catholics too. So, in his heart, had Chesterton been for many years. When he had fallen dangerously ill in 1914, Fr. O'Connor was summoned to what he expected to be Chesterton's deathbed. From that time on there was an unspoken understanding between Chesterton, his wife Frances and the priest that he would one day become a Catholic. Some of his friends have ventured even earlier dates for some sort of inner conversion – perhaps 1908, when *Orthodoxy*, his first great work of Christian apologetics, was published.

So why the delay? *Orthodoxy* represents a view of Christianity that few Catholics would quarrel with. So Chesterton's reservations were not about matters of dogma. But he represented a certain quirky strain of Englishness – Samuel Johnson perhaps epitomizes the tradition – which felt an instinctual suspicion of foreign ways. Chesterton spent many years consulting priests, friends and his wife, Frances. His dilemma was finally resolved, on Belloc's advice, by imploring the intercession of the Virgin Mary. Chesterton's readiness to do this supports the view that he had been a 'cultural Catholic' for some time. It is often the case with converts that they experience the moment of reception not as a departure in a new direction, but rather as journey's end, a sense of coming home at last.

Shaw was appalled by Chesterton's move. The teachings of the Church 'do not strike on the knowledge box of the modern intellectual', he wrote in a letter to Chesterton in early 1923. 'I believe that you would not have become a professed official Catholic if you did not believe that you believe in Transubstantiation; but I find it impossible to believe that you believe in Transubstantiation . . . You will have to go to confession next Easter; and I find the spectacle – the box, your portly kneeling figure . . . all incredible, monstrous, comic, though of course I can put a perfect literary complexion on it in a brace of shakes.'[21]

Shaw was wrong in underestimating the power of Christian ideas to penetrate the knowledge box of the contemporary intellectual. The mid-twenties would see the beginning of a revival of religion among the intelligentsia that would gain impressive momentum. In 1927, T. S. Eliot was baptized into the Church of England, to the chagrin of Bloomsbury. At around the same time C. S. Lewis was heading in the same direction. Lewis acknowledged that he was shocked out of his atheism by Chesterton's *The Everlasting Man*, published in 1925. For Lewis and Eliot, religion would have a direct effect on the future direction of their work, as it would for Graham Greene, who converted to Catholicism in 1926, and Evelyn Waugh, who became a Catholic in 1930. But the very fact of these conversions had a more immediate impact. It signalled that the etiquette of the intellectual class had changed. It was no longer a serious solecism to believe in the supernatural. By the time W. H. Auden declared himself a Christian in 1940, it was not even particularly remarkable.

Much of the drive behind the revival of religious ideas in the 1920s came from an ever widening Catholic network centred on the 'Chesterbelloc' – the Shavian tag for this 'double-headed pantomime elephant'.[22] A leading member of their circle was the letterist and sculptor Eric Gill, who had founded a community of craftsmen at Ditchling in Sussex in 1907. When he became a Catholic six years later the project began to take on a religious flavour, and reconstituted itself as the Guild of St Joseph and St Dominic, a community of Dominican Tertiaries. The members practised the simple life, being self-sufficient in food and even fabrics for clothing. The various artists and craftsmen would set aside their work at the prescribed hours to meet in the chapel and sing the daily office according to the monastic rule. Visitors would come by the coachload to gawk at these strange, bearded men in their dusty smocks at Vespers.

The Ditchling community included Hilary Pepler, who ran the St Dominic's Press – whose books were hand-printed on hand-made paper; the painter, Philip Hagreen; the weaver Valentine KilBride; the engraver Desmond Chute, and various stone-cutters, metalworkers and silversmiths. Apart from Gill himself, the most talented member of the commune was David Jones, who became well known as a painter, illustrator, poet, critic and theoretician of Catholic aesthetics, and was described by Kenneth Clark as the best watercolourist since Blake.

The Ditchling community's spiritual guide was the Dominican Fr. Vincent McNabb. The motto of the Dominican order is '*Veritas*,' and as primarily a preaching order, its commitment is to communicating important truths. Ditchling was about preaching by example. The Guild's members were not just opposed to commercialism; they were living out its alternative. Fr. McNabb did the same. He would tramp enormous distances rather than take any form of modern transport, sometimes walking from Leicestershire to London to deliver his copy to Chesterton's desk. Fr. McNabb did not post his articles because he always had another appointment in town. He had a lively slot at Speakers' Corner in Hyde Park, with regular hecklers sent along by the Rationalist Association. Every movement has its fundamentalists and Eric Gill and Fr. McNabb became Distributism's fundamentalists.

Gill had arrived at Catholicism with a head full of Nietzsche and Marx. He would always remain a man of the left and in the 1930s was regarded as a Communist by the Church authorities. He had been radicalized in the usual way: he was beaten up by the police in Whitehall while taking part in an orderly procession to hand in a petition at 10 Downing Street. Like many others who have shared that political baptism, Gill was more articulate in his denunciations than in his manifestos. He detested the modern capitalist economy. He despised industrialism. He regarded the upper classes and bankers with an equal loathing and had a Bellocian scorn for politicians. Indeed, it had been Belloc's writing that first led Gill to question his Fabianism and search for an alternative code to live by.

Gill's conversion to Catholicism was as much as anything the simple acknowledgement of an affinity. He found the Church's ideas surprisingly similar to his own. 'I invented a new religion,' he wrote in his autobiography, 'and then discovered it was an old one.'[23]

Soon after his conversion the Church authorities awarded Gill the commission to carve the Stations of the Cross for Westminster Cathedral. Having completed the job and, as he saw it, set the style, Gill began to lambast the bishops for their poor taste. The other decorations in the cathedral were too gaudy; the plaster saints in parishes up and down the country were sickly and sentimental. Gill felt he was fulfilling a sacred trust, one described by Patrick Allitt as 'trying to do for Catholic art what Newman and Chesterton did for Catholic literature and Pugin for architecture: to elevate its standards and give Catholicism aesthetic pride of place in British life'.[24] In the mid-twenties Gill, who held a 7 per cent shareholding in *G. K.'s Weekly*, became the paper's art critic, and with David Jones championed the importance of the sacramental and transformatory in the making of art. Jones challenged the tendency to empty out meaning from art and obliterate symbolic resonance. He particularly inveighed against self-expression, which he said was as undesirable in the painter or the writer as it is in the carpenter or the cook.

Gill left Ditchling after a few years, with Jones in tow, and tried to repeat the experiment, first at Capel-y-ffin in Wales and later at Piggotts in Buckinghamshire. Gill's former assistant, Desmond Chute, would abandon the simple life and become a priest. Being very rich – his family owned the Prince's Theatre in Bristol – he was able to be ordained on his own patrimony. This meant that he received no salary from the Catholic Church, but was free to live how and where he chose and did not have to take orders from any local bishop. Chute took himself off to Rapallo, Italy, where he set up a literary and artistic salon and became a friend of Ezra Pound and Max Beerbohm. Ditchling, rather amazingly, struggled on into the late 1980s.

Eric Gill's work remains familiar to the British public mostly through his typeface, Gill Sans Serif, used on the London Underground and in the logo of the BBC; and for his statues on the façade of Broadcasting House in London. It is remarkably hard to spot any religious significance in the Broadcasting House work, yet the artist claimed he had outfoxed the Corporation's managers. They commissioned him to carve Prospero and Ariel from *The Tempest*; but Gill had his own ideas. 'It didn't seem to me unduly straining the play to see in the figure of Prospero much more than a clever old magician, or in the figure of Ariel more than a silly fairy. I took it upon me to carve God the Father and God the Son. Even if that were not Shakespeare's meaning, it ought to have been the BBC's.'[25]

When Gill was invited to carve an enormous frieze for the foyer of the League of Nations building in Geneva, his first choice of theme was the turning-out of the moneychangers from the temple. 'That more than anything was what the League of Nations should be engaged upon,' he told his patrons, '– ridding from Europe and the world the stranglehold of finance.'

Unsurprisingly, the idea was received coldly, not just by his Swiss hosts, but by the American delegation as well. His plan was vetoed – with the excuse that so Christian a theme would upset the Jews and the Turks. But when Gill adamantly refused to carve anything secular, it was agreed that he could choose something from the Old Testament. 'So I proceeded along those lines and the result is there. In the middle of that monstrous exhibition of dead architecture and pseudo-modernity is a colossal representation of the recreation of Adam with a great text proclaiming the overmastery of God, and in smaller side-panels, children and animals echoing the same sentiment.'[26]

Both these examples hint at a kind of desperation on Gill's part, a railing against the dying of the religious light in art. For all their own successes, neither Eric Gill nor David Jones stimulated any great movement or succeeded in changing the course on which art was already set. Any idea of art as 'service' or as a channel of divine grace would remain unfashionable for the rest of the century. Indeed, the world of the visual arts would be at best an uneasy no-man's land, and most of the time, enemy territory for those wishing to advance the Catholic idea.

In 1991, Fiona MacCarthy published a biography of Eric Gill that revealed astonishing details of the artist's sex life, including diary records of incest. Subsequent commentators have connected these crimes with an idea put into Gill's head by the American monk Ambrose Holly. 'Cast all things on to the rock that is Christ' is a respectable theological proposition, drawn from the sixth-century Rule of St Benedict. For Gill, however, it became a spiritual ruse, a way of transcending feelings of self-disgust and self-reproach by pretending he was making a gift of his sins to Christ. Sex and religion became hideously confused as Gill convinced himself that the basest acts could be rescued from their exploitative or egotistical functions simply by being offered up as acts of 'thanksgiving' or 'celebration'. Gill's twin obsessions were the enduring subject of his work. Fr. McNabb was scandalized by an erotically charged portrayal of Christ embracing his Church. And Gill's 1923 engraving *The Nuptials of God*, produced for a commemorative card to mark the ordination of the Dominican Gerald Vann, showed the crucified Christ embraced by a naked woman.

MacCarthy's revelations coincided with a surge in public concern over the sexual abuse of minors. The Catholic Church was involved, with a number of priests facing allegations of pederasty. A group of Catholic women called for Gill's Stations of the Cross to be ripped out of Westminster Cathedral, on the grounds that they were 'paedophile art'.

Catholics were divided between those who wanted the Church to make some dramatic show of solidarity with the victims of abuse, and those who thought that tearing apart the fabric of a cathedral as a gesture to appease the media would be both cynical and futile. Auberon Waugh toured the television and radio studios pointing out that if the work of every sexual deviant were to be removed from public view the nation's art galleries would be virtually bare.

In his memoirs, the publisher Tom Burns, a close friend of Gill, recalled a story David Jones told him about a trip the two artists had made to Jerusalem. One day Jones was watching from his hotel-room window as Gill came up the street and saw him stop beside a leper squatting on the pavement. Gill, unaware that he was being observed, gave the man some money and then took him in both hands and kissed his face. 'That,' wrote Burns, 'puts paid to critics of his morals.'[27]

The universities offered more fertile ground for the Catholic revival than the world of the visual arts. Most Catholics had been prevented from attending university during the penal years. Only a few, such as George Petre who went up to Cambridge with a personal chaplain in tow, could afford the fines levied for non-attendance at Church of England services. But even after legal impediments were removed in the 1850s Catholics were warned off Oxbridge by their own bishops, who were afraid they would lapse. It was not until 1896, when ambitious plans for a Catholic university failed to mature, that Cardinal Vaughan relaxed his prohibition.

Hilaire Belloc took a first-class degree in modern history at Balliol in the 1890s and went on to sit the examination for All Souls. The selection procedure for this all-graduate college required a candidate to write a series of original essays, translate passages from three or four languages, and satisfy the fellows over dinner that he had decent table manners and a gift for conversation. Belloc possessed the necessary intellectual and linguistic abilities required for a fellowship, and certainly knew how to dispose of the cherry stones in his pudding. But, to his own great surprise, he was turned down.

He blamed anti-Catholic prejudice for his rejection – something he had recklessly invited by sitting his papers with a statue of the Virgin Mary on the desk – and he may have been right. Some years later an Anglican bishop objected to the admission of a Jew to All Souls, arguing that the college was exclusively a Church of England institution. But Belloc did hold very firm views and tended to express them forcefully. Most likely, he passed the exam but failed the dinner – his manner, as much as his Catholicism, alienating the dons, who were hardly able to get a word in edgeways.

Belloc subsequently failed to win a fellowship at his own college, Balliol. Once again he blamed anti-Catholic sentiment. But on this occasion he was probably wrong as Balliol became, in 1896, the first college to elect a Catholic fellow since the reign of James II. Francis Urquhart was, moreover, the first Catholic to be awarded both an undergraduate scholarship and a fellowship since the Reformation.

'Sligger' Urquhart was a social don. In his rooms friendships were forged and cliques took shape. His conspiritorial gatherings would be remembered by generations of undergraduates, as Graham Greene put it, 'down to the last draught of dry sherry'.[28] Among those who fell under Sligger's influence over the years were the old-Etonian son of the Bishop of Manchester, Ronald Knox, the cleverest undergraduate of his generation; the future prime minister Harold Macmillan; his friend Guy Lawrence, who would become a Catholic before being killed in the First World War; and the Catholic writer Christopher Hollis.

Knox, who converted in 1917 and became a Catholic priest two years later, joined the Chesterbelloc set in London before returning to serve as Catholic Chaplain at Oxford in 1926, Sligger Urquhart having discreetly contrived his appointment. During his thirteen years in the post, Knox established himself as the best-known priest in Britain through his journalism, books and broadcasting. Just as Chesterton's paper relied on the earnings of Father Brown, so Knox paid the expenses of the Chaplaincy out of the royalties of his detective stories.

Belloc tried to recruit Knox to his twin political projects: the transformation of Britain's social system and the remaking of Europe. But Knox considered these schemes far too worldly and secular. Nevertheless, he did see his vocation as one of polemical combat. 'Ever since I was received I have been incurably propaganda minded,' he wrote, 'and the question "What will Protestants think of this?" has never been absent from my thoughts.' He was anti-ecumenical, regarding the reunion of the Catholic and Anglican churches as 'unthinkable', but his opponents were more often atheists, agnostics and those indifferent to religion than members of the Church of England.[29] Knox relished throwing down challenges to religious debates, sometimes staged as exchanges of correspondence designed for publication.

One of the most famous of these was with his old Balliol contemporary, Arnold Lunn, who had developed a fierce scorn for religion. Lunn thought he had honed the atheist argument into a lethal debating weapon. But Knox's counterblasts were so effective that Lunn surrendered and became a Catholic himself. Indeed, he went on to become a dogged defender of the faith, producing a vast number of books and pamphlets. After the Second World War Lunn enlisted in the ranks of the Catholic Cold Warriors and became an associate of that right-wing American Catholic megaphone William F. Buckley, Jr.

Knox's interest in Catholicism had in part been prompted by Hugh Benson's writing. Benson, together with Monsignor 'Mugger' Barnes, was the keeper of the flame in Cambridge for several years. Under their influence Shane Leslie became a Catholic in 1908. Descended from the adoptive daughter of Mrs Fitzherbert, the Catholic 'wife' of George IV, Leslie came from a staunchly Unionist Anglo-Irish family and was a cousin of Winston Churchill. To the horror of his relations Leslie became an active Irish Nationalist before settling down in St John's Wood as a 'Catholic man of letters', collecting an anthology of Catholic verse, publishing his own books and essays and providing a discreet conduit for secret diplomacy between the Vatican and the Foreign Office in the years leading up to the Second World War.

As early as 1912, Hilaire Belloc had seen that for the Catholic idea to succeed in Britain, it must become not just intellectually but socially fashionable. 'We can spread the mood that we are the bosses and the chic,' he wrote, 'and that a man who does not accept the Faith writes himself down as suburban.'[30] During the twenties and thirties Catholicism came to be associated with a certain aristocratic glamour, one that would gain a purchase in the public imagination with the publication of Evelyn Waugh's *Brideshead Revisited* in 1941. But just as the Marchmains, the central family in Waugh's novel, are not 'old Catholics', this new mood, in which the Catholics were, if not quite the bosses, then certainly chic, owed little or nothing to the former recusant families.

Katherine Asquith was the widow of Raymond Asquith, son of the Liberal Prime Minister. Both her husband and her brother had been killed in the trenches. In 1919, she discovered in Belloc – a friend of Raymond from Balliol days – a partner in grief. 'I think you are the only person I know who has been unhappy in the way that I am,' she told him.[31] Katherine became interested in how Belloc's faith had survived the loss of Elodie and Louis. The two would meet and talk for hours and wrote long letters to one another, examining and explaining their feelings.

When Katherine decided to become a Catholic, she faced opposition not only from the Asquith family – it was said of Herbert Asquith that he found two things repugnant: stewed rabbit and the Catholic Church – but also from her mother, Lady Horner, who had a policy of banning Catholics, including Belloc, from her house at Mells in Somerset. Eventually, overwhelmed by the persistent charm of the fashionable Jesuit Father Martin D'Arcy, Lady Horner relented and the Manor House at Mells became, along with the Herbert family's house Pixton and Lady Lovat's Beaufort Castle in Scotland, one of the favourite weekend destinations of the Catholic smart set.

Fr. D'Arcy had a hand in nearly all the newsworthy conversions of the period: Evelyn Waugh, Frank Pakenham (later Lord Longford), the actor Robert Speaight, Edith Sitwell and many more. It was Olivia Plunket-Greene, a great-niece of Baron von Hügel, who introduced D'Arcy to Waugh. 'Blue chin, slippery mind,' was the writer's first impression of the priest who would receive him into the Church and later officiate at his marriage to Laura Herbert.[32]

Martin D'Arcy had a surprising number of friends who were not Catholics. He would lunch with W. H. Auden and Stephen Spender, knew Albert Einstein and Isaiah Berlin, sat for portraits by Wyndham Lewis and Augustus John, and enjoyed teasing the man he dubbed 'the most dangerous man in Oxford', the young A. J. Ayer.

He hired Lutyens to build the new Campion Hall, the Jesuit college in Oxford, and invited Eric Gill to supply a carving. Gill chose to portray St Martin of Tours handing half his cloak to a beggar. Originally he planned to give Father D'Arcy's features to the figure of the saint, but when he found out that his 'customer' had no intention of paying for the work, Gill gave D'Arcy's face to the beggar instead.

The grand opening of Campion Hall took place in June 1936. A group photograph of the VIP party on the steps includes: Evelyn Waugh, Lady Horner, Katherine Asquith, the Hon. Mary Herbert, Sir Edwin Lutyens and the guest of honour, the Duke of Berwick and Alba. This latter, Jimmy FitzJames Stuart, was the premier nobleman of Spain and a descendant of James II. D'Arcy, like many Catholics of his class, was a Jacobite; but the Duke's presence was also a reminder that however chic Catholics may have become, it remained unthinkable that a member of the British royal family should perform the opening ceremony at a Catholic institution, even an Oxford college.

Not that anyone needed reminding. Twelve days earlier G. K. Chesterton had died at Beaconsfield. His last cogent conversation was, by coincidence, about St Martin of Tours. 'The point is that he was a true Distributist,' Chesterton said. 'He gave *half* his cloak to the beggar.' After that Chesterton lapsed into delirium, his last words sounding eerily like an editorial from *G. K.'s Weekly*: 'The issue is now quite clear. It is between light and darkness and everyone must choose his side.'[33] Fr. Vincent McNabb sang the Salve Regina as Chesterton's life slipped away.

Thousands turned out for the funeral and Ronald Knox preached to a packed memorial service at Westminster Cathedral. The Pope sent a telegram describing Chesterton as a 'Defender of the Faith' – but *The Times* refused to print it on the grounds that, in Britain, that title is reserved for royalty.

Through their writings and journalism Chesterton and Belloc united an extraordinarily diverse group of people. They never held meetings and had no elected leader yet, in a sense, they constituted a movement. The inner circle included the writer and traveller Maurice Baring, a member of the City banking family, whose social connections helped spread the mood of 'the bosses and the chic'. There was a Fleet Street group of which J. B. Morton and Dominic Wyndham-Lewis, each at different times writers of the 'Beach-comber' column, were members. Frank Sheed and Maisie Ward were activists in the Catholic Evidence Guild, which trained ordinary people to explain the Catholic faith in plain language and take the message out on to the streets. One of their recruits, Tom Burns, subsequently described the conspiratorial atmosphere of the organization:

We were an odd lot, from barristers and bank clerks to a remarkable charlady who had reputedly read the whole of the *Summa* of Saint Thomas Aquinas and could trot out Aristotelian concepts in her Clapham cockney as easy as pie. As I went on speaking assignments anywhere from Speakers Corner to the Round Pond on Hampstead Heath . . . it was like being a secret agent in a foreign land. The pick-up point for a platform had been indicated – perhaps a little newsagent in a drab back street – and it would be a meeting point for my companion-conspirator. One talked to be heckled, so as to draw a crowd. Not a few of the hecklers were professionals from the Protestant Alliance or the Rationalist Association. With their bowler hats and mackintoshes and loud rasping voices, I imagined them as KGB men.[34]

Burns later joined Frank Sheed's publishing house, Sheed & Ward, which played a crucial part in broadening and deepening the Catholic literary revival and introducing the work of the French neo-Thomists Jacques Maritain and Etienne Gilson to a British readership. Burns was the most outstanding Catholic publisher of the century. He edited G. K. Chesterton, Hilaire Belloc, Graham Greene, Evelyn Waugh, Eric Gill, Roy Campbell, Arnold Lunn, Christopher Sykes, Christopher Hollis, Frederick Coppleston and Ronald Knox. Another of Sheed & Ward's early authors was Christopher Dawson, who would lead the Catholic assault on totalitarianism in the following two decades.

The Catholic community's response to Fascism was ambivalent. Chesterton and Belloc, for instance, had taken an early and sympathetic interest in Mussolini. Belloc visited the dictator in Rome in 1924 and came away impressed. 'What a contrast with the sly and shifty talk of your parliamentarian!' he enthused; 'what a sense of decision, of sincerity, of serving the nation . . .'[35] Chesterton followed five years later and was flattered to discover that Mussolini was a fan of his novel *The Man Who Was Thursday*.

Chesterton had come to interview the dictator. But Mussolini insisted on asking all the questions, so Chesterton obliged him with a lecture on Distributism. He left rather more sceptical than Belloc about Mussolini's merits, but found that he and Il Duce disapproved of some of the same things: capitalism, usury and Communism. Moreover, the Lateran Treaty of 1929, which recognized the Vatican as an independent state and clarified the Church's relationship with Italy, was a shrewd move on Mussolini's part. It was welcomed throughout the Catholic world and Mussolini was hailed as a more reasonable and conciliatory leader than the anti-clerical liberals who had preceded him.

Catholic sympathies for Italian Fascism inevitably raise the issue of anti-Semitism, an accusation frequently levelled at both Chesterton and Belloc. Jewish anxieties about Catholic anti-Semitism deserve to be addressed. For centuries, Jews throughout Catholic Europe would stay at home on Good Friday, when to venture out was to risk being beaten up in retaliation for Christ's crucifixion.

Thousands of Jews were massacred during the Crusades, and the Spanish Inquisition especially targeted suspected 'secret' Jews. Moreover it was not the Brownshirts or the SS but the Fourth Lateran Council of 1215 that had first proposed that Jews should wear yellow stars sewn into their clothing to distinguish them from Christians.

Chesterton was certainly aware during his lifetime that Jews found some of his opinions objectionable. He complained after returning from a lecture tour of the United States that he had been followed about by a mob of indignant rabbis. Chesterton saw the Jews not as a non-Christian religious denomination but as a displaced and landless nation. They had, he thought, all the appurtenances of nationhood: a shared history, language, literature, culture and religion. All they lacked was a homeland. He declared himself a Zionist and told the West End Jewish Literary Society in 1911 that he did not think that Jews were capable of having the same kind of patriotic feelings towards their country as Englishmen and that they owed their prime loyalty to their own people.

This might be seen as foreshadowing Norman Tebbit's famous cricket test, where the fact that supporters of Asian or Caribbean background sometimes cheer for the visitors rather than the England team is held to be of enormous sociological significance. But Chesterton was not implying any fault or shortcoming on the part of Jews. He did not think they should be expected to regard their British citizenship as anything other than provisional. It was merely the convenient expedient of the exile.

When it emerged a few years later that a very small number of Jewish bankers and merchants in the City of London had continued to do business through family networks with siblings or cousins in Berlin and Frankfurt during the First World War, Chesterton thought his view had been vindicated. But by the time of the armistice the casualty records showed that a very large number of British Jews had gallantly given their lives *pro patria* in the trenches, proving Chesterton conclusively wrong.

A number of his campaigns, particularly those against capitalism and usury, brought Chesterton into conflict with prominent Jews in the City. A newspaper report paraphrased one of his speeches as saying that poor Jews were nice, but rich Jews were nasty. Chesterton would probably not have quarrelled with that synopsis, since the idea of 'racial stereotyping' did not exist within the conceptual framework of his time. Equally Chesterton's belief that Jewish assimilation was neither desirable nor possible seems absurd to us largely because we have experienced mass immigration and witnessed the evolution of multiculturism, which he had not.

On the other hand, because of their belief in moral absolutes, Catholics are rather more constrained than others in pleading 'the climate of the times' in mitigation of anti-Semitism. Those things that are always and everywhere wrong would have been just as wrong in 1911 as they are today. It becomes important, therefore, to distinguish between moral failings and mere breaches of good manners, and to take particular care not to project back into the past contemporary standards of social behaviour that are informed by more recent historical events. To have insulted a Jew in 1920 would not have been regarded as any more outrageous than to have insulted a German. Our awareness of the Holocaust alters that.

Certainly Chesterton used epithets that today would be thought to signal an anti-Semitic outlook. But he was not a man given to hatred or malice of any kind. Nor has any serious literary critic found in Chesterton's work evidence of a sensibility corrupted by prejudice, as some have discovered in the writings of T. S. Eliot. He bore a personal grudge against only one Jew: Godfrey Isaacs, the businessman at the centre of the Marconi scandal. But in a curious and unexpected coda to the affair, Isaacs converted to Catholicism and Chesterton welcomed his old antagonist with a generous heart. When Chesterton died, a senior American rabbi paid tribute to his political and moral judgement. 'When Hitlerism came he was one of the first to speak out with all the directness and frankness of a great and unabashed spirit. Blessings to his memory!'[36]

In the case of Hilaire Belloc, things were quite different. When, at the time of the Marconi affair, someone suggested that it was chiefly a prejudice against Jews that drove him and his colleagues to expose the scandal, Belloc replied that it would be hard to imagine a man less like a Semite than David Lloyd George. This deft deflection was typical of Belloc's behaviour whenever such accusations were made. On another occasion he called for any Jew who could claim ever to have been insulted by him to step forward. None did. But this was largely because Belloc kept most of his anti-Semitic diatribes for dinner parties where Jews were not present; though on one occasion his hosts did beg him to tone down his conversation because a lady further down the table was Jewish. On such occasions Belloc is said to have rivalled even Virginia Woolf and Maynard Keynes in the vehemence of his anti-Semitic denunciations.

Why this should have been the case has proved something of a puzzle for his biographers. A. N. Wilson suggests that Belloc acquired anti-Semitic attitudes during his year of national service as an artilleryman in the French Army. Certainly there was a soldierly coarseness in his language and a French focus to at least one of his fixations: his stubborn refusal ever to accept the innocence of Dreyfus. But when Nazi persecution of Jews began, Belloc, like Chesterton, spoke out at once. Later he would censure Pope Pius XII for his reluctance to issue an unambiguous condemnation of the atrocities. Had he been forced to answer the accusation in his lifetime, Belloc would most likely have said that he was anti-Semitic when he thought it did not matter, and pro-Semitic when he believed it did.

Many people down the years have taken for granted that there is an anti-Semitic streak inherent in Catholic doctrine and culture. One of them was Sir Oswald Mosley. On forming the British Union of Fascists (BUF) in the autumn of 1932, he gave instructions that Catholics should be especially targeted for recruitment. He also took pains to prevent his less tactful subordinates from provoking any anathema from the bishops. Thomas Moloney, who has made a close study of the Fascist press in the 1930s, remarks that 'the boots which trampled weekly over many facets of current British intellectual and social life tiptoed with a clumsy delicacy around the fringes of theology and doctrinal belief, particularly if they were Roman Catholic'.[37]

Perhaps Mosley had made another common mistake: that of assuming that because Catholics believe quite extraordinary things, they are by nature credulous people, and consequently would more readily believe in him. He succeeded in recruiting fewer Catholics than he hoped, partly because the Archbishop of Westminster, Arthur Hinsley, made a point of referring to Jews as 'members of the race of Our Lord and his Blessed Mother' in order to discourage anti-Semitism. When he made a well-publicized speech critical of Mosley, Hinsley received precisely five complaints from correspondents styling themselves 'Catholic Fascists' – four from London and one from Bognor Regis. In the East End, the Blackshirt invasions increased the solidarity between Catholic dockers and the Jewish community, who fought side by side at Cable Street and took it in turns to send out patrols in Poplar and Stepney to see off the Biff Boys.

Not even the *Catholic Herald*, which under the editorship of Count Michael de la Bedoyere was sympathetic to Mussolini, flirted with Charles Maurras's Action Française and was not above publishing the odd anti-Semitic contribution of its own, managed to marshal any enthusiasm for the BUF. Indeed, there is a letter in the archives of the Archdiocese of Westminster dated 8 April 1936 from William Joyce demanding that Hinsley rebuke de la Bedoyere for his impertinent description of the Blackshirt leader as 'an ageing actor with a bald patch' who speaks in 'a tarnished Oxford accent'.[38] Joyce was at this time Mosley's propaganda chief and the man behind the Blackshirts' bid for Catholic support. He would become familiar to wartime radio audiences as the plummy Lord Haw Haw, calling from Germany to vaunt with spiteful glee the achievements of the Luftwaffe throughout the Blitz.

Joyce was born in New York of an Irish father and a Lancastrian mother and was brought up in Galway. After the Second World War, he tried to cheat the hangman by claiming citizenship of neutral Ireland, but he made the mistake of applying for a UK passport, thereby supplying the British with the pretext to try him for treason. Beyond his family, Joyce received little sympathy during his last months except from Fr. Edmund, another former Mosleyite who swapped his black shirt for a monk's habit and retreated to a monastery on Caldey Island. As Joyce was awaiting a decision on his fate, Fr. Edmund entreated him to make a solemn vow to become a priest if his reprieve was granted; but the condemned man refused. Soon afterwards Joyce was hanged.

Joyce may have been the voice of Lord Haw Haw, but Francis Stuart, the son-in-law of W. B. Yeats's muse Maud Gonne, wrote most of his scripts. Stuart got off comparatively lightly. Released after nine months in the custody of the French occupation forces, he moved to London and got a job packing hampers at Harrods. In 1958 he was permitted to return to Dublin, and to writing. In his ninety-fifth year, Stuart was awarded the Republic's highest national honour for literary achievement. Of course, no mention was made in the citation of what was arguably his best-known work, *Germany Calling*.

Meanwhile, Joyce's body lay mouldering in unconsecrated ground in the yard of Wandsworth Prison. In 1976, after a petition from his family, it too was allowed to make the journey home to Ireland. As a toddler, Joyce's daughter Heather had strutted round Mosley's Chelsea HQ giving stiff-armed Fascist salutes in innocent parody of the grown-ups. Later, as a devout Catholic, she felt she had something to expiate and began visiting synagogues to pray. Determined that her own daughter would never feel any misplaced loyalty to Fascism, she sent her off to spend two years on a kibbutz.

Insofar as Mosley and Joyce made any headway in suborning the Catholic community in England, their successes tended to be among the new, grammar-school-educated lower middle class. There was, however, one notable exception.

In February 1936, Archbishop Hinsley received a letter from a young lawyer asking for some advice on a personal and somewhat sensitive matter. The surname of his correspondent, Charles Wegg-Prosser, was one that Hinsley would immediately have recognized as belonging to a prominent Catholic family.

A century earlier, Francis Wegg-Prosser was a Member of Parliament and keen amateur astronomer who became a world-renowned expert on Galileo. In the 1850s, he gave up a tranche of his extensive estate in Herefordshire to the Catholic Church for the foundation of the Benedictine monastery, Belmont Abbey.

As he read the letter, the Archbishop discovered that what was required from him was a straight answer to the question: can someone be both a Catholic and a Fascist? He also saw that a reply was needed rather urgently, as Wegg-Prosser had already been selected as the British Union of Fascists' candidate for Limehouse in the forthcoming London County Council elections. The lawyer had not signed up with the Blackshirts for any ignoble reasons. Disillusioned with the petty, small-minded ways of mainstream democratic politicians, he hoped to find in Mosley a leader with a more expansive vision. The Depression years had witnessed an alarming growth in crime that he believed only Oswald Mosley could arrest.

Limehouse, in London's East End, had sizeable Jewish and Catholic minorities. It was immediately apparent that the strategy the Fascists were likely to follow involved whipping up anti-Semitic feeling among the Irish dockers. This the Archbishop was particularly anxious to avoid. He wrote back to Wegg-Prosser warning him against the 'pagan principle' that the state was supreme and pointing out that 'Jew-baiting is not law and order, nor is it justice and much less so is it charity.'[39]

At first, Wegg-Prosser appeared to ignore Hinsley's advice. But after wrestling with his ethical dilemma for a few months, he split with the Blackshirts and agreed to deliver an unequivocal condemnation of Mosley's rascist tactics to a meeting organized by a Jewish community group in the East End. Wegg-Prosser was a Fascist for a very short time and his public recantation more than compensated for any harm he may have caused by joining in the first place. The Blackshirt leader discovered that while he might be able to attract English Catholics to his movement by appealing to their misguided idealism, once the moral choices were starkly drawn, he could not rely upon their continuing allegiance. Another young lawyer who dropped out of Mosley's circle the same year was Frederick Lawton, who had been selected as a parliamentary candidate for the Hammersmith North by-election but at the last minute declined to stand. He went on to be one of the most prominent Catholics among the judiciary, ending his career as a Lord Justice of Appeal.

The Leader of the London County Council at the time of the 1936 election was Herbert Morrison, grandfather of the Labour politician Peter Mandelson. Mandelson's political assistant when he entered government was Benjamin Wegg-Prosser, grandson of one of the few British Fascists with a functioning conscience.

Cardinal Hinsley – as he became in 1937 – kept a framed photograph of Franco on his desk during the Spanish Civil War. The Caudillo sent it to him through the Herbert family and it was not removed for several years. Hinsley may not have cared much for Mosleyites, but he liked Communists even less. He shared this view with the majority of educated, middle-class Catholics. In fact it was a prominent Catholic layman, the publisher Douglas Jerrold, who chartered the aeroplane that flew Franco from the Canaries to Morocco to begin his insurrection. Another Englishman involved in arranging that fateful flight was a mysterious Major Pollard, about whom little is known except that he was spotted years later by Tom Burns slipping out of the SIS section of the British Embassy in Madrid.

A number of influential Catholic families had strong Anglo-Spanish links. Alfonso de Zulueta, the Count of Torres Diaz, was a curate at St James's Spanish Place in Marylebone. One of Cardinal Merry del Val's nephews was the Nationalists' press officer at Burgos, and the Duke of Berwick and Alba turned up as Franco's ambassador in London. Such people had no great attachment to the Falange, but saw in the Nationalist cause a chance of restoring the monarchy. Many Catholics of diverse backgrounds duly went to Spain to cheer, or even to join Franco's anti-Communist crusade. Gabriel Herbert drove an ambulance at the front. Eoin O'Duffy, a former chief of staff of the IRA, led a battalion of more than six hundred volunteers to fight. The poet Roy Campbell – according to his own unreliable account – alternated between the role of Nationalist rifleman and war correspondent of the *Tablet*.

Campbell, a convert of South African extraction, with a taste for strong liquor and exaggeration, used to describe himself on official forms as a 'mule trader' – a profession he did practise for a while in Provence before relocating to Spain in the early 1930s. His wife Mary had been the lesbian lover of Vita Sackville-West (before Virginia Woolf took her place) and Campbell claimed to have fought off the homosexual advances of Harold Nicolson. His *Georgiad* is a scathing, satirical attack on Bloomsbury, inspired in equal measures by jealousy and disgust. At the outset of the Spanish Civil War, Campbell was living in Toledo, where he witnessed Republican atrocities and was himself beaten up because of his friendship with the local Carmelite friars. More than a dozen of these Carmelites would be among the 7,000 Catholic clergy shot by Republican forces during the conflict. Before they were dragged in front of a firing squad, the monks entrusted to Campbell the treasures of Toledo's medieval library, including the papers of St John of the Cross, which he managed to smuggle out of the burning city in the nick of time.

Father D'Arcy spoke for most English Jesuits when he said in a BBC radio broadcast that the Nationalists were fighting to keep the name of Christ alive and on their children's lips. Arnold Lunn, mindful of the forced collectivization and the massacre of the Kulaks in the Soviet Union, hoped Franco might turn out a Third Way Distributist. In the meantime, he saw the choice to be made as one between an authoritarian government that would protect Christianity and an equally authoritarian government that would persecute it.

Not all Britain's Catholics took the same view. The *Christian Democrat*, the organ of the Catholic Social League, advised neutrality. A substantial number of working-class Catholics, particularly readers of the *Catholic Worker*, judging the conflict as essentially political rather than religious, accordingly took the Republican side. James McGovern, the Independent Labour MP for Glasgow Shettleston, was alone among Catholic MPs in speaking out in the Commons against the Church's support for the Nationalists. When Eric Gill also came out for the Reds, an annoyed Hinsley gently chided the wayward artist, telling him he must learn to see with the right eye as well as the left.

Throughout this period, British Catholics drew a sharp distinction between Latin forms of Fascism and the Teutonic variety. While the former could sometimes be a useful bulwark against the Soviet Union, the latter was a pagan phenomenon and in many respects regarded as the moral equivalent of atheistic Communism. In recent years, it has been widely alleged that the Catholic Church remained silent during the Holocaust. This is not strictly true. The Holy See chose not to issue a clear, public denunciation of Hitler's persecution of the Jews. But the Catholic Church is not the same thing as its Vatican headquarters. The Catholic Church in England – and in Germany itself, for that matter – certainly did not remain silent.

However, these allegations have recently received a fresh impetus with the publication of John Cornwell's *Hitler's Pope*. The author was given access to some, but by no means all, of the Vatican papers relating to the period. What he found gave him reasonable grounds for concern about Pius's character and convinced him that certain political interventions by the Holy See – particularly the decision to wind up the Catholic Centre Party in Germany – helped the Nazis achieve and consolidate power. Sometimes Cornwell seems unsure whether he is accusing the Pope of actual wrongdoing or merely of not having been blessed with the gift of hindsight. Pius's reasons for refusing to condemn the Holocaust in clear terms remain a mystery, and one unlikely to be resolved until scholars (especially Jewish scholars) are given free and unlimited access to all the documents in the Vatican archive. One fact, however, emerging from the flood of rebuttals, concerns Pius XII's personal role in saving the 8,000 Jews of Rome from extermination by the SS. When this fact is taken together with other such actions and the Holy See's provision of baptismal certificates to thousands of Hungarian Jews, it could plausibly be claimed that the Catholic Church saved more Jewish lives from the Nazis than any other non-Jewish organization.

In Britain, there was no hint of ambivalence in the Catholic

Church's position. Straight after Kristallnacht Cardinal Hinsley joined the Chief Rabbi on a platform to make a speech in which he compared Hitler to Nero 'revelling in the persecution of Jews' and commended to the German people the advice of Immanuel Kant, 'the philosopher of Nordic race and blood' who said 'be a person and treat others as persons'. In Germany, Hinsley's intervention was met with angry denunciations. One Nazi newspaper sneered that he had once been 'a missionary to Negroes', a fact it adduced as the only credible explanation why a Catholic cardinal should make common cause with the Jews.[40] Hinsley continued to make speeches and broadcasts critical of the Nazis, many of which were relayed to audiences in the United States in an effort to overcome isolationist sentiments among American Catholics and encourage the US to enter the war.

In the summer of 1941, Count von Galen, the Catholic Bishop of Münster, delivered a series of sermons denouncing the Gestapo, the persecution of Jews and other minorities, and the genetic cleansing of the mentally ill. These were smuggled to England via a Catholic underground network, printed in bulk and delivered to the Royal Air Force, who dropped them by the tens of thousands over German cities with substantial Catholic populations. In the summer of 1942, the Polish government in exile made public the first reliable estimates of German atrocities in Poland – including the figure of 700,000 Jews murdered since 1939. Within days of this early intimation of the enormous scale of the Holocaust, Hinsley was in front of a BBC microphone denouncing the killings. It is worth noting that most of the massacres were perpetrated during the period of the Hitler-Stalin Non-Aggression Pact and that those maintaining radio silence about the slaughter were not Catholics, but those on the political left who took their cues from Moscow. It is also worth noting that Nazi propaganda was unremittingly anti-Catholic as well as anti-Semitic, and that senior Gestapo officers argued in successive memoranda that the Third Reich would never be safe until the Catholic Church was extirpated.

Cardinal Hinsley was the instigator of the 'Sword of the Spirit', a remarkable campaigning organization that brought together British

Catholics with exiles from France, Holland, Belgium and Poland to fight the battle of ideas. The Sword was also an early experiment in ecumenism, forging links with other Christian groups, especially the Church of England – although it soon stumbled over the obstacle of communal prayer, which was forbidden by the Catholic teaching of the time.

The Sword worked with the Ministry of Information, disseminating leaflets and organizing meetings designed to provide a moral and spiritual dimension to propaganda on the home front. Hinsley entrusted its running to Christopher Dawson, who was assisted by Barbara Ward, later well known as an economist, Brains Trust panellist and adviser to Presidents Kennedy and Johnson. Lady Jackson, as she became, also served as a governor of the BBC, and was an all-purpose member of the Great and the Good. She was for a long time the most influential Catholic woman in British public life. But all that belongs to another period – one after 1945, when the Catholic Party, the great social, intellectual and literary momentum that Catholicism had built up in Britain in the inter-war years, would seem like a spent force.

4

'In this country,' wrote Graham Greene in 1941, 'Catholicism, which should produce revolutionaries, produces only eccentrics.' The artist Eric Gill was right, Greene said, to insist that 'Catholicism and Conservatism should be as impossible bedfellows as Catholicism and National Socialism'. But at the outbreak of the Second World War upper- and middle-class Catholic opinion clearly favoured the Tories. Even the rebellious Gill, Greene concluded, had become merely another curiosity: 'the overpowering tradition of eccentricity simply absorbed him'.[1]

Greene arrived at this judgement ignorant of the wild extent of Gill's idiosyncrasy or the kind of fetishism the artist's cult would later engender. Gill kept a collection of his spermatozoa mounted on laboratory slides, which he liked to show to his closest friends under a microscope. Each sample was carefully labelled, indicating the precise spot – often on Ditchling Common – where the sin of Onan had been committed and the seed put under glass for posterity. Perhaps Gill knew that one day his seminal work would fetch as fancy a price as any of his monumental carvings. Recently the entire batch came into the possession of the Notting Hill art dealer Rupert Otten, who sold them on to a buyer he will only identify as 'a very, very famous pop star'.[2]

The figure Greene had in mind as epitomizing the tradition of Catholic eccentricity was Charles Waterton, the nineteenth-century traveller and naturalist. Waterton was a Yorkshire squire, descended on his father's side from the martyred Lord Chancellor, St Thomas More; and on his mother's from the Bedingfields of Oxburgh, one of a very small number of East Anglian recusant families.

In 1812, Waterton embarked on a series of madcap adventures in South America, including a ride on a ten-foot crocodile. 'Should it be asked how I kept my seat,' he wrote, 'I should say I rode some years with Lord Darlington's foxhounds.'[3] Waterton returned from his expedition with an exotic bestiary – stuffed birds and suchlike – part of which today lines the galleries of his old school, Stonyhurst. He also brought back a strange, anthropomorphic creature he called the 'Nondescript'. Covered in rough hair like a gorilla, this curious hybrid had an unmistakably human face. Fearsomely feral at first glance, on closer acquaintance its features suggested a sardonic intelligence. Waterton was an expert taxidermist and had fashioned the freak out of a monkey's skin as a practical joke against the London scientific Establishment. It worked a treat. He was reprimanded by his fellow naturalists for having flayed and stuffed a native.

Waterton has long held a special place in the affections of the Catholic gentry, as much for his defiance of mundane social conventions as of man-eating caymans. Quite extraordinarily devout, he slept on bare boards with a solid oak pillow, rising at midnight and at 3.00 a.m. to say his prayers. Thackeray wrote of him, 'I could not but feel a kindness and admiration for the good man. I know his works are made to square with his faith; that he dines on a crust, lives as chastely as a hermit, and gives his all to the poor.'[4] But though Darwin was a close friend, Waterton was considered a laughable figure by most of his increasingly atheistic contemporaries in the scientific community, for his was a very Catholic brand of eccentricity.

Even into his eighties, the sprightly Waterton loved to shin up a tree. He had a lifelong compulsion for scaling things – on a visit to Rome in 1818 he had annoyed Pope Pius VII by climbing St Peter's. When he was journeying down the Orinoco, the jungle had represented not so much an obstacle to travel as the very reason for it. No less in Yorkshire, Waterton looked for signs of God in the world by physically engaging with nature and observing it at close quarters. He also had a gift for projecting himself into the minds of animals, the better to understand their thought processes and behaviour. To discover what it was that made the canine species tick, Waterton would spend hours on all fours snuffling about under tables, wagging his bottom and barking when strangers approached. By achieving such an intimacy with creation, he felt himself ever closer to its Creator. And it was because of his profound respect for Divine design that Waterton took a particular shine to animals that others shunned. The repulsive Bahia toad, for example, a hideous animal that the superstitious thought fashioned by the Devil himself, and looked to the unbeliever like some ghastly genetic accident, became one of Waterton's favourites. As one of God's creatures, the miserable toad was entitled to dignity and respect. Waterton's decision to turn the grounds of his house – Walton Hall, near Wakefield – into the world's first wildlife sanctuary, was neither motivated by sentiment nor by the interests of pure science, but can perhaps be best understood as a priestly action, the preparation of a solemn sacrifice.

Waterton, of course, remained indifferent to the mockery of his detractors. Not giving a hoot what anyone thinks was part of his recusant patrimony. The gene of eccentricity was most likely inherited from his mother's family. The Bedingfields have been consistently odd. One – 'Whisky Dick' Bedingfield – went West as a young man to become a gunslinging compadre of Wild Bill Hickock; and in 1992, the present occupant of Oxburgh Hall, Henry Paston-Bedingfield, was appointed York Herald at the College of Arms. From the perspective of twenty-first century Britain it is a moot point whether it was the cowboy in his Stetson and snakeskin boots or the genealogist with his unicorns couchant who pursued the more eccentric career.

Over the years, a certain amiable dottiness became required of the upper-class English Catholic. In particular, those who shared the dissident bloodline of the martyrs were expected to hold the puritanical censoriousness of the middle classes in high contempt. Even those who did not share the bloodline would often affect the style or ape the gesture. Whether in real life or in fiction, the tradition had to be kept up. Hence Sebastian Flyte's teddy bear and, perhaps, Monsignor Gilbey's violet gloves.

Alfred Newman Gilbey, whose life almost spanned the twentieth century, conformed to – and to a large extent helped to shape – a media stereotype of retro-Catholicism. For twenty-five years he was a resident of the Travellers' Club in Pall Mall. Few gossip columnists were up and about at half-past seven in the morning to see him toddling off to the Brompton Oratory in frock coat, gaiters and broad-brimmed hat to celebrate Mass in the Tridentine Rite, or even to witness his return down Piccadilly on a number 14 bus (until 1990, when a well-wisher supplied him with a car and driver). Nevertheless, down the years the newspaper diarists were kept plentifully supplied with the precious detail of the Monsignor's routine. Similarly, Gilbey was widely – if not universally – known as the author of *We Believe*, a book he had published under a pseudonym.

Not that Gilbey was given to anything as vulgar as self-promotion. He had no need. His reputation was carefully tended by members of an extensive fan club. Some were society women eager to have him grace their drawing rooms as a living conversation piece or add lustre to a relation's memorial service. A mention in the Court and Social that 'Monsignor Gilbey was robed and in the sanctuary' was a sure sign that the dear departed had indeed arrived. But in the main, the monsignor's acolytes were whey-faced young men in three-piece tweeds, of mildly misogynist bent, and representative of the type that used to gather at Fisher House in Cambridge during Gilbey's 100-term stint as University Chaplain – lasting from 1932 until 1965, the year he fled 'the monstrous incursion of women'.

That phrase – of which Gilbey was over-fond – was no ecumenical nod towards John Knox but a borrowing from Arthur Machen's lament for the 'old tavern life, now gone; utterly and forever'. Gilbey tried to revive something of that lost atmosphere in his Chaplaincy: the blazing fire, 'port that *was* port', 'a certain genial habit of the mind and soul congruous with good men, good books and choice poetry'.[5] Convivial though this bibulous literary bachelordom may have been, it lacked the easy, democratic spirit of the tap house. The Chaplaincy had, in fact, once been a pub, the Black Swan; but with its new furnishings, largely paid for out of Gilbey's own wallet, Fisher House came to resemble one of the smarter St James's clubs. From his leather-upholstered chair, Fr. Gilbey would dispense a somewhat esoteric course of instruction. His young men learned that flounder was 'a dish better served at the Athenaeum than anywhere', and that Lord Holland would always commend to a gentleman 'duck, green peas and apricot tart to follow'.[6]

After dinner came the 'penny readings' round the fireside. Chesterton, Belloc and Dickens were staples. But as he increasingly felt the need to 'keep the jungle at bay', Gilbey's chosen texts became more defensive. After 1945 selective quotations from *Quality or Inequality*, by the Catholic Conservative Christopher Hollis, provided his disciples with a subtly argued defence of privilege against encroaching egalitarianism. Foxhunting, from which Gilbey was instructed to desist by the Church, was another literary and conversational obsession among the Chaplaincy set. It was a world away from the Oxford Catholic scene with its theological pyrotechnics from Ronald Knox and the coruscating table talk of Martin D'Arcy, philosopher of love. Yet it was Gilbey who supervised a record number of conversions; so Fisher House must, occasionally, have served up some stronger meat than Lord Holland's duck.

Aside from a taste for aristocratic company, Gilbey shared with Father Knox a fondness for the works of R. H. Benson. It seems odd that a man of such unpunctured serenity as Alfred Gilbey should acknowledge that pulpit hysteric as a model. Yet he used to insist that Benson 'had more influence on me than anyone I've never known'.[7] Gilbey followed Benson's example in having himself ordained under his own patrimony. Educated by the Jesuits at Beaumont, he had witnessed the full rigour that vows of poverty and obedience imply. With a drinks-trade fortune behind him, Gilbey was able to fulfil his priestly vocation free from the close supervision of the Church authorities and from compulsory asceticism. Though he vigorously asserted the theoretical merits of 'the infinite and merciful gradations of a hierarchical society', in his own career Gilbey chose to remain a free agent.[8]

Yet, as he would unfailingly point out, privilege has its price.

Gilbey believed he paid that price daily by defending the conservative values that made his version of civilized living possible. He thought others should do so too. But in his time he saw Cambridge invaded by 'new men' demanding an equal slice of a cake they had had no part in baking. He used to say that it was not the hunger for the cake he found repugnant so much as the stridency with which the egalitarian claim was asserted. Similarly, he protested it was not women he disliked but feminists; and not fairness he repudiated but political correctness.

There was, no doubt, something of the tease about Gilbey. He was not the first Catholic – nor by any reckoning the last – whose way of declaring himself *contra mundum* was to assume a provocatively reactionary pose. The attitudes he struck were often detectably half-hearted. His case for capital punishment, for instance, hung upon the flimsiest thread of logic. If he were ever found guilty of murder, Gilbey insisted, he would much rather be hanged than incarcerated for life. And so – it did not quite follow – would the vilest criminal, assuming his sensibility could master his cowardice.

Gilbey may well have been in earnest about his own preference for the rope. For sure, the thought of an extended confinement among the great unwashed would have produced one of those frissons of fastidious distaste to which the monsignor was susceptible, and which once led him to make a shocking comparison between High Mass at Lourdes and a Nuremberg rally. Unlike Fr. Martindale, the Farm Street Jesuit who prayed for a drunken sailor to convert but reluctantly made do with a duchess, Alfred Gilbey would for ever give thanks for the duchess. But she would prove a rare enough beast. The Monsignor's customary milieu consisted of that seemingly unchanging coterie of callow adolescents who turned up to serve Mass in the boot room at the Travellers' Club – superior, effete, giggly, given to a certain kind of ecclesiastical camp which, with its coy whispers of copes and chasubles and choirboys' bottoms, sits more comfortably in the Anglo-Catholic than the Roman tradition.

One can only speculate how bored Gilbey must have been by

their adulation, how frustrating it must have been for a man of high intelligence to hear every thumping banality that dropped from his lips scavenged up and passed around as a precious pearl of wit or wisdom. And how limiting for a priest, whose stock-in-trade was moral instruction, to be a man who himself could do no wrong. He never escaped that, even in death. 'There was a certain asceticism to Alfred Gilbey,' wrote his *Times* obituarist. 'He might counsel a dinner companion against ordering a certain dish and then choose it for himself, as a gentle exercise in self-mortification.'[9]

Out of the hollow credulity of that observation reverberates an echo of the true Gilbey. The force of his charm and, no doubt, the preservation of his self-respect relied upon an adroit straddling of the ironic line. He was canny enough to know that his delicately balanced ambiguities were lost on the clubland boobies with whom he dined, and that it had been into the fellowship of monumental snobs that the English Establishment had deigned to welcome him. In his heart, Gilbey knew well enough that he had been put on earth not for the cultivation of an Edwardian persona but for the cultivation of his immortal soul. And towards the end, having perhaps seen which way the wind was blowing, he made a plea to posterity to judge him not by his *Commonplace Book*, a self-serving anthology of nostalgic treats; nor, by implication, the frock coat, the gaiters or the violet gloves; but by *We Believe*, his simple exposition of Catholic doctrine, something he considered 'a very serious book indeed'.[10]

But by that time it was too late: Monsignor Gilbey had become an icon. That overpowering tradition of eccentricity had absorbed him as well. Greene had rightly recognized that eccentricity thrives on social inequality. It thrives on media attention too. By the time Fleet Street had finished with him there was little left of Gilbey's mission to instruct the young in Catholic truth; instead he was enshrined as a Catholic curiosity. The general reputation of Catholicism suffered as a result, the faith commonly represented as not much more than fogey's pantomime, an excuse for appropriating Grandpapa's wardrobe together with his threadbare social prejudices.

The Gilbey style could not have been better tailored to appeal to Americans. On a whirlwind tour of the United States in 1995, Gilbey dined with Judge Robert Bork, lunched at the offices of the *Wall Street Journal* with President Reagan's former speechwriter Peggy Noonan and plugged one of his books on Mother Angelica's Eternal World Television Network in Birmingham, Alabama. 'The audience was swiftly oohing and aahing over the monsignor's clothes,' reported his cousin, Emma Gilbey, his companion on the trip. 'If the long black purple-trimmed robe tied with a wide sash, also in purple, was admired, the black shoes with silver buckles were adored. One woman asked where she could buy them.'[11]

Apart from a stream of converts, Gilbey could also count on the credit side a successful disarming of the English upper class that Belloc had identified as the chief enemy of Catholics in this country. The descendants of the Reformation kleptocrats found in this too, too clubbable priest a man so like themselves that it became impossible any longer to sustain their generalized aversion to Catholics. But the real price of Gilbey's indulgent privilege was the alienation of a substantial section of his co-religionists. The very word 'exclusivity', after all, implies a bolting of the doors. A rising generation of Catholics found Gilbey's snooty posturing distasteful. In her memoir of a Catholic upbringing, *Holy Smoke*, the writer and broadcaster Libby Purves devotes an entire chapter to 'Forgiving Monsignor Gilbey'. She remembers the 'impotent fury' the mere mention of his name used to provoke in her and how even she, a middle-class girl educated at an expensive convent, found herself inexorably driven from the practice of her faith by the cliquey attitudes of 'posh *Cath*olics' during the 1960s. 'These people with their country house attitudes, their substitution of "civilized values" and the "art of living" for charity,' Purves writes, 'can do real damage to the name of religion; as much damage as any bent or avaricious US TV evangelist.' But Purves goes on to warn against reflexive inverted snobbery too:

We who mock the reedy pretensions of aristocratic religion should go very carefully, individual by individual, when we judge. The time to point the finger and shout 'hypocrite!' is when we actually catch the possessor of a watered-silk soutane being haughty and unkind to a less classy co-religionist, or visibly oppressing the poor. We should not, as good Catholic teenagers, have allowed ourselves to become alienated from the Church merely by the dispiriting observation that while the Anglicans had Bishop Trevor Huddleston taking on apartheid, we had Monsignor Gilbey in a silly hat keeping an enviable cellar.[12]

It would be invidious to measure the life of Monsignor Alfred Gilbey against that of Father Michael Hollings in terms of relative worth. Each had his particular calling; and while the two may have interpreted the notion of the 'social apostolate' rather differently, the Holy Spirit has a knack for matching horses to courses. Though their careers could not have been more different, each, in his way, was one of Purves's 'posh *Cart*holics'.

Hollings, had he wanted to, could easily have out-snobbed Gilbey. Through his mother, Agnes Hamilton-Dalrymple, he was a cousin of the Duke of Norfolk and related to the Welds, a family of Catholic landowners from Dorset. By contrast, Gilbey was born into the drinks trade. His father was one of the gin Gilbeys and his Spanish mother was from the Gonzalez-Byass sherry dynasty; though he liked to boast a slight connection with the recusant Vauxs of Harrowden.

Hollings followed Gilbey to the Jesuit public school Beaumont. During the Second World War he served with the Coldstream Guards in North Africa and was awarded the MC after a particularly daring raid in Tunis, during which he was wounded in the throat. Although the injury was subsequently found to require major surgery, Hollings dismissed it at the time as a trivial flesh wound and refused all medical attention until he had successfully led his men back behind their own lines.

In the early years of the war, Hollings drifted from his faith. Nobody was ever sure quite what brought him back, although he always insisted that it had nothing to do with coming close to death in the Tunisian desert. Years afterwards, Hollings would sometimes allude to an epiphany in Palestine; but a personal encounter with

Padre Pio in Italy may have been just as significant. Either way, his army friends were surprised by his sudden resolution to become a priest on returning to civilian life.

He went to Rome for his seminary training and spent four years at Westminster Cathedral before being posted to Oxford as University Chaplain. There, Hollings struck up a relationship with ITV, becoming one of Britain's first 'telly priests'.

When he returned to London in 1970, Hollings began to acquire a reputation – as both an eccentric and a revolutionary. First in Southall and then in Notting Hill, he opened his doors to modern society's waifs and strays. Dossers, heroin addicts, raving alcoholics and the mentally ill – all the wretched of the streets were guaranteed a meal or a place to stay.

There were no rules and no business hours at the parish house. Hollings would cheerfully get up at half-past two in the morning to admit an inebriate rapping at the door. For years he slept in an armchair in front of the fire, having surrendered his own bedroom to the more pressing claim of the homeless.

Hollings saw his guests as the Bahia toads of the human race and offered them not just shelter and sustenance but a respectful hearing as well. On one occasion he surprised a burglar in his kitchen and instead of calling the police put on the kettle and heard the man out – every angry and frustrated detail of his life. The thief became a regular churchgoer.

Somehow Hollings also found time to be active in public affairs. He sat on the Rampton and Swann committees looking into the educational under-performance of West Indian children; he was a member of the Press Council and Chaplain to the Catholic Institute for International Relations, and he was on the board of Christian Aid. At a local level he involved himself in trying to improve race relations, and in the 1980s saved the Notting Hill Carnival by negotiating a deal between fractious cliques on the organizing committee.

Twice it looked as if Michael Hollings was in line for promotion. He was considered a likely choice when the abortive idea of appointing a bishop to the universities was discussed in 1969. Then, in the mid-1970s, he was the bookies' favourite to succeed Cardinal Heenan as Archbishop of Westminster, while rather longer odds were offered on Basil Hume. But Hollings was often in trouble with the Church authorities. He received a stiff reprimand after agreeing to bless the marriage of the divorcé David Frost to Lady Carina Fitzalan Howard. Hollings took the view that since the marriage was going to go ahead anyway, it would be better blessed than unblessed and he complained that canon law was stifling the Church. He was also admonished for preaching in favour of the ordination of women, an issue he obdurately maintained Rome had got completely wrong.

Hollings's devil-may-care attitude to authority combined with an utter indifference to material wealth and a totally self-sacrificing lifestyle made him an oddball amongst the Westminster clergy. Some younger curates dreaded working with him, afraid that if they went out for the evening they would come home to find a tramp in their bed. A number of parishioners found his spiritual intensity hard to endure. Hollings, though wholly at ease in the company of dukes and Rastafarian dope-dealers, could turn gruff with self-important members of the English middle class.

Despite his subversive views on women priests, it would be a mistake to label Hollings as a liberal or a progressive. In liturgical matters, for instance, he was profoundly conservative. Though disdaining the high flummery of Westminster Cathedral ('dressing and undressing the Cardinal to music', he called it) he was a staunch supporter of the Tridentine Rite in its minimalist, Low Mass variety. Nor, according to the Catholic writer Damian Thompson, was Hollings 'one of the growing breed of grey-shirted, nondescript Catholic priests for whom any notion of class distinction is theologically abhorrent'. On the contrary, Thompson says, 'he had a patrician Englishman's keen sense (and enjoyment) of the subtle gradations of the class system. In the end, though, what he liked most about the social order was the fun he had turning it on its head, a mischievous activity which lay at the very heart of his understanding of the Gospels.'[13]

That impish (yet theologically informed) inversion begs the

question: what should be the Catholic's attitude to social class? Did Michael Hollings' genial acquiescence in the English game of charades represent the only civilized response; or might Damian Thompson's greyshirts be on to something? The question has become important because the media nowadays focus almost exclusively on blue-blooded Catholics. And taking their cues from this, the Church's enemies claim they have identified another example of Catholic hypocrisy, demanding to know how class distinction can be reconciled with notions of universal brotherhood or equality before God.

Some Catholics take the relaxed view that snobbery is simply a form of social taxonomy, a harmless and enjoyable pastime like pinning butterflies to green baize. There is, they say, real satisfaction to be had in observing and classifying the infinite degrees of rank established by tiny clues of dress, speech and manner. Admittedly, these tend to be people who themselves would never be turned down for a job for having the wrong number of buttons on their cuff. Others (and not all of them can fairly be described as 'chippy') argue that it deserves to be equated with racism on the moral scale. Their case rests upon the fact that, fundamentally, both involve indefensible discriminations based on trivia.

Secular morality is on the side of the snobs. Though racism is rightly denounced as a very serious evil, class hatred is barely regarded as a solecism. 'Classism' – unlike 'speciesism', 'sizeism' or 'ableism' – barely figures in the catechism of political correctness. That is probably because to outlaw it would involve proscribing its inverted form as well. This kind of inconsistency generates a pervasive scepticism among Catholics about the theoretical coherence of secular, humanist morality. To the Catholic mind, questions of right and wrong should not be contingent upon political fashion.

As might be expected, Rome offers its own guidance in this matter. The Catechism of the Catholic Church has a section in its article on social justice devoted to 'Equality and Differences Among Men'.[14] Here, serious discrimination, whether on the grounds of race, colour or social conditions, 'must be curbed and eradicated as incompatible with God's plan'. Men are enjoined to look upon their neighbour as 'another self' and by cultivating a charitable disposition try to eradicate 'the fears, prejudices and attitudes of pride and selfishness that obstruct the establishment of truly fraternal societies'.[15]

This is not to argue that the same cant and pseudo-moral posturing should be brought to the practical consideration of class issues that are so often brought to racial questions. Indeed, the Catechism goes on to say that the fact of the existence of social differences is part of God's plan – He wants to hand us the opportunity to be generous to one another. But clearly this is an area where careful moral discernment is required. When class distinction involves unkindness or injustice, it is sinful – as Michael Hollings understood. His social antennae were no less sensitive than Alfred Gilbey's, but no one would ever accuse Hollings of being a raving snob.

He was, however, accused of being a predatory homosexual. In September 1995, a man identified only as 'John' claimed that Hollings attempted to molest him more than twenty years previously, when, as a seventeen-year-old, he had been referred to the priest by social workers. 'John', it was subsequently revealed, was acting in collusion with one of the Sunday tabloids. During this confrontation, Hollings said something to the effect that he never meant to cause the young man harm and had only intended to offer comfort and assistance. This statement was pounced upon as an admission of impropriety, though it might equally have been read as a denial.

Unfortunately for Hollings, the story surfaced at a time when the Catholic Church worldwide was facing a series of scandals involving the cover-up of sexual offences by priests. In the past, when complaints of wrongdoing were made, bishops tended to deal with them 'within the family', sometimes taking no action except to remove the priest concerned from temptation. In the United States a number of paedophiles had thus been allowed to continue their depravities for many years, leaving the Church open to accusations of gross negligence. During the early 1990s, more than $400 million were paid out in settlement of lawsuits based on this sort of claim. The crisis also prompted an institutional examination of conscience – bishops now admitting that the old system of settling complaints put too high a priority on safeguarding the Church's reputation, to the detriment of justice for the victims. New guidelines were introduced at the behest of the insurance companies, placing priests on the same footing as teachers, social workers and other caring professionals – that they would be treated as guilty until proven innocent. Father Hollings was suspended from his parish duties and sought refuge with his cousin at Arundel Castle.

The Church of St Mary of the Angels is located on the borders of Bayswater and Notting Hill. The parish has changed a great deal since Michael Hollings first moved there in the 1970s. The winos and dossers are still in evidence and the district still has a wide ethnic diversity, but the immediately surrounding streets nowadays house media grandees, cabinet ministers and bonus-fat brokers from the City. The area has also become a magnet for many of London's richer Catholics. Rupert Otten's art gallery, with its collection of Ditchling woodcuts, lettered stones and spermatozoa, sits within the church's shadow. The writer Paul Johnson lives just around the corner. As the inquiry into the Hollings affair dragged on month after month, a cadre of articulate and well-connected parishioners began to speak up on behalf of the beleaguered priest they regarded as a local saint.

Julia Stonor, member of the Oxfordshire recusant family that once sheltered Edmund Campion, deplored the secrecy and delay that characterized the inquiry. Paul Johnson said, 'The Spanish Inquisition would have made a better job of it.'[16] Some of Hollings supporters even suspected a conspiracy involving a group of progressives around Cardinal Hume, who, they said, despised Hollings because he was a supporter of the Tridentine Mass.

Ironies abounded. One prominent religious conservative who finds it difficult to formulate the word 'homosexual' without sneering in distaste was prepared to back Hollings, guilty or not guilty; while self-styled liberals were one minute confiding their support for reducing the age of gay consent to sixteen, and the next demanding the full rigour of the law be brought against the priest over his alleged involvement with a seventeen-year-old.

The Metropolitan Police were indifferent to the sour recriminations passing to and fro between the rival Catholic factions. They focused on the deposition in hand. The worst that 'John' had alleged was that Hollings made a clumsy pass at him, which once rebuffed was not further pressed. There was room for doubt whether 'John' had mistaken an arm-around-the-shoulder display of solidarity for a sexual come-on. It seemed unlikely that the experience 'John' described would have caused him lasting psychological trauma, so why had he come forward now, a quarter of a century later, arm in arm with a reporter from the *News of the World*? In the end, the prosecuting authorities decided not to press charges. Cardinal Hume turned up for Sunday Mass at Hollings's church to announce the news in person. The entire congregation burst into applause. But it came too late. The long, anxious wait for his reinstatement had broken Michael Hollings's health. He died a few months later.

It was a source of great pleasure to Monsignor Alfred Gilbey to be styled 'Grand Cross Conventual Chaplain Ad Honorem of the Sovereign Military Hospitaller Order of St John of Jerusalem, of Rhodes and of Malta'. The Knights of Malta are the third oldest order in the Catholic Church after the Augustinians and the Benedictines, but they are distinct from other orders on account of their 'military' or chivalric status. Founded as hospitallers in 1099, the Order provided care, assistance and protection to groups of pilgrims travelling to the Holy Land. Inevitably it was drawn into battle with the Saracens and eventually became militarized. A degree of nostalgia for this period amazingly persists, evident in the Order's public relations handout, which begins: 'The Crusades, for better or worse, are a thing of the past . . .'

After the fall of Acre, the Knights escaped via Cyprus to Rhodes, finally arriving in Malta in 1530, the year in which they were granted sovereignty over the island by the Holy Roman Emperor, Charles V. There they fought off the besieging Turks, under the command of Suleiman the Magnificent, with remarkable tenacity and a certain ruthlessness. When they ran out of ammunition for their cannons, the Knights would bombard the enemy lines with the severed heads of their Turkish prisoners. In 1571, at the Battle of Lepanto, the Knights helped to break Ottoman seapower in the Mediterranean, effectively saving Europe from Turkish domination. The Order was eventually expelled from the island by Napoleon and it began a period of peripatetic exile before settling in Rome.

Today the Order of Malta remains a sovereign state, represented at the United Nations and issuing its own passports and postage stamps. Like the Vatican City, the Palazzo Malta on Rome's Via Condotti is formally independent of the Italian Republic. The Order's Grand Master is internationally recognized as a head of state and is properly addressed as 'Your Eminent Highness'. In Catholic protocol he is the Church's highest-ranking layman, with the rank of a cardinal or a prince of the Holy Roman Empire. A number of other heads of state – King Baudoin of the Belgians, King Juan Carlos of Spain and Prince Rainier of Monaco belong to the Order as more junior members.

A Scot, Fra' Andrew Bertie (pronounced Barty), Grand Master since 1988, was the first Briton to be elected to the post since Hugh de Revel in 1277. Bertie should have no trouble lording it over the European royals. His maternal grandfather was the Marquess of Bute; and he is connected by blood to the Earl of Abingdon and Lindsey, through him to the journalist Sir Peregrine Worsthorne, and, in a roundabout way, through the Stuart genealogical maze, to the Queen herself. Educated at Ampleforth and Oxford, Bertie served in the Scots Guards before becoming a schoolmaster at the Catholic public school Worth. There he excited the interest and curiosity of the boys with his proficiency in more than half a dozen languages, including Tibetan, and with his black belt expertise in judo. Bertie always seems to amaze people with his feats. Four years after becoming Grand Master he created a sensation in Naples when he caused the premature liquefaction of the blood of St Januarius. For the past 600 years, the blood of the fourth-century saint had adhered to a rigorous schedule, liquefying only on certain appointed dates, three times a year. According to Neapolitan superstition, should the miracle ever fail to occur, an earthquake will level the city. In May 1992, Bertie paid an out-of-season visit to the church where the congealed blood is kept on display. Kneeling before the reliquary, he began to pray. Within seconds the blood changed state.

From his office in the Palazzo, the Grand Master controls an organization of over ten thousand Knights and Dames (the Order admits women) and many tens of thousands more volunteers in its ambulance services, clinics and hospices throughout the world. The Knights of Malta have been active in most of the recent wars and emergencies, establishing field hospitals in Lebanon, Rwanda and Bosnia, relief operations in Thailand and Cambodia, as well as the world's best equipped maternity hospital, located appropriately enough, in Bethlehem.

Like any quasi-military body, the Order has a complex hierarchy. The more senior 'professed' Knights take vows of poverty, chastity and obedience and live according to monastic rule. Knights of Honour and Devotion and Knights of Magistral Grace live as ordinary members of society. The Order is distinguished from comparable social and philanthropic organizations by its emphasis on Catholic spirituality. The Pope personally nominates a representative to serve on its governing council and is consulted before important decisions are made. In 1993, Pope John Paul II granted permission for the restoration of the Grand Priory of England, which was first suppressed by Henry VIII and then again by Elizabeth I. Henry also seized the Order's lands, including the manors of Knightsbridge and St John's Wood, then just outside London.

Before the restoration could take place, a quorum was required of five professed 'Knights of Justice' – men who had taken all their vows and were prepared to live a quasi-monastic life. Eventually seven such Knights were found, including Matthew Festing, a Sotheby's auctioneer, Frederick Crichton-Stuart and the writer Alfred Marnau.

There are over two hundred Knights in Britain and approximately forty Dames. Among the well-known names associated with the Order in recent years have been the Conservative MPs Bill Cash and Edward Leigh; Brigadier Andrew Parker Bowles; Hugh van Cutsem, a Suffolk landowner and a close friend of the Prince of Wales; Prince Rupert zu Loewenstein, the business manager of the Rolling Stones; the historians Desmond Seward and John Keegan; Edward Stourton, a presenter of BBC Radio 4's *Today* programme; and a large number of peers including the Duke of Norfolk, Lord Camoys, Lord Mowbray, Lord Hesketh and the late Lord Craigmyle. In Scotland, those associated with the Order have included Peter Drummond-Murray of Mastrick (the Slains Pursuivant at Arms), the late Lord Lovat and Cecilia McEwen of Bardrochat.

Traditionally the Order has preserved its social exclusivity by requiring members to meet rigorous social conditions. In theory, Knights of Honour and Devotion, such as Edward Leigh, should be of 'unsullied noble blood' and be able to show sixteen quarterings, the equivalent of two to three hundred years of armigerous pedigree. Knights of Magistral Grace, a discretionary degree, pass into the Order across a lower social threshold, with no need for staggering proofs of nobility. But like all others, they have to agree to live according to the tenets of the Catholic faith.

In Europe, the Order still finds it easy to maintain a generally aristocratic membership – in Britain about 80 per cent of Knights are of noble blood. But this is clearly impossible in the United States. There the Knights of Malta are associated with the political and business élites, recruiting powerful figures such as the New York financier Peter Grace; William Flynn, the chairman of Mutual of America; John Coleman, one-time head of the New York Stock Exchange; the former Secretary of State Alexander Haig; and Ronald Reagan's CIA director, William Casey. The Order's American Association has always inclined to the political right. One of its founders, John Raskob, the chairman of General Motors, plotted to seize the White House in protest at Roosevelt's New Deal. It broadened its membership base during the 1930s, recruiting Joseph Kennedy, who, if not exactly a progressive, was at least a Democrat. Today the Association is closely involved with the right-of-centre think tank, the Heritage Foundation. The relationship between the Foundation and the Order owes a good deal to the work of a former Treasury Secretary, the late Bill Simon, a particularly devout Knight of Malta, who left $350 million to charitable causes in his will. In 1989, President Reagan, though not a Catholic, was presented with the Order's Grand Cross of Merit Special Class in recognition of his stand against abortion, and his support for the institution of the family and for prayer in schools.

The American Knights have stooped to levels of vulgarity that make their European confrères wince. In the late 1970s, their southern Association held a spectacular fundraising ball in Palm Beach, Florida. The setting was the Breakers Resort Hotel, a kitsch pastiche of the Villa Medici in Rome, where an enormous ice-sculpture of the Maltese cross was erected for the occasion. Douglas Fairbanks and Rose Kennedy were among the guests, each of whom was given a complimentary bottle of scent before being asked to write out cheques to pay for a new hospice in Fort Lauderdale. The Duke of Norfolk, who had been flown in to lend some aristocratic tone to the proceedings, found himself cornered by a predatory socialite. 'I think,' she said, 'we both represent power . . .'[17] The amiable and self-deprecatory Duke had some difficulty convincing the woman that he exercised only limited authority and was in fact merely the Chief Butler of England. That title, though genuine, always foxes wealthy Americans. But if the US Knights are more used to counting their dollars than their quarterings, they at least can claim to be racially inclusive. The American Association recruited its first black member as early as 1973, when many other blueblood institutions were still operating a colour bar.

Some traditionalists argue that the Order should think carefully before relaxing any further its quaint attachment to old-fashioned proofs of chivalry. The aristocratic connection, they say, prevents the Knights of Malta from turning into just another networking opportunity for businessmen on the make, a slightly classier Catholic version of the Freemasons, Rotarians or Kiwanis. Nevertheless, the Order has begun to consider alternatives to armorial quarterings as criteria of admission. The aim is to find some formula that recognizes families that have traditionally contributed to society by providing judges, doctors and so on. One day, perhaps, proof of 300 years of vaguely defined 'public service' will suffice. But the Order still remains deeply attached to the idea that lineage is important, that virtue and honour are somehow transmitted down the generations. 'They provide the last defendable bastions of hereditary nobility,' writes Desmond Seward in *The Monks of War*. 'They alone preserve the mystique of rank and birth in a world which finds aristocracy not merely alien but incomprehensible.'[18]

The Order's social exclusivity sometimes causes it inconvenience. Seward reports that numerous crooks, charlatans, Masons and others have appropriated the Knights of Malta's symbols to set up counterfeit orders of their own. The Venerable Order of St John, despite its royal patronage and the valuable work done by its volunteer ambulance crews, is one such inauthentic, Victorian copy. The Internet has spawned many more. Day after day, a procession of poor saps turns up at the Palazzo Malta demanding dining rights or an audience with the Grand Master, waving bogus certificates conferring worthless titles. The accountants charged with settling the affairs of the fugitive tycoon Asil Nadir discovered amongst his effects one such certificate of knighthood, resplendent with ribbons and seals, for which the supposedly canny fraud had paid a tidy sum. In the United States, a number of these dubious orders have turned, over the years, into quite substantial organizations in their own right, boasting such luminaries as Frank Sinatra and Dewi Sukarno as members, and holding lavish 'knighting ceremonies' in Las Vegas ballrooms.

The real Order of Malta has tentatively modernized some of its practices. Notoriously secretive in the past, it is now much more forthcoming about its activities around the world, if only to distinguish itself from the proliferating fakes. It has opened up its Grand Priory, a villa on the Aventine, giving the public a chance to see for the first time in decades one of Rome's secret architectural treasures: Piranesi's church of Santa Maria del Priorato, along with Piranesi's own tomb in the grounds. The Order now admits women to its Sovereign Council, a change made, according to a spokesman, 'in accordance with the authentic spirit of Christianity and humanitarianism'.[19]

Public perceptions of the Order vary from country to country. In Italy, the revelations of political and financial corruption associated with the Masonic lodge Propaganda Due have left many people suspicious of all secret or exclusive societies, particularly those that recruit figures prominent in public life. There has been speculation in the press that senior politicians and industrialists including Giulio Andreotti, Francesco Cossiga and the Fiat boss Gianni Agnelli are, or have been, Knights of Malta, along with extremely suspect figures active in right-wing politics and intelligence work whose names have been linked with various neo-Fascist groups and P2.

During the Cold War, the Knights of Malta bestowed medals on the spymasters Reinhard Gehlen and James Jesus Angleton, and honoured the French politician Antoine Pinay, the founder of a secretive 'circle' where statesmen swapped ideas with spooks. The Knights were also active in securing the Christian Democrat victory in the crucial 1948 general election in Italy, using funds supplied by US intelligence. It is not at all surprising that Catholics were involved in winning the Cold War for the West. But nor is it surprising that leftist journalists in Italy have consistently portrayed the Order of Malta as a surrogate of the CIA.

Moreover, Italians are aware that for many years before Fra' Andrew Bertie was elected Grand Master, the Order's wealth made it the object of rivalries and turf battles within the Roman Curia. The wily Cardinal Canali, one-time controller of Vatican finances, was accused of conniving with New York's Cardinal Spellman to divert cash from the Order's American Association into Curial coffers. Another persistent theme of the scandal-mongering sections of the Italian press has been the allegation that senior Curial officials practise Freemasonry, which is forbidden by the Catholic Church. The Order's origins in the time of the Crusades, its use of titles such as 'Grand Master' together with certain elements of its institutional aesthetic have something in common with the Masonic tradition.

Furthermore, the rituals followed by the Freemasonic Knights Templar allow for formal welcomes to visiting 'Hospitallers' and 'Knights of St John'. However, the Order of Malta denies having any connection with Freemasonry whatsoever. Given that Freemasons in Italy and France have been fiercely anticlerical, and in Scotland and the United States strongly Protestant, it would be very odd if the Knights of Malta did have anything to do with them. It is more likely that a number of the bogus orders of St John, those which have borrowed some of the Knights of Malta's traditions, are connected with Royal Arch Masonry and with the Templars – themselves a dubious 'revival' of an ancient military order suppressed by the Pope in 1312 on trumped-up charges of buggery. That explanation is unlikely to satisfy conspiracy theorists, of course, their excitement further fuelled in recent years by a succession of real-life dramas resembling scenes from a Michael Dibdin novel, an investigation by David Yallop, or even one of the more improbable histories of Baigent and Lee.

Consider, for instance, the murder of Enrico Sini Luzi, an Italian aristocrat, a Gentleman of the Pope's Antechamber and a Knight of Malta. Sini Luzi was found in his flat, face down on a velvet cushion, dressed only in his underpants and a cashmere scarf. He had been battered to death with a candelabra. Then there was the case of the leading candidate for the mayoralty of Cannes, found shot by his own hand in a cemetery, dressed in full Knights of Malta regalia. Or, going back to the late 1980s, the murky affair of Mauro Casagrande, who was exposed – only days before he was due to be installed as a Knight of Honour and Devotion – as spy for Fidel Castro's intelligence service. The Cuban dictator, it transpired, had been keeping the Order under surveillance since 1961, when he discovered that a senior Knight, the Honduran coffee baron Roberto Alejos, had lent his estates to the CIA to train Cuban fighters in preparation for the Bay of Pigs invasion. It is but a short step in the paranoid imagination from all this to the dozens of websites now claiming to link the Knights of Malta to organized crime and sinister political plots aimed at global domination. All baseless, of course; but the involvement of some European Knights with the Falange, the Vichy regime and with Mussolini during the middle part of the twentieth century, and with the vigorous pursuit of 'Western goals' in the latter part, is undeniable.

In Britain, the Order excites no such unease in the public mind. It seems almost like a home-grown institution. The Knights, kitted out in their chivalric chic, are perfectly in keeping with the British upper class's obsession with fancy dress. It is all of a piece with formal dinners at high table in the ancient universities, or the officers' mess of the Household Cavalry. Many of the Knights are former army officers. They are mainly drawn from the country gentry and, more often than not, educated at Ampleforth. A large number are of recusant stock, and most can trace descent from one or another of the English martyrs. Their annual fund-raising gala, the White Knights Ball, is a considerably more decorous affair than the Palm Beach extravaganza, despite its name. The British Knights are discreet, if not downright secretive, about their affairs.

The only Knight who attracts much media attention is Prince Rupert zu Loewenstein. Christened 'Rupie the Groupie' by the gossip writers, he is often spotted out and about with his music business clients, the Rolling Stones and Pink Floyd, and his daughter Dora (Maria-Theodora), the Stones' official biographer. But Loewenstein is not a natural rocker. In dress and manner he conforms more to the style of a City gent than a music-business mogul. Indeed, before he got his hands on Mick Jagger's investment portfolio in the late 1960s, Loewenstein worked as a nine-to-five pinstriped broker at Bache & Co, before teaming up with the buccaneering Jonathan Guinness to buy out the ailing merchant bank, Leopold Joseph.

In most other respects Loewenstein is the typical Knight of Malta – Ampleforth, Oxford, very long pedigree. In the *Almanach de Gotha* he is Prince Rupert Ludwig Ferdinand zu Loewenstein-Wertheim-Freudenberg, and counts among his antecedents the Elector Palatine Friedrich I. Only he knows his net worth, but suffice it to say, if we still had super-tax, he would be paying it. It is men like Loewenstein – with noble lineage combined with pots of money and a wealth of social contacts – that the Knights of Malta like to recruit. Money attracts more money; and the Order requires a great deal of it to fund its hospitaller work.

In England, the Knights have supported the hospital of St Elizabeth and St John in north London and are the largest provider of sheltered housing for the elderly outside the public sector. In Scotland, they operate a dial-a-ride service for the disabled and help paper over the cracks in the welfare system by supporting drink and drug rehabilitation projects. The British Knights also fund a leprosy centre in Uganda and a medical centre in Tanzania, as well as contributing to the costs of the Order's various hospitals and field ambulances in war zones. But giving money and fund-raising is not all there is to being a Knight of Malta. Fra' Andrew Bertie is adamant that the duties of his Knights Hospitaller should extend far beyond their chequebooks. It is a requirement of the Order that each Knight should give up some of his time to personal service to the poor and the sick. So it is that city brokers, landed toffs from the shires and the occasional Tory MP can find themselves attending for hours at the bedsides of dying AIDS patients in hospices. It is through such corporal acts of mercy, as well as through prayerful pilgrimages to Lourdes, Fatima and Walsingham, that the petty snobbery of counting quarterings and the intrinsic silliness of prancing about as a caped crusader is more than adequately redeemed.

One of the most energetic Knights of Malta, and President of the British Association for six years, was the late Lord Craigmyle. He inherited from his mother a large tranche of the Inchcape shipping fortune, much of which he gave away in a series of anonymous donations. As well as working with the handicapped through the Order of Malta, Craigmyle ran a charity for the home-less on the south coast. He would often go out on the soup run, and, believing that his clients needed stimulating company as much as hot food, would sit and chat for hours, introducing himself only as 'Jock'. The next morning might find him closeted with Cardinal Hume discussing how the Catholic Union could best lobby minis-ters to secure some amendment favourable to the Catholic interest; and in the afternoon, on his feet in the House of Lords putting the

Catholic perspective on school buses. If the Duke of Norfolk was the unofficial leader of the Catholic peers, Donald Craigmyle was his chief whip.

Eventually Craigmyle succeeded the Duke as President of the Catholic Union and took on most of the day-to-day political work himself. Since Victorian times, the Union has been the main conduit of discreet Catholic influence upon the upper echelons of government, and an even more discreet channel of communication between Archbishop's House and Buckingham Palace. Throughout the twentieth century, successive Dukes of Norfolk, or their kinsmen, have been leading figures in the Union. During the Second World War, Lord Fitzalan, uncle of the then Duke of Norfolk, was the intermediary between the Church and Winston Churchill's government. Part of his job was to relay to Cardinal Hinsley Lord Halifax's disappointment at the reluctance of Pope Pius XII to be openly critical of the Nazis. There was very little Hinsley could do about the Vatican's stance. But he tried to make up for its deficiencies by being unequivocal on the issue himself.

Miles Fitzalan-Howard, who succeeded to the Dukedom of Norfolk in 1975, follows the family tradition. He has done a great deal of work to advance the cause of Catholic education and protect Catholic schools from blundering ministers – most of them Conservative – who have failed to think through the implications of their proposals for the Catholic community when drafting their bills. On more controversial subjects, such as abortion and embryo research, he has preferred to conduct his campaigns in the open. In one of his more memorable speeches, he declared: 'The embryo is the start of life and must be given the same status as a child, a grown-up person, or a member of the House of Lords.'[19] The Duke has adopted a pragmatic approach to Catholic moral teaching, something that occasionally gets him into trouble with the authorities. He once described the rhythm method of contraception as 'absolute nonsense', revealing that he and his wife had tried it '. . . and it didn't bloody work'.[20] His common-sense approach extends to the issue of euthanasia. Sceptical of proposals to clarify the law in this area, he said: 'If I were to see a comrade in mortal agony on the battlefield, of course I would feel compelled to put him out of his misery, and trust to the mercy of God. But I wouldn't then try to pass an Act of Parliament about it.'[21]

The Duke is a former professional soldier who achieved the rank of major-general and commanded a division on the Rhine. He rounded off his army career as Director of Military Intelligence. As a brigadier in the late fifties he served with the buccaneering Brixmis unit, which was allowed to go behind Warsaw Pact lines in East Germany to report on manoeuvres and take photographs of the latest Soviet hardware, and which frequently had to outrun the GRU and the KGB to bring their information safely back to the West. Partly because of this background, and on account of his extraordinarily extended family, which seems to penetrate almost every sphere of life, the Duke is regarded with suspicion by those uneasy about Catholic political influence.

He is sometimes said to sit at the centre of a vast Catholic intelligence service of his own. Since the ghost of one of his forebears, the 4th Duke, is known to haunt the premises of Coutts Bank on the Strand (and has defied teams of ghostbusters sent in by the management to expel him), some say the overdraft balances of most of the landed families in England are regularly reported to Arundel Castle. In fact the Duke is one of the least conspiratorial of men, seeing himself as just a simple soldier. The only halfway mysterious organizations with which he has been associated are the Roxburghe Club, an association of millionaire bibliophiles, whose members have included Sir Paul Getty, Paul Mellon and Christian, Lady Hesketh; and the 15 club, a Catholic dining society whose members must be able to trace their lineage back to the reign of Henry VII. Confusingly, thirty people sit down to each of the club's dinners.

Though there is nothing sinister about the 'Catholic mafia' over which the Duke presides as honorary godfather, it has been powerfully effective. Before the first phase of the Labour government's reform of the House of Lords in 1999 there were eighty-seven Catholics in the upper house, forty-six of them hereditary peers. Although they spanned both sides of the House, as well as the crossbenches, when questions of importance to the Catholic community came up they were able to work together in a bloc as their sixty or so co-religionists in the Commons never could. Until the establishment of the papal nunciature in 1982, the Catholic peers played an even more important role as indirect channels of communication between the Vatican and the state. Before this date, the year of Pope John Paul II's visit to the UK, the Vatican was represented only by an Apostolic Delegate, who had a purely ecclesiastical function and no diplomatic status. According to Cabinet papers released in 1990, the then Duke of Norfolk had applied in 1959 to have this situation reviewed, but a memorandum from Selwyn Lloyd, the Foreign Secretary, argued that to upgrade diplomatic relations with the Vatican risked re-igniting religious controversy in cities such as Liverpool and Glasgow.

It is doubtful whether many Catholics in Liverpool or Glasgow ever knew about the off-stage manoeuvrings of senior members of the House of Lords on their behalf. But the leadership roles of successive Dukes of Norfolk were acknowledged throughout the community, and surprisingly rarely challenged. It is a long-established status, dating back before Catholic emancipation, which was itself, largely brought about through a Duke of Norfolk's efforts.

With the universal decline of social deference, one might have expected Catholics to question aloud in what sense they were ever really 'led' by the Duke, as the media have always insisted. Though Catholics are no more given to tugging their forelocks than anyone else (indeed, bearing in mind the Irish ancestry of the majority, they might be thought to be of more rebellious spirit than most), they do seem to be fond of their own toffs. This attitude is probably the result of Catholic education – at least as it was dispensed during the ghetto years.

Children would be taught to revere the post-Reformation martyrs. Teachers explained that the upper-class Catholics were in most cases descended from these souls who had made the ultimate sacrifice for the faith in the sixteenth and seventeenth centuries. Before a more ecumenical tone was prescribed for the teachers of

Catholic history, it was also insisted that Catholic titles were more authentic. Catholic lords, the argument went, were twenty-four-carat noblemen who had come over with the conqueror and represented a genuine tradition of *gentillesse* and chivalry; while non-Catholic aristocrats had got their wealth by cattle rustling and pillaging monasteries, and their titles by currying favour at court or bribing Lloyd George. It was as if the familiar, contemporary distinction between the *nouveau riche* vulgarian and the 'real gentleman' could be projected back across history in denominational terms. Such tendentious teachings would have become quickly discredited had they not been borne out by experience. The fact was that Catholic noblemen usually turned out to be harmless, if not always benevolent. They certainly seemed to lack the customary rapacity of their class.

Occasionally, a Catholic family would throw up a 'wrong'un'. Raymond de Trafford came from a Lancashire recusant family on whose ancestral estates Manchester United's football ground now stands. Thrown out of Downside and the Coldstream Guards, he fetched up in Kenya in 1926, where he joined the dissolute set that congregated around Lord Erroll in Happy Valley. Evelyn Waugh, who met de Trafford in the early 1930s, described him as 'v. Nice, but so BAD; and he fights and fucks and gambles and gets disgustingly drunk'.[22] On one occasion Waugh recorded in his diary that de Trafford had brought 'a sluttish girl back to the house. He woke me up later to tell me he had just rogered her, and her mama too.'[23] De Trafford fell in love with Alice de Janzé, a beautiful American separated from her husband. The pair planned to marry, but de Trafford's family prevailed on him to break off the relationship. When he told her that he could not go against the teaching of the Catholic Church by marrying a divorcée, Alice, outraged by what she saw as a sudden and inexplicable access of moral scruple, pulled out a pistol and shot her lover, before turning the gun on herself. Both, remarkably, survived the incident and eventually they married. They did not, however, live happily ever after – the marriage only lasted a few weeks. Raymond wound up in prison for manslaughter, having knocked down a pedestrian while driving blind drunk. De Trafford was a rare black sheep among the recusant families, though Downside comes second only to Harrow in turning out public-school jailbirds. Like so many Catholic lives, de Trafford's seems almost to have been deliberately contrived to illustrate a moral point. But the most important lesson that Monsignor Gilbey, the Knights of Malta and the old recusant families can teach is a political one: that the conversion of England is hardly likely to be achieved from the top down.

On a broiling Saturday in July 1999, 20,000 men converged on Drumpellier Park in the predominantly Catholic town of Coatbridge in Lanarkshire. Knots of musclebound toughs lolled against the walls of the corporation housing along Moss Park Road, swigging bottles of strongbrew. Shaven-headed and extravagantly tattooed, they might have been mistaken for young offenders out on day release. In a bid to dispel the pervasive torpor, one member of the group shinned up a wall to a commanding parapet and struck a mock-heroic pose. With one hand he raised a white standard emblazoned with the Red Hand of Ulster. With the other he pointed to the legend on his T-shirt: 'SEE ME? I DON'T GIVE A FUCK.'

This improvised tableau was a mere sideshow. The real spectacle could be seen a short distance away in Sunnyside Street, where a barmy army was marching behind flutes and the Lambeg drum to the tune of 'Men of Harlech'. The crowd belted out their chorus with raucous gusto: 'Fuck the Pope and the Virgin Mary.'

Scotland's 1,000 Orange Lodges had mustered in Coatbridge to express solidarity with their brethren in Northern Ireland. For a good number of those in attendance the occasion was a dry run for the stand-off at Drumcree, due to begin two days later. For the purposes of their dress rehearsal, Catholic Coatbridge had become Scotland's Garvaghy Road.

It is often wrongly believed that Ulstermen bringing specialist skills from the Belfast shipyards to the Clyde in the late nineteenth century introduced the Orange Lodges into Scotland. In fact, Scottish Orangeism is almost as old as the movement itself. Ulster Protestants founded the Orange Order in Armagh in 1795 as 'a religious and patriotic fraternity'. When Scottish regiments were despatched to help put down the Irish uprising three years later, many of the soldiers were initiated into the Order, establishing lodges on their return.

Orangemen generally deny that they are anti-Catholic or that their parades are displays of Protestant triumphalism. The July marches, they claim, are innocent commemorations of William of Orange's victory over James II, symbolic re-enactments of an historical event, no more laden with religious bigotry than a meeting of the Sealed Knot. But when they remove their shirts, their tattoos tell a different story – sometimes one where religious bigotry and white supremacism are elaborately intertwined.

The Battle of the Boyne took place in 1690, more than a century before the Order's foundation. Catholics suspect that the movement was really conceived to manipulate the memory of the Boyne in order to strengthen a Protestant social and economic ascendancy and suppress agitation for land reform: in short, to keep the troublesome Catholic in his place.

Today the Grand Orange Lodge of Scotland boasts a membership of 50,000. This figure doubtless exaggerates the movement's active support, but the Order comfortably outstrips every political party in Scotland. The Scottish Labour Party, for instance, the senior partner in the nation's ruling coalition, has fewer than 33,000 paid-up members.

Like the political parties, the Orangemen reach out to a wider community who share their values. The boy in the 'SEE ME' shirt wore none of the Order's official regalia. Most likely he was a member's son or younger brother, or just along for fun. In a few years' time, when he has learned to pass himself off as an upright citizen, they will initiate him into the lodge. For now, he has to submit with a deferential nod when an older man, dapper, respectable even, in bowler and suit, asks him to tone it down a bit. Not too stern, mind; these lads are the Order's future.

Some commentators dismiss the Orangemen as a genetic residue, the sediment left in working-class communities after a process of social distillation, in which the best have evaporated off to the University of Strathclyde or to well-paid jobs in Silicon Glen. But such an analysis fails to take account of the alarming number of educated, professional men prepared to join in a full-throated rendition of 'The Sash'.

Besides, to descend to crude eugenic theorizing is to adopt the traditional mindset of the bigot. When the first starving refugees from the Irish famine arrived in Scotland in the late nineteenth century, many literally disfigured by poverty, some Scottish doctors declared them genetically abnormal. The slur stuck. In 1905, a Scottish sports paper published a cartoon portraying two footballers, one from Celtic, the other from Rangers. Over the caption 'Apes & Aryans' the Celtic player was drawn as a degenerate, simian creature; the Rangers player as tall and fair with an aquiline nose. The idea that the Catholic Irish were liable to pollute not only Scotland's culture but also its bloodstock was widespread during the first quarter of the twentieth century. As a fresh wave of Irishmen arrived, threatening the job prospects of native Scottish Protestants, the press and the politicians conspired to portray the 'bhoys from the bog' as both physically malformed and intellectually backward, suited only for the most menial employment. In 1923, the General Assembly of the Church of Scotland commissioned a report that considered wholesale repatriation of the Irish immigrants, branding them racially inferior.

Following the Reformation and the 'War of the Three Kingdoms' (as the Scots more accurately style what the English parochially reduce to the 'Civil War' or the 'English Revolution'), Catholicism had struggled to survive in small pockets in the Highlands, the Western Isles and Galloway. After the failure of the Jacobite rising in the eighteenth century, any broad resurgence looked extremely unlikely. By 1800, there were fewer than one hundred Catholics resident in the city of Glasgow. In 1870, twenty years after Cardinal Wiseman's triumphant return to Westminster, there was still no restored Catholic hierarchy north of the Tweed.

But mass immigration from Ireland swiftly boosted numbers. Soon Catholics would account for one in four of Glasgow's population. Nowadays there are more than 750,000 baptized Catholics in Scotland, nearly three-quarters of them living in the west or the economically dynamic central belt. The majority are of Irish descent, but the total includes immigrants from Italy, Poland and Lithuania as well as Scotland's native Catholic survivors. In terms of active membership and Sunday observance, Catholics now constitute Scotland's largest religious denomination, if only because with its great Disruption and its further schisms over the Declaratory Act of 1892 Protestantism has fragmented into a multiplicity of sects with bewilderingly similar names. Chief, by virtue of numbers and social authority, is the Church of Scotland (the 'Kirk'). Then there are the United Free Church, the Free Church and the Free Presbyterians – all stemming from the Calvinist tradition of John Knox. The Episcopalian Church in Scotland is part of the Anglican Communion.

On the fringe are a few thousand Baptists and freelance Evangelicals. It is possible for anyone to equip themselves with a degree in divinity from some obscure university in the deep south of the United States and set up in the religion business on their own. Usually the award of these diplomas is conditional upon a certain amount of distance learning; but sometimes all that is required is payment of a fee. Once qualified, the spiritual snake-oil salesman goes in search of a bourgeois congregation, his ambitions being to found a church where you cannot hear coins rattling in the collection box, just the reassuring rustle of paper tithes. In Northern Ireland personal and political fortunes have been made this way and in Scotland too many have prospered by taking a leaf out of Elmer Gantry's book.

Pastor Jack Glass, known as the foremost scourge of 'Romanism' in Scotland, does not quite fit this stereotype. For sure, he founded his own sect, the Zion Baptist Church. And it is true that its premises in Glasgow's Calder Street did brisk enough trade in their better years to earn the pastor four or five times the salary of a Catholic priest. But Glass studied hard for his academic credentials, spending three years at the Free Church College in Edinburgh. Indeed, he used to tease his one-time friend and associate Ian Paisley with the jest that the Ulsterman had purchased his doctorate from a trailer park attendant in South Carolina for $10 in cash. In fact, Dr Paisley obtained his degree from Bob Jones University perfectly legitimately, even attending in person. Glass and Paisley finally fell out over one of those esoteric points of theology, utterly baffling to outsiders but a frequent cause of acrimony among Presbyterian divines. While most Catholics consider Paisley an incorrigible figure, the very epitome of Protestant Ulster's 'No Surrender' mentality, Jack Glass thought him far too freely given to compromise. Paisley, he claimed, was an unwitting agent of the Pope.

Dr Paisley was not the only eminent preacher whom the pastor found wanting in Calvinist rigour. When the American evangelist Billy Graham visited Scotland in 1991, he was surprised to find Glass picketing his Glasgow rally. As an ecumenical gesture, Celtic Football Club had made its stadium available for the event. But it was not just the choice of venue that provoked Glass's holy wrath. He accused Graham of 'backsliding' from his 1948 declaration that Communism, Roman Catholicism and Islam represented three equal menaces to Christian civilization. In the intervening years, Graham had met the Pope and abandoned intemperate rhetoric. There would be no denunciation of the Mass as a blasphemy, no caustic parodies of Marian piety, no condemnation of papist idolatry at Parkhead that day. Billy Graham, Glass believed, had sold out.

Pastor Jack sees himself as the guardian of a pristine tradition. 'John Knox is dead, but the God of John Knox is alive and the God of John Knox is the God of Jack Glass.'[1] An innocuous enough motto, you might think; but the turbulent pastor has adopted Knox's manner along with his theology. Although he was not suspected of any involvement with the Loyalist paramilitaries who threatened to respond with bombs and guns if the papal Mass at Bellahouston Park went ahead, he was undoubtedly behind the political agitation against Pope John Paul II's visit to Scotland in 1982.

Jack Glass's brand of violence consists of a ferocity of speech and gesture. One of his signature interventions was staged in 1990 at St John's Kirk in Perth, where Archbishop Winning (as he then was) had been invited to preach at an ecumenical service.

For four centuries, St John's was a Catholic church, until John

Knox hijacked its pulpit in 1559 to deliver a sermon against idolatry. Knox's inflammatory preaching incited a mob to desecrate the sanctuary, before going on an iconoclastic rampage through the town. No Catholic bishop had returned to St John's since. The Knox connection made the church a particularly suitable venue for a service of reconciliation; but it also provided a fitting stage for one of Pastor Jack's famous displays of recalcitrance. It was certainly more appropriate than St Peter's Square in Rome, where, during the Easter celebrations in 1975, to the bafflement of pilgrims from around the world, Glass had turned up sporting a sandwich board inscribed, front and rear, with the slogan: 'No Popery!'

Winning was about to deliver his historic message of ecclesiastical rapprochement when an indignant figure appeared in the church doorway. Pastor Glass had rehearsed his histrionics with care. First there was a loud clatter as he flung down thirty pieces of silver for the Judases on the church council who had allowed a popish prelate across the threshold. Then, as the onlookers recovered from their surprise, Glass vanished, only to reappear with a plaster bust of Pope John XXIII, father of modern Catholic ecumenism. With both hands, he raised the figure above his head, holding it poised until – having finely judged the peak of anticipation – he hurled it down to shatter against the ancient flagstones. The elders of the kirk hurried to shoo the troublemaker out of the door and Winning tried to persevere with his address without acknowledging the interruption. But more provocateurs had been planted among the pews and they rose up as one, shouting that the Pope was the anti-Christ and Thomas Winning a wicked blasphemer.

Mark Scott was sixteen years old, a pupil at the prestigious Glasgow Academy. He was one of the five children of Niall Scott, one of the city's most successful corporate lawyers. Mark was a Celtic supporter and on the afternoon of 7 October 1995 had watched his team beat Partick Thistle. He did not go drinking after the match and was not looking for a fight. Instead, he and two friends set off along London Road in the direction of their homes in Glasgow's West End. Their route took them past Bridgeton Cross, an area known as 'Little Shankhill', on account of its gable ends decorated with Loyalist murals. According to witnesses at the scene, at approximately half-past five, a man ran up behind Mark, seizing him by the head with one hand, and with the other drawing a knife across his throat with such vehemence that it cut clean through the flesh as far as the spine. Mark staggered, spurting blood, for more than twenty-five yards before he collapsed. Dozens of people looked on, but no one tried to catch his assailant.

Gary Horne, a local market trader, was pushing his child in a pram a short way down the street. He was the first to react, pulling the blanket off his infant son and rushing to help staunch the flow of blood from Mark's gaping throat. He was joined by a group of drinkers from a pub who tried to cram beer mats into the wound, but to no avail.

After the police arrested Mark's murderer, a youth called Jason Campbell, the accused man was described in the press as a 'Rangers supporter', as if that fact alone represented sufficient motive for the crime. But Campbell, it later emerged, was a self-styled 'Bridgeton Billy Boy'. He was proud of the fact that his father had been imprisoned for his part in Scotland's only instance of sophisticated sectarian terrorism – the bombing of two Catholic pubs in Glasgow in 1979. The murder of Mark Scott could no longer be glibly ascribed to the rivalry between football tribes.

At his trial, Campbell proved a clever and mendacious defendant, concocting an alibi, rejected by the jury, that his mother gave evidence to support. His defence counsel tried to discredit Gary Horne's evidence, suggesting that he had only co-operated with the police in identifying the killer to get himself rehoused in a better district. Certainly, Horne would never be safe on the streets of Bridgeton again after appearing as a prosecution witness; but he did not relish the prospect of eternal exile from his community and was certainly not perjuring himself. Indeed, several independent witnesses corroborated his testimony. Nevertheless, the jury took what seemed an unconscionably long time in their deliberations and had to be sequestered for a night in a hotel before finally reaching a guilty verdict.

Although Jason Campbell received a life sentence, this was by no means the end of the affair. Campbell watched events in Northern Ireland carefully, taking note of the paramilitaries' demands for prisoner release in exchange for their various ceasefires. Despite having no family in Northern Ireland and no personal history of paramilitary involvement, he applied to be transferred out of the Scottish prison system to the Ulster Volunteer Force (UVF) wing at the Maze prison. Astonishingly, ministers consented to his request. Scotland's Catholic community was appalled that the government should accept the murder of a Celtic supporter as a 'political' offence that might qualify for early release under the terms of the Northern Ireland peace process.

Letters of complaint were sent to 10 Downing Street, but no one could say for sure who had made the decision. The then Scottish prisons minister, Henry McLeish, denied having any part in it. Was it, perhaps, the East Kilbride MP, Adam Ingram, a junior minister at the Northern Ireland Office? If so, it could have been very embarrassing for the government. As a young man Ingram had been a member of the Orange Order. He had also held a recent meeting with the Progressive Unionist Party's David Ervine, a politician with close links to the UVF. Tony Blair insisted that the Northern Ireland and Scottish Secretaries resolve the matter without further delay. Consequently Mo Mowlam took responsibility for the mistake, while Donald Dewar, having reviewed the application, denied Jason Campbell his transfer and his chance for an early ticket of leave.

The murder of Mark Scott did not prompt any exercise of national self-examination in Scotland of the sort the racist slaying of the black teenager Stephen Lawrence did in England. As far as most commentators were concerned, the tragedy merely supplied further proof that Glasgow's youth are football crazy. The Scottish media like to marshal all consideration of sectarian issues within the perimeter of the football stadium, and it is an iron rule that everyone maintains a scrupulous even-handedness between the teams, even though this reflexive assumption of equal culpability is entirely specious.

Celtic Football Club has not, traditionally, discriminated on religious grounds when recruiting players. Its famous manager Jock Stein was a Protestant. But until the signing of Mo Johnston in 1989, Rangers used to discriminate as a matter of policy. (There had, in fact, been one Catholic on the books at Ibrox in the 1950s, but Don Kichenbrand cannily kept his religion a secret from team mates and club officials.) The Manchester United manager, Alex Ferguson, though himself a Protestant, was eased out of Rangers in 1969 when it was discovered he had committed the unpardonable treason of marrying a Catholic.

Rangers' signing of Johnston was presented as evidence of a high-minded determination to stamp out sectarianism. But the policy was resisted by many of the club's supporters, who mobbed Ibrox when the news of it got out. Flags were burned, sabres rattled and a spokesman demanded that the Rangers directors formally rededicate the club to 'God, the Union and the Protestant religion'.

Nevertheless the Scottish media insist on promoting the fiction that the two clubs are, and always have been, as bad as one another. The veteran football correspondent Alex Cameron is as objective as anyone can be when it comes to Old Firm rivalry. He has had his windows broken by supporters of both teams. 'Celtic, like Rangers,' he wrote in a recent memoir, 'seemed to realize that there was a vested interest in sectarianism. Celtic didn't mind being different and, in fact, nurtured the notion. Celtic, while not discriminating in one sense, were still keen to flag up their Catholic status.'[2] Here Cameron is making a category error that disfigures much Scottish commentary on this subject, drawing a false equivalence between affirming Catholic identity and discrimination or religious hatred.

To maintain marks of difference should not be an offence in a multicultural society; indeed it could be said to be the very point of multiculturalism. But in Scotland, Catholics can stand accused of being 'provocative' for simply being themselves. Scottish football supplies many instances of this, such as the booking of Partick Thistle's Rod Macdonald (an English Catholic) for making the sign of the cross at a tense moment during a match against Rangers. Some years earlier Dundee United's Argentine striker Victor Ferreyra had been taken to task for doing the same thing, as had Mo Johnston in his time at Celtic.

Celtic Football Club has been criticized not only for being too Catholic, but also for being too Irish. Since it was originally founded to serve an Irish immigrant community, it has not taken the criticism too much to heart. During the 1950s, the club put up determined resistance to attempts by the authorities to force it to remove the Irish Tricolour that traditionally flies above its ground. According to the Labour MP Brian Wilson, who has written a history of the club, Celtic had to face the serious threat of being driven out of business if it would not comply. Nevertheless, Celtic remained firm, just as it did when the campaign was renewed in the 1990s. A defiant piece of oratory from the club's chairman, Robert Kelly, stiffened the resolve of officials and supporters alike. 'It is necessary that Catholics should become more and more organized,' Kelly said, pointing out that the community was still failing to punch its weight in Scottish society. 'We have no need to be ashamed of our fathers,' he went on; 'nor have we any cause to be ashamed that Celtic's founders came from that country that has provided protagonists for liberty wherever they have settled.'[3]

But Celtic has not been insensitive to criticism. Recently it launched a campaign called 'Bhoys Against Bigotry', in a gesture to show willing. Fans were genuinely puzzled, and some even affronted by the move. Most Celtic supporters deny they are prejudiced and say they are heartily fed up with the pundits' line that Scottish sectarianism is a two-way street. They invite independent observers to consider the evidence. The songs that Rangers fans sing on the terraces, they point out, are rollicking, bellicose celebrations of Protestant supremacy, spiced up with insulting references to the Pope or the Virgin Mary. By contrast, Celtic's tunes are mostly old rebel songs from the Easter Rising with no religious reference at all. Their principal anthem, 'The Fields of Athenry', is a poignant lament, narrating the story of a young man parted from his lover and transported in chains to

Australia because he has the temerity to demand social justice. Where, they ask, is the sectarianism in that?

Almost two years after the murder of Mark Scott, Sean O'Connor, a nineteen-year-old Cambridge undergraduate, was walking along London Road after a match between Celtic and Motherwell. He was almost at the very spot at Bridgeton Cross where the fatal attack on Mark Scott had taken place when he too was attacked and his throat slashed wide open. He put his hand to his neck and found that his fingers reached into the wound as far as the knuckle.

The police later arrested Thomas Longstaff for the assault. Longstaff, it turned out, had been a close friend of Jason Campbell, whose father, the one-time pub bomber, sat in the public gallery during Longstaff's trial. Longstaff employed the same defence barrister who had acted for Campbell; and once again, the defendant denied being present at the scene of the crime. Prior to taking part in an identification parade Longstaff had asked a detective constable for a glass of water, sloshed a liberal measure into his cupped hands and used it to plaster down his hair, saying as he did so, 'Thank God for the not-proven verdict.' But not even Scotland's most successful criminal advocate could shake the assured and certain testimony of the prosecution witnesses. Longstaff was sent to prison for ten years.

Donald Findlay QC made his name in 1984 representing the gangster Joe Steele, who despatched six victims during Glasgow's notorious Ice-cream Wars. He successfully defended another mobster, Paul Ferris, accused of killing 'Fat Boy' Thompson, the son of Arthur Thompson, Glasgow's *capo di tutti capi*. With his mutton-chop sideburns, fancy waistcoat, fob watch and pipe, Findlay used to cut a ridiculous figure for a man so young (he was born in 1951); but he calculated early in his career that sartorial quirks and antique props could help establish him as one of Scotland's media treasures, alongside the quixotic MP Nicholas Fairbairn, whose Tory politics he shared.

Never an Establishment man – he is by nature too demotic and too irreverent, Donald Findlay often appears ill at ease among the bigwigs at the Faculty of Advocates, as if determinedly struggling to resist assimilation into the bourgeoisie. He has never forgotten that when he first went to the Bar his father warned him not to acquire a posh accent, for fear of losing his soul. He disdains many of the customary professional pieties. It has been reported that he sat at the hotel piano after a Bar dinner and belted out 'The Sash' under the reproving gaze of seniors. Some were surprised to hear him sing such a song. He is not a native Glaswegian, having been born and brought up in Fife, where Orange sympathies are far less common. Findlay has, however, long been a passionate Rangers fan, and was proud to be appointed as the club's vice-chairman.

Findlay's first foray into sectarian controversy was harmless enough. He made light of Paul Gascoigne's flute-miming antics on the football field and somewhat disingenuously described the Loyalist anthems favoured by Rangers supporters as 'folk songs'.[4] Although he was widely criticized for his insensitivity at a time when the club was trying to outlaw sectarianism on the terraces, he could still plausibly claim to hold no prejudice against Catholics in general, only against Celtic Football Club. But in 1998, Findlay published a controversial novel. Its title, *Three Verdicts*, alludes to the 'not proven' verdict that is a peculiar feature of Scottish law, and upon which Thomas Longstaff's hopes of an acquittal had vainly reposed. Mr Findlay's casebook contains many celebrated trials that have ended this way.

The hero of Findlay's novel, James Muirhead QC, is urbane and good-looking, perhaps a somewhat idealized version of Findlay himself. The book pillories senior figures in the Scottish judiciary, portraying the Lord Advocate as a grossly incompetent old booby. But the book provoked offence beyond the Scottish legal circle. The villain is called Doyle, the family name, as it happens, of the six murder victims in the Ice-cream Wars. (A tendency to reverse the positions of perpetrator and victim would emerge as a leitmotif in the Donald Findlay story.) Significantly, all the criminal or nefarious characters in the novel were given Catholic names and the book portrays a Catholic priest who accepts a bribe – something that earned the author a mild rebuke from Cardinal Winning's spokesman and alerted a number of Catholic journalists to mark Findlay's card.

On the last Saturday in May 1999, Rangers beat Celtic 1–0 in the Scottish Cup Final at Hampden Park. After the match, the Rangers team returned to Ibrox to attend a celebration party in the Edmiston Suite, next door to the stadium. Late in the evening, clearly having had quite a lot to drink, Donald Findlay stepped forward to the microphone to congratulate the players on their performance during the competition. Adopting a heavily ironic tone, he said, 'You know, at Ibrox we don't have anything to do with that sectarian stuff any more . . . You have to be very careful or you end up on the front page of the *Daily Record* . . . but if you promise not to tell anybody, join in . . .' With that he launched into a medley of anti-Catholic ditties, most of which were of the usual, crude 'Fuck your Pope and the Vatican' variety.[5] But in the light of the subsequent excuses offered by Findlay's apologists – 'harmless fun', 'it was a private function' and so on – the words of one particular jingle that Findlay sang that evening demand special consideration. 'The Billy Boys' is arguably the nastiest number in the Rangers repertoire. It contains the line 'We are up to our knees in Fenian blood. Surrender or you'll die – for we are the Bridgeton Billy Boys.'[6]

As QC for Jason Campbell and Thomas Longstaff, Donald Findlay had sat day after day in the courtroom listening carefully to all the evidence at the trials of both defendants. He would have known that in each case the victim was attacked at Bridgeton Cross; that Sean O'Connor was called 'Fenian scum' just before his throat was sliced; that Mark Scott's blood sprayed the pavement for twenty-five yards, issuing from his ruptured artery with such force that it defied the efforts of men with blankets and beer mats to staunch it. Is it possible that not a single one of those key words in the Billy Boys song – 'Bridgeton', 'Fenian', 'blood' – sparked any synaptic connection in Findlay's brain with the memory of Mark Scott's death?

That question goes to the heart of the issue, yet it appears never to have been asked by the Scottish press. Scottish society remains in denial on the issue of anti-Catholic prejudice. It would rather the charge not be brought at all; and when events force a consideration of the evidence, Scotland always returns the third verdict.

As Findlay was on his feet, dancing his sweaty jig at the microphone, a few miles across Glasgow three young Celtic fans lay in hospital. Liam Sweeney had been trapped by Rangers supporters in a café and badly beaten. Karl Roarty had been shot in the chest with a crossbow bolt. Roarty was unlucky. He had gone to the Cup Final wearing a plain T-shirt, but a friend he met at the match gave him a Celtic jersey for his twentieth birthday and persuaded him to put it on. The green and white hoops would be the bowman's archery target, Karl's heart the bull's-eye, narrowly missed. Thomas McFadden was unluckier still. The doctors at the Victoria Infirmary had already made arrangements to transfer his body to the morgue.

McFadden, sixteen years old, had not even been at the match. His mother, afraid there would be violence, persuaded him to stay away and watch the game on television at the pub where she worked. After it was over, still in his Celtic colours, young Thomas left to meet his sister. In the street two Rangers supporters, David Hutton and Peter Rushford, set upon him. As Rushford punched and kicked, Hutton drew a knife, stabbing McFadden four times, twice piercing the heart. The victim remained on his feet and watched by the crowd, pulled up his shirt to reveal his wounds and, as his lifeblood drained away, began to sing in a faltering voice 'The Fields of Athenry'.

Hutton and Rushford had watched the Cup Final at a flat down the street that Rushford shared with his girlfriend, Emma Skett. The two men had stoked themselves up with beer and temazepan to get in the right mood for the game. They put on Rangers shirts and trailed bunting out of the window. Emma wore a Rangers jester's hat.

'Did you get him?' Emma asked when the two men returned after the attack.

'Aye,' replied Hutton, 'we got the wee Fenian bastard.'

Emma noticed that Hutton had blood on his hands. 'You didnae plug him, did ye?'

'Aye, right to the hilt.'[7]

They decided to break out some more beer. The policeman who arrived at the flat a few minutes later reported that he found the group in a relaxed and convivial mood. The constable discovered the murder weapon hidden inside the grill in the kitchen; the killer had not even bothered to wash it up. Hutton was subsequently sentenced to life imprisonment for murder. Rushford received a short custodial sentence for assault and has already been released. At the trial, both men were described as unemployed and of no fixed abode, reinforcing the stereotype of the sectarian thug as a member of a near-feral underclass. In fact, when the crime was committed, Rushford was the head chef at a fashionable Glasgow eaterie, and Hutton a skilled pipe-fitter.

By the morning of Monday, 31 May, barely thirty-six hours after he died, Thomas McFadden was no longer the lead story on the news. Something much bigger had broken. As he feared, Donald Findlay had made the front pages of the Daily Record. His act had been captured on amateur video and clips would soon be running on network television. The broadcasters faced a dilemma. Those parts of the performance that demonstrated the enormity of Findlay's behaviour were not suitable for family viewing; but by screening only sanitized excerpts they risked reinforcing the argument that the incident was essentially trivial, and not a matter of real public concern. Less impactful than the sectarian display, yet powerfully poignant in their way, were the sequences showing Rangers' Catholic player, Neil McCann, clearly uncomfortable and embarrassed, together with a number of the team's European signings, who appeared utterly bemused by the whole spectacle.

Findlay would own up to no moral fault, admitting only to an 'error of judgement'. When he resigned from his position at Rangers, the club's chairman David Murray said Findlay had paid 'a high price'. That phrase would surface again and again in newspaper reports. It was the cliché of choice when Findlay was fined £3,500 for bringing the Faculty of Advocates into disrepute, and when St Andrews University withdrew its offer of an honorary degree. It prefaced the reports, seeded by sources close to Findlay himself, that he had become so depressed as a result of the scandal that he was contemplating suicide.

The complicity of the Scottish press in the indecently hasty rehabilitation of Donald Findlay presented an object lesson in what would come to be termed Scotland's 'sleepwalking bigotry'. Of the major titles, only the *Daily Record* seemed to take a clear-sighted view of the issues. It says something very disturbing about the condition of a national press when a sensationalist tabloid outstrips the pack in moral discernment. Most of the papers appeared chiefly concerned to make excuses for Findlay. In a series of interviews over the next twelve months, readers were invited again and again to feel sorry for Donald. His girlfriend had left him; he had been spat upon in the street; he had paid 'a high price'. Increasingly he would make light of the sing-song that got him into trouble. Donald Findlay, it is fair to say, left the dock of public opinion showing no remorse.

Two weeks after his initial disgrace, the *Sunday Herald* published an article under the headline 'In Defence of Donald'. It argued that the public outcry against Findlay was something largely got up by Celtic supporters: 'If you can't beat [Rangers] on the pitch, then using their vice-chairman against them will do nicely.' It was also attributable, the article said, to a Catholic cult of victimhood, Catholics being always alert and 'anticipating insults and bigotry while reserving the right to sing their own songs at their own private functions'.[8]

Nowhere in this 1,200-word article was there any mention of Thomas McFadden or the synchronicity of his death and Findlay's performance. There was an extraordinary reluctance among Scottish commentators to ask whether prominent people who take part in sectarian displays might share some responsibility for the crimes men such as Campbell, Longstaff and Hutton commit. It was as if Findlay's grotesque musical celebration of Billy Boys wallowing in

Fenian blood and the act of slashing or stabbing 'Fenian scum' had taken place in two quite separate moral universes.

The *Sunday Herald*'s daily sister, the *Herald*, probably has a higher proportion of religious bigots among its readership than any other full-format newspaper on the UK mainland. Until a recent re-vamp of the paper and the appointment of a new editor, that unhappy truth was more than adequately reflected both in its letter page and its comment section. The American writer Richard Hofstadter once described anti-Catholicism as 'the pornography of the Puritan'.[9] Though never remotely hard-core, quite a lot of what the paper used to find fit-to-print could seem, at least to the Catholic eye, like the soft porn of the Presbyterian. One of the *Herald*'s columnists, John MacLeod, is often ostentatiously disrespectful towards the Pope and unpleasant about Catholicism in general. Writing about the Catholic bishop Roddy Wright, who absconded with a girlfriend in 1996, Macleod wrote: 'Nothing would give me greater pleasure than to seize on the scandal as a club to batter Romanism, a system I regard as profoundly evil.'[10] A London sub-editor would sit up smartly at that 'profoundly evil' and perhaps substitute 'wrong-headed' or 'misguided' to avoid causing offence to Catholic readers. What is at issue, after all, are the theological differences between two Christian denominations. But in Scotland, the rhetorical parameters within which religion is discussed are stretched to accommodate anti-Catholic sentiment, and such hyperbolic language is commonplace.

For some of his readers, MacLeod's teases are clearly a source of titillation and pleasure. 'If ever I was proud to be a Scotsman it was this morning when John MacLeod's article arrived on my desk,' wrote a correspondent from Santa Cruz, Bolivia. 'If ever I was proud to be a Glaswegian,' he went on, 'it was when I saw the *Herald*'s courage to print such an article when many of its readers are Roman Catholics. Down here in Latin America drug trafficking and corruption is dominated by Roman Catholics and completely ignored by the Pope. This is understandable because he has never known the in-dwelling of the Holy Spirit in his life.'[11] And so it goes on.

When Arnold Kemp, a former editor of the *Herald*, took up his post in the early 1980s, he found that it had long been the practice at the paper to throw away all job applications from Catholic journalists unread. Kemp changed that state of affairs and his successor, Harry Reid, rigorously pursued a fair recruitment policy. To its credit, the *Herald* tries hard to remain impartial in important areas of controversy. It goes to extravagant lengths to be even-handed between Labour and the Scottish Nationalists, at one time employing two political editors, one for each party. Labour is seen in the west of Scotland as largely a Catholic party, so this policy has proved reassuring for Catholic readers. The paper also reflects a broad range of opinions on religious questions, commissioning many essays and features from Catholic writers. But on the issue of sectarianism the *Herald*, like the rest of the Scottish media, has tended to exercise only a spurious kind of even-handedness.

The facts simply do not support the media's insistence that there is little to choose between the two sides of the sectarian divide. Glasgow's Catholics do not prowl the entries of the city's tenements in search of Protestants so that they can slit their throats. Nor do prominent Catholic lawyers get up at parties and sing anti-Protestant songs. When a Celtic supporter refers to a player who has signed with Rangers as a 'traitor' that is not, as one Scottish newspaper put it, 'a sickening display of Catholic bigotry';[12] that is football. When a player, whether he hails from Argentina, Liverpool or Govan, makes the sign of the cross he is not being sectarian, he is being Catholic. When a Scot of Irish extraction sings an Irish anthem and waves the Tricolour, he is not being sectarian; he is being Irish. He is doing nothing essentially different from a Scot who sings 'Flower of Scotland' waving the Saltire. Whenever Catholics complain about Orange marches, it is invariably observed that Catholics have flute bands of their own. And so they do. The difference is that no one has ever heard the members of the Hibernian Association chanting 'Fuck the Moderator of the General Assembly'. It is just not their kind of song. Unless the Scottish media begin to respect these distinctions they are in danger of perpetuating an unconscious, institutionalized bigotry of their own.

It was against this background that in August 1999, a little over a month after the opening of the Scottish Parliament, and two months after Donald Findlay's resignation from the Rangers' board, the composer James MacMillan delivered a lecture at the Edinburgh Festival on the subject of bigotry in Scotland. MacMillan's paper examined Scottish society in the round. He began by regretting that the Reformation in Scotland had involved such an abrupt repudiation of the country's Catholic heritage. It was, he said, as if the reformers had declared a cultural Year Zero. Were Scots to revisit the past, MacMillan suggested, all sorts of buried treasure might be found. Though he gave no specific examples, it is likely that the sort of thing he had in mind was the music of Robert Carver. Few Scots have ever heard of this composer, who lived and worked in Stirling in the sixteenth century. His Renaissance polyphony was simply 'too Catholic' for what came to constitute Scottish taste and ever since has failed to match the narrowed criteria of authentic Scottishness that the Reformation imposed. Only very recently, since Cappella Nova resurrected his work, has Carver's music been available in recorded form.

MacMillan discussed his own work as a composer, acknowledging a Catholic inspiration,

whether in its theology and philosophy, or in its liturgy, or simply in the encultured experience of my own upbringing in the west of Scotland. Since childhood I was brought up to deal with reflective abstract concepts like the metaphorical, the metaphysical and the sacramental. In later life there was a thankfully smooth transition of these concepts from the purely religious sphere to the artistic sphere, although these two things are one and the same thing for me. And in my fruitful engagements with other artists, regardless of their own religious beliefs, I have found these to be common concepts. It is almost as if on one hand, the adherent of a sacramental religion and on the other the artist, although they may speak different 'languages' and to different purposes, they nevertheless share a common 'linguistic' root. The Catholic and the Artist, at a fundamental level, can understand each other because the origins of their most precious metaphorical concepts are the same.[13]

Turning to his experience as a citizen, MacMillan set out a number of examples of the expression of anti-Catholic bigotry in Scottish life today. He cited a recent exhibition on the history of immigration into Scotland mounted by the Public Records Office. Various colourful stands had celebrated the cultural enrichment brought to the nation over the centuries by Flemish weavers, Jews, Asians, Chinese restaurateurs and many other national and ethnic minorities. Only the story of Irish immigration was given short shrift, dismissed in a cursory note on a wall panel: 'An increasing number of seasonal Irish labourers who worked in the summers in lowland Scotland stayed over due to poor economic performance in Ireland. Many of them became a burden on the local Parish Poor Laws.'[14]

Addressing the fraught issue of Scottish football, which he considers a 'metaphor for a more deep-seated malaise', MacMillan discussed corruption among officials and referees. The last Catholic to venture on to this slippery turf was the Celtic player Paolo Di Canio, who told the Italian sports magazine *Guerin Sportivo* three years earlier that many Scottish match officials are 'shameless' in their bias against Celtic and in their favourite handling of Rangers. 'I like everything in Scotland except the refereeing,' Di Canio said. 'Ninety per cent of the referees are Protestant and I am playing for a Catholic club. It shouldn't matter but it does.'[15] The Scottish media contemptuously dismissed Di Canio's complaints, accusing the player of temperamental instability. MacMillan demonstrated how subsequent investigations into the practices of the Scottish Football Association suggested that, if anything, Di Canio had underestimated the degree and prevalence of official wrongdoing.

Surveying the wider society MacMillan detected an anti-Catholicism that 'even when it is not particularly malign is as endemic as it is second nature . . . Our professions, our workplaces, our academic circles, our media and our sporting bodies are jam-packed with people like Donald Findlay.'[16]

Some years previously Magnus Linklater, a former editor of the *Scotsman*, had attended a memorial service for the Marquess of Bute. Afterwards, someone remarked how odd it was that the Queen had not thought fit to admit Lord Bute to the Order of the Thistle, despite his long record of generous service to the arts and heritage in Scotland. Linklater was intrigued and looked into the matter further. He found that not only were there no Catholics among the current members of the Order, but that the Queen had never honoured any Catholic in this way in all her years on the throne. An official spokesman said they thought there had been one Catholic at some time or other during the past three hundred years, but nobody could remember the name.

It is unlikely that the Queen was personally to blame for this omission. But those senior figures in the Edinburgh Establishment who are discreetly canvassed regarding the suitability of candidates are almost certainly at fault. Few Scottish Catholics, though, give a hoot about honours, and beyond being raised by Linklater as a curiosity, the matter excited little comment.

On other occasions, elements of the Scottish Establishment have shown themselves to be unduly suspicious of Catholic motives. Glasgow University was established in 1451 by Papal decree, a fact some of its lecturers nowadays prefer to forget. In 1992, to mark the quincentenary of the appointment of Robert Blacader as the first Archbishop of Glasgow, a group of Catholic notables raised £250,000 to endow the first Catholic chair at the university since the Reformation. The St Kentigern Chair for the Study of the Child was not expected to be controversial. The incumbent would head a multi-disciplinary project studying all aspects of childhood in contemporary society. Both the government and opposition had given it their blessing. The Scottish Secretary, Ian Laing, and Donald Dewar, his Shadow, had agreed to join the Pope's special representative Luigi Barbarito at the installation. But then came voices of dissent. A senior lecturer from the university said that the move represented 'a step backwards into the Middle Ages'. Inevitably, the spat attracted the attention of Pastor Jack Glass, who joined in the denunciations, claiming that the Catholic Church was insinuating itself into university life so it could exert an influence over academic affairs.[17] What should have been a joyous anniversary celebration for Glasgow's Catholics was soured by prejudice. More recently, a similar furore greeted proposals to merge St Andrew's College, the Catholic teacher-training college, with the university. A former head of the education department, Professor Eric Wilkinson, alluded to 'a right-wing faction of the Roman Catholic Church' who, he alleged, wanted to 'turn the clock back to before the Reformation'.[18]

The legal profession too has been disturbed by the occasional sectarian flare-up. The Catholic Lord Advocate, Lord Hardie, revealed that earlier in his career he faced a whispering campaign when standing for election as Dean of the Faculty of Advocates. Such examples lend weight to James MacMillan's argument that anti-Catholic feeling is by no means confined to the football terraces or the mean streets of the industrial west.

The writer Andrew O'Hagan grew up in the same Ayrshire town as James MacMillan. One day, O'Hagan found himself sitting at a literary dinner between a Scottish poet and a foreign author. 'The foreign author began asking the poet about discrimination against Catholics in banking and insurance, and about Masonic influence in the police. And why no writers? The foreigner wondered if Scotland was now the only place in the world where to be a Catholic was a distinct disadvantage. The poet was not enjoying himself. "No," he said eventually, "it's not like that. You're asking the wrong questions."' As O'Hagan concludes: 'There are no wrong questions in a civilized society.'[19]

Inevitably, Donald Findlay was sent MacMillan's lecture to review. He dismissed it as 'anecdotal and parochial'.[20] Although clearly intended to be pejorative, it is not clear what precise critical judgement these words are meant to convey. Faced with detailed evidence drawn from real human experience, people tend to call it 'empirical' if they approve, 'anecdotal' if they do not. As for 'parochial', one can only guess that Findlay was playing to the Edinburgh gallery, the high-minded burghers of Scotland's capital who like to pretend that sectarianism is a Glaswegian vice.

Findlay denies being a bigot. Indeed, he has threatened to sue anybody who calls him one. In Scotland he would probably win; and not only on account of his legendary forensic skills. Nothing, perhaps, so convincingly proves MacMillan's argument than the fact that were someone to swear foul oaths at Nelson Mandela, or exult in wading through Negro blood, he would have some difficulty persuading a Scottish jury that he was not a racist. But when similar insults are directed against Catholics, the very same jury is likely to take them as proof of nothing more than one whisky too many. Bigotry is a very old-fashioned thing. What Findlay and his ilk are about is altogether more post-modern. His sing-song was not so much an expression of sectarian hatred as a teasing allusion to its place in the sub-culture of Rangers FC specifically, and maybe of society at large. It was a half-ironic tribal dance, a reckless play of emotive cultural signifiers. To the secular mind something so elusive may be thought beyond culpability or censure; to the Catholic mind it is not. Nor, judging from the fact that Findlay was censured by his professional association, the Faculty of Advocates, and from the decision of St Andrew's University to withhold their honorary degree, is the singing of sectarian songs still acceptable to the more respectable elements of Scottish society.

But Findlay represented the broad consensus of Scottish punditry towards MacMillan's lecture when he declared that the whole issue of sectarianism was 'thirty years out of date'.[21] This was odd, since nearly all the concrete examples offered by the composer were drawn from the previous three to five years. Yet, despite such attempts to banish MacMillan's complaints to the margins of public space, the lecture was effective. The comment section of the *Herald* has become the main forum for debating the forbidden questions. In one contribution Peter Lynch, of the University of Stirling, suggested that the Scottish Parliament should set up an equivalent of the South African Truth and Reconciliation Commission to examine, without time limit, allegations of sectarian bigotry.

Anti-Catholic feeling saturates Scottish history. It drips from the founding charters of Scottish nationhood and culture. 'We detest and refuse,' says the National Covenant of 1580, 'the usurped authority of that Roman Antichrist.'[22] Part of the problem is that Protestantism (as its name implies), and particularly its Calvinist variant, largely defines itself in terms of its rejection of certain elements of the Catholic faith. Scotland's history has been, with good reason, described as theology interrupted by homicide. With that heritage, it would be extraordinary if old antagonisms did not, in some measure, persist today.

The 'Scotland's Shame' debate has not only stimulated wider consideration of the issue, but also clarified the terms in which the discussion should continue. The problem of workplace discrimination, for instance, can now be seen in its proper context.

For most of the twentieth century it was a matter of acute concern for Scotland's Catholics. Serious discrimination was practised in the shipyards along the Clyde and in many of the old smoke-stack industries. It was also common in proprietor-run small and medium-sized manufacturing companies, where the boss was often a Freemason or a member of the Orange Order. It did not abate until economic change swept away much of the heavy industry and globalization ushered in foreign (frequently American) management in the light-manufacturing sector.

Nowadays Catholic school leavers are just as likely, in fact slightly more likely, to end up in managerial or professional jobs than those from non-denominational schools. At the other end of the scale, however, unskilled Catholics are more likely to remain unemployed.

According to Professor Tom Devine of Aberdeen University, the economic betterment of the Catholic community has resulted in a significant shift in political attitudes. Where twenty-five years ago Catholics tended to be uneasy about independence or devolution, they are now more likely to favour independence than Protestants. This enabled Cardinal Winning to play off Labour against the Scottish Nationalist Party (SNP). When Labour politicians disappointed him, he would hint a tilt towards the Nationalists. The former SNP leader Alex Salmond made a reciprocal *démarche*, becoming a columnist in the Catholic magazine *Flourish* and standing up for the right of Catholic parents to send their children to denominational schools.

Some commentators emphasized the dangers of Winning's strategy, pointing out that the historic links between Labour and Catholicism have proved fruitful. More than a third of Scotland's MPs are Catholics and all the past nine provosts of Glasgow have been Catholics too.

But in Scotland, just as in the rest of the UK, the old ghetto Catholicism has given way to a looser and more open arrangement. Catholic identity now coexists with a range of other identities – political, social, national and those derived from popular culture. At its most extreme this can result in a Celtic supporter declaring himself a Catholic 'in the football sense; but not at all religious'. In such circumstances, Cardinal Winning's political steers, though still listened to with respect, were not felt to be binding.

The brouhaha over the retention or repeal of Clause 28 has given Scottish Catholics cause to doubt the Cardinal's political judgement. Many believe the debate was mishandled. The ostensible purpose of the clause was to prohibit local authorities from promoting homosexuality or the teaching of the acceptability of homosexuality as a family relationship in any maintained school. On the face of it, the clause would seem to be irrelevant to Catholic schools, which are free to determine their own sex education policies, and do so under the guidance of the bishops.

When the Scottish Executive first mooted repeal of the clause, they consulted the leaders of the main religious denominations. At this time Cardinal Winning had good channels of communication with the political leadership. (Donald Dewar's political adviser, John Rafferty, was a Catholic; indeed, his previous job had been as Director of Development for the Archdiocese of Glasgow.) Winning sat across the table from Dewar and received an assurance that the repeal would not lead to the promotion of homosexuality in schools. He left the politicians with the impression that he was satisfied with the assurances he had received. The first the press got to know of the plans for repeal was when they were briefed that the church leaders had been squared.

Quite why Winning changed his mind and joined the entrepreneur Brian Souter in a campaign against the repeal remains unclear. Some observers floated the unworthy suggestion that Winning had conceived papal ambitions and wished to send a signal to the more conservative electors in the Sacred College of Cardinals. Others reported that he had been profoundly shocked by video material and teaching aids involving thirteen-year-olds taking part in role-playing exercises, including one where children were invited to play the part of a man caught performing a homosexual act in a public lavatory.

Whatever the reason, the result was that Winning was branded a reactionary and a homophobe. Neither of these descriptions was fair. Thomas Winning was nothing if not orthodox; and the orthodoxy of the Catholic Church is the 1992 Catechism, in which unfair discrimination against homosexuals is explicitly outlawed. But Winning found his every statement twisted out of context and a speech he made in Malta misrepresented as having equated homosexuals with Nazis.

There is no doubt that the controversy spun out of control, dividing the Catholic community against itself. Frank McAveety, the Labour deputy minister charged with seeing the repeal through the Parliament, is himself a Catholic. John Rafferty, having left the First Minister's office, wrote an article in the *Scotsman* criticizing the Cardinal's stand: 'It is his use of the language of sin, condemnation and perversion which have no place today. I am certain that parents want to hear the language of love – the central message of the New Testament. It is loving that matters whether in straight or gay relationships.'[23] Father Gordon Brown of South Queensferry came out as a homosexual and announced that a support group of gay priests would campaign against the Cardinal.

In his Malta speech Winning had focused upon an issue of great importance to him. 'Marriage is not an institution of the Church,' he said, 'Marriage is from the Natural Law. The Church, realizing how essential to children is the stable union for life between a man and a woman, has made it one of the events in human living that can expect special and continuous help from Jesus Christ. Marriage is, for the Church, a sacrament.'[24] The Cardinal had for some time been concerned by a tendency common among right-wing libertarians and New Labour alike to treat gay partnerships, heterosexual cohabitation and elective single-parenthood as mere lifestyle choices that could claim equal validity with Christian marriage and between which public policy should remain neutral. It was the intention of many of those around Winning, and probably of the Cardinal himself, to initiate a public debate that would challenge these assumptions and affirm the special and sacramental status of marriage. But somehow the Cardinal found himself caught up in a sterile and ill-tempered row about homosexuality that left the Church looking insensitive, authoritarian and rather out of touch. This led to a weakening of the Catholic Church's political position in Scotland, leaving it dangerously exposed over the issue of denominational schooling.

The battle to retain control of its own schools is the most important issue facing Catholics in Scotland. It is a battle that has had to be fought and re-fought on scores of occasions in the past. Today there are more than 60 Catholic secondary schools and over 350 Catholic primary schools in Scotland, with some 130,000 pupils enrolled, representing 16 per cent of the total school population. Virtually 100 per cent of Catholic children of primary school age attend Catholic schools. In the west of Scotland, where Catholic secondary schools are plentiful, some 90 per cent of children transfer to them. (Where there is a drop-out, it is usually in affluent suburbs where socially ambitious parents select a prestigious, non-denominational alternative.) The Catholic schools are vital to the maintenance of a Catholic ethos and to the transmission of a common cultural tradition and sense of Catholic identity. Without them, it is unlikely that anything resembling a cohesive Catholic 'community' would survive for more than two or three generations.

That is precisely why there has been a sustained campaign to destroy them. The prototypical campaigner against Catholic education was Alexander Ratcliffe, an admirer of Hitler, who founded the Scottish Protestant League in the 1930s. He coined a slogan that is still in currency today, when he campaigned against 'Rome on the Rates'. The notion that Protestants' tax pounds are used to inculcate religious ideas of which many citizens disapprove is sustained by the myth that Catholics tend to be welfare scroungers who make little contribution to the exchequer themselves.

Through the second half of the twentieth century members of

the Free Church and the Orange Order kept up Ratcliffe's cry. The Orangemen, at least, have not tried to disguise their motives. David Bryce, Grand Secretary of the Orange Order until December 1994, has made perfectly plain where he expects the abolition of Catholic schools to lead: to the steady erosion and ultimate disappearance of the Catholic faith in Scotland.[25]

Nowadays, however, a large number of people in the political and religious mainstream, often ostensibly liberal in outlook, make common cause with extremists in calling for abolition. The notion that denominational education is one of the primary causes of sectarian hatred has put down stubborn roots. In response, Catholics point out that Catholic schools exist side-by-side with non-denominational ones throughout England and Wales, across much of Continental Europe, and in the major towns and cities of the United States, without generating any ill feeling whatsoever. Indeed, the only places where sectarianism remains an acute problem are Scotland, Northern Ireland and those parts of the old Confederacy where the Ku-Klux-Klan's writ still runs. That fact alone should direct anyone honestly seeking to identify the true causes of the phenomenon towards the cultural assumptions and institutions of Protestant fundamentalism, rather than those of the Catholic Church.

Unlike the Church of England, the Church of Scotland runs no schools of its own. At the Kirk's General Assembly in 1998, a Dumbarton minister appealed for an end to what he emotively termed 'segregation'. The Reverend John Cairns called for an education system that reflected 'an ethos of a nation that shares many things'.[26] Scotland's Catholics have no quarrel with the idea of sharing. Indeed, they regard their own cultural distinctiveness as a gift they can bring to enrich Scotland's national life. Real sharing requires an element of cultural exchange, the potential for which is seriously reduced by the imposition of uniformity in education. Catholic schools may be separate, but they are by no means exclusive. They welcome pupils from other denominations and faiths. Glasgow's Muslims, for instance, show a marked propensity to opt for Catholic education.

A new and insidious argument seeks to make Scotland's Catholic schools victims of their own success. The schools have proved to be powerful engines of social mobility, bringing a socially disadvantaged immigrant community up to parity with the rest of the population. A group of activists within the Educational Institute of Scotland (Scotland's largest teachers' union) claim that the economic and social indicators show that the schools have completed their task and they are, therefore, now redundant. It seems extraordinary that teachers, of all people, should see schools in narrowly functional terms and as such readily disposable items. This kind of brutally dismissive disrespect for the institutions that embody the shared experience and collective memory of the Catholic community is not at all unusual. Consequently, Scotland's Catholics have begun to worry that though Scottish Protestants may steadily be losing their religion, they are not necessarily losing their reflexive anti-Catholicism; and that a new generation of secular Scots may retain the mean-spiritedness that was a feature of hard-line Calvinism. James MacMillan addressed this concern in his Edinburgh Festival lecture:

This tendency to restrict, to control and to enforce conformity and homogeneity is an obsessive and paranoid flaw in the Scottish character. It is not confined to the Presbyterian mind. It has eased effortlessly into the collective psyche of much secular discourse, so that even the humanist and liberal objections to religious belief (and to Catholicism in particular) are motivated by the same urge to restrict, control and enforce.[27]

Catholics who live outside Scotland may question MacMillan's assertion that this is a specifically Scottish trait. The face that secular humanism turns towards Catholics quite frequently wears the expression of the bully. In the United States, it is often observed that Catholics are the only minority whom it is permissible to belittle or revile in politically correct company – a fact that prompted the Yale academic Peter Viereck to term this hostility towards Catholics 'the anti-Semitism of the liberal intellectuals'.[28]

This mindset certainly constitutes a barrier to the advancement of Catholic ambitions, but not necessarily an insuperable one. The immediate task facing Catholics in Scotland is to negotiate some cultural space, to champion a richer and more meaningful definition of pluralism than the secular powers have so far allowed. This is not a job well suited to arch-reactionaries in fancy dress. But Scotland can boast a small but energetic Catholic intelligentsia, liberal in outlook and with its political centre of gravity on the left. Sadly, in 1993, it lost its unofficial leader with the death of Anthony Ross, at one time the Provincial of the Dominican Order in Britain.

Ross was an early Scottish Nationalist and a close friend of the poet Hugh MacDiarmid. 'In the impossible event of my abandoning atheism,' MacDiarmid once said, 'I will follow Ross.'[29] As a priest at the Chaplaincy Centre in Edinburgh's George Square, Ross was Scotland's Michael Hollings, ministering to the homeless, drug addicts, alcoholics and former prisoners. He was an active peace campaigner with the Campaign for Nuclear Disarmament and a pioneer in the pastoral care of homosexuals. His writing spanned an extraordinary range of disciplines – including poetry, history, theology, a biography of John Knox and studies in comparative penology.

The Dominicans also supplied the theologian Gilbert Markus, who spent the mid-nineties as Chaplain at the University of Strathclyde; and the Jesuits the moral philosopher Jack Mahoney, who returned to Scotland after retiring from his post as Professor of Business Ethics at the London Business School. Intellectually charismatic priests tend to catalyse the formation of loose networks of Catholic laymen – writers, academics, professionals, artists and composers such as James MacMillan – such that almost any moment can appear to portend a Catholic intellectual revival.

The present period is no different. James Macmillan ended his Edinburgh Festival lecture with a summons to Scottish Catholics to develop a new critique of globalized capitalism. And in advance of the opening of the Scottish Parliament, the Catholic philosopher John Haldane ventured a list of ideas Catholics could contribute to the 'new Scotland':

One is the concept of society as a moral community in which responsibilities stand alongside rights, in which material goods are produced with an eye to benefit as well as to profit, and in which the value of life is respected as well as its quality being promoted. Intellectually and culturally the Catholic contribution should be to challenge materialism, instrumentalism, hedonism and short-term gratification, and to present in a Scottish context the central ingredients of the Catholic philosophy of culture: abstract reflection, artistic endeavour and joyous good living.[30]

Persuade any Scot to step out of the shadow of his history, and he will probably drink to at least some of that.

The Catholic Church is by far the largest organization of any kind in the world, with close to one billion adherents, representing some 18 per cent, or more than one in six, of the earth's population. It has been estimated that by the year 2025 the total number of Catholics will have doubled since the 1960s. The Church employs over one a and a half million personnel, including almost 900,000 nuns, more than 400,000 priests and nearly 4,200 bishops. Despite reports of a crisis in vocations, the numbers of men coming forward for priestly ordination increased year on year throughout the 1980s, contributing to a worldwide increase of 30 per cent over the decade. Confined to the periphery, there is a long queue of women eager to be ordained, but not deemed eligible. And though there has been a noticeable tilt towards the developing world in the Church's composition, the country with the highest density of priests per head of Catholic population has remained the United States. There, the late twentieth century was a boom time for the Church. During its final decade, Catholicism was the only major denomination still growing, and by the millennium one in four US citizens was Catholic.

They speak this not in the streets of Askelon, or indeed anywhere else, for in the modern Church 'triumphalism' is the new taboo. Any number of things are covered by that word, from holding public processions to singing 'Faith of Our Fathers'; but chiefly the new mood is against taking any pleasure in the fact that the hierarchical, institutional Church survived the twentieth century more or less intact. It is not out of any religious jingoism that these facts are reproduced here; rather because they stand in striking contrast to some of the most common secular assumptions in Britain. The idea that institutional religion generally, and Catholicism in particular, is in a condition of terminal decline is one so easily and frequently asserted that it has become a false truism. An extraordinary number of people continue to believe, as their grandfathers and great-grandfathers believed before them, that religion is a picturesque oddity whose continuing presence is an embarrassment, and one that must surely disappear before too long. This view is held as stubbornly at the beginning of the twenty-first century as it was at the beginning of the twentieth. Yet, whenever the obsequies have been read over religion – at the Enlightenment; again after Darwin; by Nietzsche at the turn of the century; and solemnly after Auschwitz – God has always shown himself to be very much alive. And just as the Christian idea has survived the storm of the twentieth century, so the institution of the Catholic Church remains a force to be reckoned with, even in the most socially developed and technologically advanced of modern societies.

By all conventional measures, Catholicism reached its zenith in England and Wales, perhaps surprisingly, during the 1960s. The year 1959 saw a record 13,735 adult conversions; in 1961, almost 13 per cent of marriages took place in Catholic churches; infant baptisms were running at 15 per cent of live births until 1964; and the Catholic paper, the *Universe*, was selling 300,000 copies per week. Popular, community-based Catholicism was still able to command the loyalty of the working class. When Archbishop Heenan first arrived in Liverpool in 1957, during what he called 'a period of intense zeal in the Catholic Church', a crowd of 40,000 people turned out to attend a welcoming service on the site of what would become 'Paddy's wigwam', the new Metropolitan Cathedral.[1] As he made a tour of his parishes in the following weeks and months, Heenan found that his visits sparked spontaneous public festivities. Houses were decorated with papal flags and bunting and whole neighbourhoods spilled out on to the streets to cheer his progress.

This was a community content within its citadel. One of the effects of historic sectarianism in Liverpool had been to concentrate the Catholic minority in the city centre and the docklands. Vauxhall, Scotland, Kirkdale and Everton were identifiably Catholic districts, each with its own infrastructure of parochial schools and

Catholic drinking clubs. Priests were intimately bound up in community life. They sat on the committees of the social clubs, sometimes even negotiating deals with the brewery; they attended bingo nights and dances, supervised sports and youth activities, and taught in the schools. Most parishioners were extremely poor and many were only semi-literate. As well as visiting the sick and the elderly, the priest needed to be on hand to fill in official forms and draft job applications. He was a figure of authority as well, on occasion administering a clip round the ear to a local delinquent rather than involve the police.

Inevitably, the Church took a hand in politics. Between 1885 and 1929, the Scotland Division of Liverpool was represented by T. P. O'Connor, who continued to sit as an Irish Nationalist, even after the foundation of the Free State. By the time O'Connor died, most Catholics had affiliated to Labour. A group of Catholic families took control of the party machine in the ghetto areas, establishing the pattern of a political mafia that would influence the city's politics for generations. When a vacancy arose in the Liverpool Exchange constituency in 1970, one or another member of the Parry family represented every single ward at the selection meeting. No outsider was surprised when Bob Parry emerged as the prospective parliamentary candidate. Yet the victor had not enjoyed such a clear run as it seemed. Bob's brother Jimmy felt that the Jesuit education he had received at St Francis Xavier's College equipped him far better than his sibling for the role of representing the electors at Westminster. This view was shared by a number of influential members of the clan and caused some offstage acrimony in the pre-selection phase.

Many similar spats had taken place in earlier decades over the allocation of seats on the city council. Political squabbles would sometimes be resolved through the mediation of the parish priest; or in exceptional cases the shortlist might be sent to the Archbishop. But Liverpool's sectarian politics were never so neat and clear-cut as Glasgow's. Though the Conservative and Unionist Party held a special appeal for Protestant and especially Orange voters, with the Tories holding the majority of parliamentary seats in Liverpool until as late as 1964, non-Catholics constituted a majority in the city's Labour Party too. In the 1950s, Liverpool's politics were characterized by a complex and shifting pattern of caucuses, only some of them representing sectarian allegiances. The Catholic Action caucus was the one that worked most closely with the Church hierarchy to combat the spread of atheistic socialism. At a council election where a Communist had the temerity to stand, the parish priest patrolled the polling station throughout the day, having first ensured that the ballot box was placed at the foot of a statue of the Virgin Mary.

Assured in their leadership roles and enjoying considerable status and esteem, some of the clergy lived high on the hog. The philosopher Anthony Kenny, later to become Master of Balliol College, Oxford, worked as a curate in Liverpool during the early 1960s. Life in the presbytery provided Kenny with a foretaste of the high-table truffles to come. 'We ate good, and often expensive, food,' he remembers; 'the parish priest was generous with cocktails and there was wine several times a week.'[2] Meanwhile, their parishioners, making do on short rations and small beer, still managed a chirpy buoyancy. They did not know then that before long their communities would be ripped asunder; that their friends and neighbours would be redistributed to soulless dormitories on the city's edge; that the factories would close and no new ones would open; or that their streets would be surrendered to pimps, prostitutes and drug-dealers; and that amidst the urban blight the flame of faith would gutter and almost fail.

Indeed, a sign of the optimism and confidence that inspired Liverpool's Catholics in the decades before the old communities were dispersed can be seen in their ambitious plan for a cathedral. In 1928, Archbishop Downey had secured (over cocktails, as it happens) the services of Sir Edwin Lutyens, the most renowned architect in the country. Lutyens did not share the Catholic faith, but this did not matter to Downey, whose sole concern was to hire the best in the business. There was a nice symmetry in the fact that Sir Giles Gilbert Scott, who designed Liverpool's Anglican cathedral, a Gothic masterpiece, was a Catholic. Besides, Lutyens, as a frequent guest at Mells, was now moving in Catholic circles and displayed sufficient sympathy with the Catholic aesthetic in his conversations with his prospective patron. On Downey's instructions, Lutyens drew up plans for what was intended to be one of the greatest churches in the world. The Cathedral of Christ the King was to be twice the size of St Paul's in London and would be capped by an enormous dome, bigger even than that of St Peter's in Rome, and which was sure to dominate the Mersey skyline. A foundation stone was laid in 1933, and work began on the crypt.

When Lutyens died on New Year's Day 1944, the plans for his cathedral were found strewn around his deathbed. He had only to look about him for monuments to a successful career: a cenotaph here; a viceroy's house there; any number of houses built to gratify Edwardian grandees that grace the covers of *Country Life* to this day. But the architect's last thoughts had clearly turned to unfinished business. The Church moved heaven and earth to raise the money to complete his building. But where Pugin had his Earl of Shrewsbury and Cardinal Vaughan could look to the 15th Duke of Norfolk to stump up for Westminster Cathedral, Liverpool could find no such benefactor. The intervening years had seen a transformation of the national economy. The Catholic landed classes were simply not rich enough any more. The crisis required a great Catholic plutocrat, but none had yet emerged. Heenan tried another tack, asking Giles Gilbert Scott's younger brother Adrian to scale down the Lutyens original to more affordable dimensions. But not even in thriftily shrunken form could the great project be brought in on budget.

Hence Frederick Gibberd's wigwam. Its architectural distinctiveness has won the hearts of many of Liverpool's faithful, if largely because the Catholic Scouser will always stand up for his own when it is mocked. The bishops seem happy enough: the cathedral's form suits the post-Vatican II fashion for liturgy in the round. Most Catholics can find something good to say about it, if only that Patrick Reyntiens' stained glass is outstanding. But Evelyn Waugh detested its circular arrangement, with the congregation sitting in tiers 'as in an operating-theatre'.[3] Many like-minded traditionalists pray that one day, when the concrete crumbles and the modernist edifice collapses into dust, Lutyens's more expansive vision – a synthesis of European Catholic history combining Roman, Byzantine, Romanesque and Renaissance elements – will at last be realized, to stand solid for 2,000 years to come.

The imprecation serves as a metaphor for traditionalist aspirations for the Church more generally. Much of what has been constructed since the Second Vatican Council, whether in the fields of liturgy, theology or ecclesiology, has, like the wigwam, begun to show defects in the concrete. Already many of the innovations of the 1960s and '70s seem curiously retro. Some were dated even at the moment of their inception. The fad for folk Masses, for instance, naïvely conceived to appeal to youth, succeeded only in alienating its target demographic. Like Bob Dylan, youth had already gone electric. The class of '73 whose musical tastes ranged from Led Zeppelin to glamrock were repelled by hollow, acoustic renditions of 'Morning Has Broken'. Meanwhile, as their elders sighed for Palestrina, they shook their heads in amazement as the hallowed cadences of Church Latin were replaced (in the name of intelligibility, if you please) with the gibberish of 'Kum-bay-ya', a word whose meaning, if it ever had one, had long ago been lost in the thicket of the Benin rainforest.

The crowds that welcomed Archbishop Heenan to Liverpool surged out again to say farewell, thronging the platforms of Lime Street station, when he departed for Westminster in 1963. No Catholic bishop could attract such public displays of enthusiasm and affection today. An estimated 2,000 people gathered in the cathedral piazza and along Victoria Street during the funeral service for Cardinal Hume – a meagre crowd compared to the half million Londoners who lined the streets between the Brompton Oratory and Kensal Green to see off Cardinal Manning in 1892. No doubt jut as many mourned Hume in their hearts or watched his Requiem Mass on television, but the poor turnout was a salient demonstration of the extent to which Catholicism has withdrawn from the streets. Corpus Christi parades, once a colourful feature of every parish, are nowadays rarely seen. In London, the annual walk to Tyburn to honour the English martyrs has been discontinued. In Scotland, thousands of families from across the nation used to congregate at Carfin Grotto; today a mere handful maintain the tradition. Only Our Lady of Walsingham, it seems, can still raise a quorum. Not since the hole-in-the-wall days of persecution has so much studied discretion been brought to the practice of the Catholic faith. Its craving for social assimilation combined with an excess of ecumenical tact has rendered the Catholic community almost invisible. No wonder so many people believe it is bound for extinction.

Admittedly, the somewhat upbeat account of Catholic fortunes at the beginning of this chapter seems at odds with the British Catholic experience since the 1960s. Another column of figures could be adduced to create quite a different impression. Conversions, which stood at 12,000 in England and Wales in 1964, had fallen to just over 5,000 a decade later and have remained at much the same level ever since. Catholic marriages have declined by 60 per cent. Mass attendance has halved since 1966. Seminaries have closed down as the number of ordinations has halved. The numbers leaving the priesthood to marry has caused an even greater dearth of clergy. Extrapolate these trajectories into the future, as secular commentators frequently do with barely suppressed glee, and Catholicism will be more or less extinct in Britain by about 2030.[4]

As usual, the reality is rather more nuanced than the bald figures suggest. The drop in Mass attendance is often presented as evidence of a wholesale abandonment of religious observance. Yet if Catholics today were discovered to be only a tad less punctilious than the generation of 1966, turning out to Mass on average once a fortnight rather than every single week, that alone would almost wholly account for the halving in churchgoing over the period. Should Catholics become even less conscientious in the future, putting in an appearance only one week in four, the headlines would scream that attendance had plummeted by 75 per cent and Catholicism was in free fall. But though someone who goes to church once a month may be something of a slacker by traditional Catholic standards, he cannot be branded an apostate.

Recent evidence suggests that this pattern of irregular worship is precisely what is happening. A survey in one London parish identified 1,000 different faces coming through the church doors over a three-week period; yet in no single week did the congregation exceed 600. Elsewhere priests have found they have to distribute census forms over six consecutive weeks in order to compile a comprehensive register of 'regular' Mass-goers.

A variety of social factors affect the frequency with which Catholics attend Mass. Father Michael O'Halloran SJ, the parish priest at Farm Street, Mayfair, has identified a phenomenon at the top end of the market that he calls 'playing the squire'. Affluent thirty-somethings acquire manor houses in the country to which they head off most weekends. Those from recusant families who inherit their properties may find that their house comes with a chapel attached. But the more typical yuppie soon discovers there is scant provision for Catholic worship in many rural areas in the south of England. Often, they find themselves drawn to the village church, effectively becoming Catholic in London and C. of E. in the country. The numbers defining this syndrome in its pure form are tiny indeed. But this behaviour is mimicked down the social scale as moderately well-off Londoners buy cottages rather than manor houses, or snap up offers of discounted weekend breaks in country hotels. Take into account longer and more frequent foreign holidays, longer working hours and the relaxation of the rules on Sunday shopping, and lifestyle factors – the manifold temptations of a consumer society – emerge as more powerful determinants of the erosion of the parish averages than any surge in conversions to atheism.

Equally, it has not been the arguments of science that have undermined the piety of the Catholic working class so much as the depredations of town planners. The destruction of the old Catholic ghettos disrupted a web of social and cultural relationships that affiliated individuals to one another and to the Church.

Too much tends to be made of the coercive powers of the priest in the old ghetto community. The stereotype depicts a craven congregation driven unwillingly to Sunday Mass on pain of mortal sin. While it is true that the old-fashioned priest knew his congregation well, and once alerted that a particular family was absent, might demand to know the reason why, his concern was always as much pastoral as disciplinarian. Nor was the average Irish Catholic in the inner city so easily cowed. If the local church were full, it was because it was the focus of community life, and because it provided a potent spiritual and aesthetic experience through the liturgy each Sunday. The glow of the sanctuary lamp, the haunting echo of the consecration bell, the alto voices in the choir – even the gaudy plaster saints together exercised a powerful enchantment.

There is evidence that better-educated and better-off Catholics appear to be more dutiful in observing the Sabbath than their poorer and unemployed co-religionists.[5] Again, this challenges the idea that the decline of religious practice owes very much to intellectual progress. The persistent stop-at-home is rarely a bookish type with shelves full of Hume and Voltaire, Darwin and Dawkins, but is much more likely to be poorly educated, claiming benefit, living an isolated existence on an overspill estate and spending Sunday mornings minding the kids or doing the family shopping.

Many other factors contribute to a greater or lesser extent to the attrition of Sunday observance. Undeniably there has been a shift in attitudes among Catholics towards exercising private judgement in disciplinary matters rather than abiding by the Church's regulations. Others will have rebelled against their family background; possibly an even greater number will have temporarily abandoned the practice of religion in their late teens and twenties, only to return to it when they have children of their own. The Catholic sociologist Michael Hornsby-Smith says that during the period in question the nature of Catholic identity was transforming itself 'from something that was externally ascribed to a group to something elected by the individual'.[6] This suggests that though church-going may be less common, what remains is more whole-hearted and authentic.

Equally, the crisis in vocations is not quite what it seems. In the early 1970s, there were 7,600 priests in England and Wales; today the figure has dropped to 5,700. The number of parish churches and chapels open to the public has, however, stayed stable at around 3,600. The shortage is not so acute that any parish has been left without a priest; indeed, the overall density of clergy per head of Catholic population in the UK remains healthier than in many other countries. Yet priests complain of having to cope with a greatly increased workload. Like the doctor or the politician, the priest's casebook expands as rapid economic and social change multiply the numbers of the distressed. Even with the help of some 400 newly recruited deacons, and with the laity taking on some of the functions priests used to perform, some dioceses have all but declared a state of emergency, doubling and redoubling their prayers for vocations. The average age of the Catholic clergy is increasing alarmingly because of the dip in both retention and recruitment since 1970, a phenomenon whose implications will take decades to work through.

Once again, secular commentators have seized on the 'priest famine' as proof that faith is heading for the exit. A variety of explanations are adduced – an alleged revolt against institutional religion; the 'impossible' demands of priestly celibacy; and, from quite another camp, the supposedly baleful influence of Vatican II. Do we need such broad-brush theories to account for a shortfall of 1,900 priests over 30 years, or 63 per annum? When we experience an even more acute shortage of nurses, we do not, after all, imagine that the nation has ceased to believe in the NHS.

In the United States, by contrast, the tendency has been to seek explanations at the micro rather than the macro level. One intriguing line of enquiry has been to examine the influence of changing public attitudes towards homosexuality. Before it became acceptable to come out, the priesthood offered an attractive refuge for gay men. They did not have to explain why they were unmarried; they could enjoy an exclusively male domestic environment; and if they felt morally uncomfortable with their inclinations, the vow of celibacy offered an escape from a troubling dilemma. Like tends to recruit like. The proportion of men with a gay orientation has tended to be higher among the Catholic clergy than in the population at large.[7] It seems reasonable to speculate that the softening of society's censure of homosexuals might have led to a significant reduction in recruitment to the priesthood. But even this is too facile. While the overall enquiry has been inconclusive, anecdotal evidence has surfaced of heterosexual men deserting seminaries, claiming to have been put off by a pervasive 'gay subculture'. The lesson is that there is probably no single, readily identifiable, explanation of the priest shortage, but a host of small ones – each one elusive, more complex than at first it seems and driven by wider currents in the world beyond the Church.

In fact, the huge numbers entering the English seminaries in the 1960s were something of a freak occurrence. They were the result of a spectacularly large wave of Irish immigration during the previous decade. Instead of single men coming to find work, whole families took the boat to England. Back in Ireland it had become an established tradition among larger families for one or more sons to opt for the priesthood, usually entering the seminary during their teens. This tradition generally survived the crossing. Quite suddenly the seminaries were full to bursting point. But soon the immigration began to tail off and the newly arrived Irish quickly adapted their family planning to the constraints of small council dwellings. The falling birth rate combined with a wider provision of educational and employment opportunities made the vast, barrack-like seminaries redundant within a generation.

Today's seminarian tends to come from a very different background. He is much more likely to be a graduate and to have tried out some other career first, often reaching his late twenties or early thirties before deciding to commit himself to the Church. Andrew Pinsent was a particle physicist working at CERN before enrolling at the English College in Rome in the 1990s. Among his fifty or so fellow seminarians were a former astronomer who had specialized in the structure of quasars, three solicitors, a lecturer in chemical engineering, an IT consultant, a former local government officer and half a dozen teachers. 'It is easy to be deceived by technological and cultural change into believing that a religious calling belongs to a period that is past,' says Pinsent. 'The reality is that God is still calling, even in the world of the Internet and anti-matter accelerators.'[8]

The latest trend points to a modest increase in ordinations. There has also been a spurt in the numbers volunteering to be monks. Some of the orders that have set up websites during the past few years report that they are inundated with requests to try out the contemplative life and are having to turn people away. Even the Cistercians of the Strict Observance, who require a vow of silence, are hearing a clamour at the gates. It is far too soon to tell whether this outbreak of enthusiasm marks the start of some new cycle in the life of the Church. The bishops cannot afford to be complacent, but they need not be too pessimistic either. 'I have no time for prophets of gloom,' Cormac Murphy-O'Connor announced on the occasion of his installation at Westminster. 'I do not believe these are gloomy times for the Catholic Church in our country.'[9] The new Archbishop chose as his motto '*Gaudium et spes*' – joy and hope. The sins against hope are despair and presumption.

Who were the prophets of gloom the new Archbishop had in mind? It is possible that he was thinking of the sort of people Belloc might have called 'enemies of the Faith' in the secular press. But the Catholic community has more than enough Jeremiahs of its own, particularly on its traditionalist wing.

While it is well known that the Catholic Church in Britain is riven by strident factionalism, misconceptions abound about who is in which camp and what precisely is at issue. The impression given by the media is that the Church is divided into two. One party combines right-wing politics, theological conservatism, opposition to women priests, a distaste for homosexuals, a tendency to moral rigidity and a preference for elaborate and old-fashioned ritual, usually in Latin. By contrast, their opponents are supposed to be left-of-centre, non-judgemental, ecumenical, informal, open-minded, open-sandalled and prefer their Mass in the vernacular. The immediate appeal of this analysis is easy to see: it mirrors the familiar conservative versus left-liberal/progressive culture war in the wider society. But such a model is of little use in examining the complex antagonisms within Catholicism. Concepts such as 'tradition' and 'authority', for instance, have a quite different set of meanings and resonances within the Catholic context than in general cultural discourse. Those who venture into this treacherous territory are well advised to discard many of their preconceptions. Even when it is possible to escape the conservative/liberal paradigm, there is no alternative taxonomy to hand. One is constantly thrown back on the old vocabulary: radical, progressive, liberal, conservative, reactionary and fundamentalist.

One way or another all the players in the game end up defining themselves in relation to the Second Vatican Council. Whether Vatican II was an 'occurrence', an 'event' or a 'continuing process' is a question that is itself hotly contested. Arguably the only way of obtaining a clear understanding of what the Vatican II's implications are for the contemporary Catholic argument is to examine the Council in the light of the multiple ironies and contradictions that, forty years on, continue to attend it.

It was the twenty-first ecumenical council of the Church. Previous councils had been called only when there was some heresy to be extirpated or some new dogma to proclaim. The Council of Trent, which ended in 1563, was summoned to meet the challenges of the Reformation and to lay the foundations of the Counter-Reformation. Vatican II did nothing of the sort. It reiterated the teaching of previous councils, but added no new dogma of its own. It is described, therefore, as a 'pastoral' rather than a dogmatic council.

When, on 25 January 1959, Pope John XXIII first told his cardinals that he planned to call his bishops together, the news was received in puzzled silence. Officials in the Curia were against the idea, wary that a council might strip away many of their own bureaucratic powers. Some tried to dissuade the Pope, quoting Cardinal Manning's dictum that to call an unnecessary council was to 'tempt God'. Others were genuinely baffled and sought a fuller explanation of the council's purpose. In answer, the Pope reportedly flung open the windows of his room, saying that his motive was to 'let in some fresh air'.

There had only been one council since Trent: the First Vatican Council of 1870, which had promulgated the doctrine of papal infallibility. Little had changed in the Catholic Church for 400 years. This was not surprising, as Trent had set out to be definitive. At its conclusion Pope Pius IV issued a Bull of Confirmation that not merely discouraged but forbade anyone 'to publish any commentaries, glosses . . . or any kind of interpretation whatsoever of the decrees of the council'.[10] At Trent, the fathers had sat through twenty-five sessions over eighteen years, under five popes. Now, the Church wished to close off debate. The Counter-Reformation went on to generate its own institutional culture, and, in the Baroque, even a favoured aesthetic. It gave Catholicism a distinct identity in direct opposition to all things Protestant. The immutability of its doctrines was one of Catholicism's greatest strengths; the mannered austerity of its style, one of its greatest attractions. People loved the old Church and most of its ways.

And it was certainly successful. When Pope John called his council, the churches were full, Catholicism was expanding, the Modernists had been seen off. There was no sense of institutional panic whatsoever. If the Church was to consider its position, it would do so in a climate of confidence and from a position of strength.

Yet Pope John was not alone in having sniffed something musty and decaying in the air. For some time the practitioners of what was termed the *nouvelle théologie*, centred around a group of French Jesuits and Dominicans, promoted a movement of Ressourcement, which involved looking back before the Council of Trent to rediscover biblical, patristic and scholastic texts, and finding new meaning and significance in them. They were reacting against what they saw as a decayed or exhausted school of Roman neo-scholastic philosophy that had degenerated into sterile logic-chopping and the manufacture of petty rules. The unofficial leader of the group was Henri de Lubac, who would come to be recognized as one of the guiding spirits of Vatican II.

When he opened the Council on 11 October 1962, the Pope set the tone for the proceedings by announcing that 'the substance of the ancient doctrine of the Deposit of Faith is one thing, but the way it is presented is another'. It steadily became clear that the Counter-Reformation or Tridentine period in the Church's history was being brought to a close. The Council's job was to institute an *aggiornamento* – a bringing-up-to-date of structures and attitudes. Catholics were to emerge from their 'embattled citadel' and engage with the outside society in a new way, seeking to transform the world by teaching the truth through love. That truth would no longer be something the Church felt it monopolized; rather, Catholicism would open itself to all authentic truths, wherever they could be found. The Church would develop an expertise in what it is to be human; and reading 'the signs of the times' would interpret them in the light of the Gospel.

The Council met in four sessions, one each autumn between 1962 and 1965. It published four Constitutions, nine Decrees and three Declarations, which, taken together, are now recognized to have instituted a radical transformation of the Catholic Church and to have been the most important religious event of the twentieth century. One of its most immediate effects was to introduce to ordinary Catholics a new and sometimes baffling vocabulary. Henceforth the Church would cease to see itself as an institution belonging to the clergy where little was expected of the laity other than that they should pay and pray. Now it was to be a 'pilgrim church' made up of the 'people of God'.

John XXIII died during the Council and was succeeded by Pope Paul VI. The new Pope did not follow the example of Pius IV and seek to restrict discussion of its conclusions. Indeed, the debate has continued ever since and the documents of Vatican II have been found susceptible to numerous competing interpretations. Moreover, though the programme of the Council Fathers has still not been fully implemented, much has been carried out in the name of Vatican II that either cannot be found in the documents or is in direct contradiction to them.

The most blatant changes have taken place in the liturgy. While the Council itself reaffirmed the place of Latin as the official language of the Church and explicitly protected its liturgical use, it also permitted the vernacular. In the hands of subsequent reformers, this permission became a mandate for revolutionary change. In most local parishes throughout the country, Latin has been more or less abolished, with perhaps one or two parts of the Mass being sung or spoken in Latin on special occasions. It remains very much a living language, however, in the larger churches and cathedrals. In London, the Latin services at Westminster Cathedral, at Farm Street and the Brompton Oratory are packed out, while the vernacular services in the suburban churches are often half-empty.

The people who cram the pews to hear the Mass in Latin cannot be dismissed as nostalgic reactionaries, old fogeys or liturgical purists, for these services are celebrated in the Latin version of the Novus Ordo – the new formula introduced after the Council, which liturgical fundamentalists shun as a 'bastard rite'. A frequent cause of confusion to non-Catholics who read (or sometimes write) about Catholic affairs in the newspapers is the use of the phrase 'the Latin Mass' as a synonym for the old Tridentine Rite. The Latin Mass Society, for instance, is concerned not so much with preserving the use of the Latin tongue as with preserving and reviving the old liturgical form.

The reason many traditionalists eschew the term 'Tridentine' is because they believe that though the Mass was codified at Trent, it is to all intents and purposes the same Mass that was celebrated for 1,500 years before that. According to the liturgical historian Adrian Fortescue: 'Our Mass goes back without essential change to the age when Caesar ruled the world and thought he could stamp out the faith of Christ, when our fathers met together before dawn and sang a hymn to Christ as God . . .'[11] Many twentieth-century reformers dispute this, claiming that the new rite, devised after Vatican II, more closely reflects the liturgical practice of the early Church. Hence the long-running debate whether the priest should face the high altar or face the people. (The consensus among experts today is that the reformers of the 1960s got this wrong: the early Christian priests did not, after all, face the people, but always looked towards the East.)

In Britain, the campaign to preserve the Tridentine Rite began even as Vatican II was in progress. 'Is it too much to ask that all parishes should be ordered to have two Masses, a "Pop" for the young and a "Trad" for the old?' wrote Evelyn Waugh to Archbishop Heenan in August 1964. 'Do not despair . . .' Heenan replied. 'We shall try to keep the needs of all in mind – Pops, Trads, Rockers, Mods, With-its and Without-its. I hope you will dine with me if you ever come to London.'[12]

The Archbishop's cheerful promise of liturgical pluralism, however, was not kept for long. By 1971, the reformers were bold enough to propose that the Old Mass be effectively outlawed throughout the world. The writer Alfred Marnau set about organizing the local resistance. Archbishop Heenan had complained that the pressure for liturgical reform came chiefly from liberal Catholic intellectuals who dismissed him and his fellow bishops as 'mitred peasants'. Marnau was anxious to assure Rome that not all British intellectuals were on the side of the innovators and that those who opposed them were by no means exclusively conservative in outlook. He sought out signatories for a letter to the Pope that would demonstrate a broadly based, cross-party and ecumenical support for the Tridentine Rite. The key paragraphs of the document were as follows:

One of the axioms of contemporary publicity is that modern man in general, and intellectuals in particular, have become intolerant of all forms of tradition and are anxious to suppress them and put something else in their place. But this axiom is false. Today, as in times gone by, educated people are in the vanguard where recognition of the value of tradition is concerned, and are the first to raise the alarm when it is threatened.

The rite in question, in its magnificent Latin text, has also inspired a host of priceless achievements in the arts – not only mystical works, but works by poets, philosophers, musicians, architects, painters and sculptors in all countries and epochs. Thus, it belongs to universal culture as well as to churchmen and formal Christians . . . The signatories of this appeal, which is entirely ecumenical and non-political, have been drawn from every branch of modern culture. They wish to call to the attention of the Holy See the appalling responsibility it would incur in the history of the human spirit were it to refuse to allow the Traditional Mass to survive, even though this survival took place side by side with other liturgical reforms.[13]

Among the signatories were: Harold Acton, Vladimir Ashkenazy, Lennox Berkeley, Maurice Bowra, Agatha Christie, Kenneth Clark, Nevill Coghill, Cyril Connolly, Colin Davis, Miles Fitzalan Howard, Robert Graves, Graham Greene, Joe Grimond, Harman Grisewood of the BBC, Rupert Hart-Davis, Barbara Hepworth, Auberon Herbert, John Jolliffe, David Jones, Osbert Lancaster, F. R. Leavis, Cecil Day Lewis, Compton Mackenzie, Yehudi Menuhin, Nancy Mitford, Raymond Mortimer, Malcolm Muggeridge, Iris Murdoch, John Murray, the Earl of Oxford and Asquith, Kathleen Raine, William Rees-Mogg, Ralph Richardson, Joan Sutherland, Philip Toynbee, Patrick Wall MP and the philosopher E. I. Watkin.

A friend of Marnau's with access to the Vatican left the letter in a prominent place on a table in the Curial offices. It was soon brought to the Pontiff's attention. Any one of the names of the writers, poets, musicians and thinkers whose signatures were appended might have struck the Pope as impressive. But Paul VI was a devotee of the classic detective novel. On reaching Agatha Christie, he abandoned his perusal of the list, and with a shrug, instructed his officials to draw up an indult permitting the continued use of the Tridentine Rite in Britain.

The chief enemy of the supporters of the Old Mass during this period was a Vatican official called Annibale Bugnini. As secretary of the Pontifical Liturgy Commission, he was responsible for drafting the liturgical reforms discussed at Vatican II and was a member of the Consilium charged with implementing them once the Council had dispersed. Over the years Bugnini has been accused of being a Freemason, a secret Protestant, even – following an unguarded remark by Pope Paul that 'the smoke of Satan' had somehow entered the Church – of being in league with the Devil. His critics have rightly fingered him as a sly operator, but they mistake his co-conspirators. Bugnini was really in league with the 'Rhine

'Group' – bishops from Holland and Germany whose local experience persuaded them that there might be a real possibility of bringing about Christian unity in northern Europe if the Catholic Church could only make its Mass more acceptable to Lutherans. The Rhine bishops were the driving force for liturgical change and greater ecumenism both at the Council and afterwards. In their own countries they sought to de-emphasize all that was specifically Catholic; and through Bugnini this project was extended to the wider world.

When the 'Agatha Christie indult' had been drawn up, Bugnini tried to minimize its effect, writing a secret letter to Cardinal Heenan demanding that the measure should be given no publicity and that use of the Tridentine Rite should be strictly rationed. Some time later Bugnini's rivals in the Curia succeeded in having him removed to an unenviable posting – as Papal Nuncio in Tehran. There his ecumenical abilities would be tested to the limit when, in 1979, he was sent to plead with the Iranian authorities for the release of fifty-two American hostages, held captive in their embassy. The Ayatollah Khomeini curtailed Bugnini's attempt at 'dialogue' with a disdainful wave of his hand.

Three years later, back in Rome, Annibale Bugnini died of apoplexy – a fate one might think more likely to befall one of his more choleric critics. Aware of the accusations levelled against him and of the contempt in which he was held by a number of liturgical traditionalists in Britain, Bugnini had taken care to specify his own epitaph: '*Fidem servavi*' – I have kept the faith.

An advertisement appeared in the religious press some time ago promoting a talk by Elfrieda Harth, the spokesperson of the international movement We Are Church. Printed below the customary details of time, date, venue and ticket price were the words: 'Bring a lunch to share'. In its specific context this innocent exhortation, which might elsewhere suggest little more than the hovering presence of Brown Owl, acquires an unintended significance. It is not simply that it confirms that the progressive tendency in the Catholic Church has now entered a post-ironic phase; the

161

injunction also manages to encapsulate in five short words every-thing that makes mainstream Catholics uneasy about the ultra-liberal project. First there is the brazen show of bounty announcing that not only Are We Church, but we are the sort of people who share our lunch. Then there is the unmistakable implication that on this occasion conviviality is going to be compulsory. And in the shadow of that obligation lurks the threat of reproof. Any-one turning up to the gathering short of a sandwich to share will be found guilty not of a mere solecism, but of a kind of moral failing.

The chain of signification lengthens, leading us up the aisle to face the fundamental question of the Eucharist. Is it to participate in a sacrifice, to witness in awe and reverence as the bread and wine becomes the flesh and blood of Jesus Christ Our Lord, who is present amongst us? Or is it essentially an act of communion, where the Spirit circulates, manifesting itself as a sort of warm glow of togetherness as the group participates in a remembrance meal, *a lunch to share*? The answer to that question is in large part what has divided Catholic and Protestant since the Reformation. It is one of the marks of Catholicity that has proved most difficult to de-emphasize. It is said that Annibale Bugnini once ventured that the word 'Mass' be changed to 'Meal', but was overruled by the Pope. It is not only the hardline traditionalists who worry that some of the more progressive Catholics are really Protestants at heart.

Groups such as We Are Church also entertain ambitions to democratize the Church, making the bishops and even the Pope accountable to the people of God. In part this is because Rome has proved unsympathetic to substantial parts of its agenda. For the greater part of the 1990s the whole question of women's ordination, for instance, was closed down by the authorities. Even bishops seeking to raise the matter privately with the Pope during their *ad limina* visits to the Vatican were told John Paul II simply did not want to discuss it. But the movement also reflects a revival of the Modernist George Tyrrell's vision of replacing the institutional structures with an 'art school of Divine Majesty'.

If the hierarchy is alarmed by this kind of radicalism, it does not show it, despite recent research conducted in Ireland indicating that a majority of Catholics there favour the election of bishops by the laity. Perhaps the English bishops are too preoccupied in defending themselves against groups wholly antithetical to We Are Church – organizations such as Pro Ecclesia et Pontifice and the magazine *Christian Order*.

These are the self-appointed guardians of Catholic orthodoxy. Their strictures are, as often as not, directed at the hierarchy itself. Rod Pead, the editor of *Christian Order*, is a former civil servant from Australia, and a fiery public speaker. At the Faith of Our Fathers Conference in 1999, he lambasted the bishops for their lack of obedience to Rome and their tolerance of disobedience in their own dioceses. Not even Scotland's Cardinal Winning was spared. He was denounced as a trimmer, a stripper of altars and an enemy of the Tridentine Mass. Pead invokes the authority of St Augustine and St Thomas Aquinas for his onslaught on 'recalcitrant bishops' and despite his magazine's tiny circulation, boasts that it is the linchpin of a 'British counter-revolution'.[14]

'*Christian Order* leaves the rest to worry about the celebrated "conversion of England". We are more concerned about the re-conversion of Catholics!' Pead says. 'Obedience to Catholic doctrine and discipline – to Papal and Magisterial authority – matters above all else. All the heartfelt social justice documents and fretting about the state of the world by churchmen will come to nought without a self-confident, orthodox Catholic laity faithful to Tradition.'[15]

No one has invested so much as Pead in the idea that the Catholic Church in Britain is in a state of crisis. He is almost certainly the most likely candidate for Archbishop Murphy-O'Connor's idea of a prophet of gloom.

The spiritual heir to the late Fr. Paul Crane SJ, Pead accepts his mentor's analysis that almost every aspect of Catholic life has declined as a direct result of Vatican II.

Along with Daphne McCleod of Pro Ecclesia, Crane had been highly critical of the falling standards of religious education in schools after the Council, where comparative religion was emphasized in place of teaching Catholic doctrine. He also took the battle to those whom Cardinal Heenan had dubbed 'ecumaniacs', resisting any compromise of Catholic belief and practice for the sake of a spurious unity.

Paul Crane was someone whose attitudes to Church affairs may have suggested that he was a political reactionary; in fact, he was not. An economist by training and a graduate of the London School of Economics, Crane spent the decade prior to Vatican II as general secretary of the Catholic Social Guild and the editor of the magazine *The Christian Democrat* – both dedicated to the furtherance of Catholic social teaching. He also founded Claver House in Victoria, a college where students from the Third World could learn development skills.

What Crane created through *Christian Order* (as *The Christian Democrat* was renamed), and is nowadays continued by Rod Pead, was not, in the end, something that can properly be called 'right wing' or 'reactionary'. Rather, it was a kind of Catholic fundamentalism. Its partner in this enterprise, *Pro Ecclesia*, is believed to be the prime source of 'delations' – a form of authorized 'sneaking' whereby activists monitor the words or actions of the clergy, watching for any deviation from the Vatican line or hint of Modernist heresy. Reports are made to the appropriate office in the Curia, sometimes to Cardinal Ratzinger himself.

These organizations have in common a shared reverence for 'the Truth', something they see as readily available in its entirety through the *magisterium*, or teaching authority of Rome, and the Tradition that has been bequeathed from the early Church. But the question of whether the way in which the Church understood and expressed that truth in the Counter-Reformation period, when the dominant challenge was Protestantism, should be the very same way that the Church understands and expresses that truth in the modern world, where the challenges are agnosticism, atheism and indifferentism, needs sober consideration.

While these small, but vocal factions have squabbled noisily over issues of liturgy, religious education and ecumenism, a quiet revolution in Catholic attitudes has been taking place in the mainstream. The impetus was the publication in 1968 of the Papal Encyclical *Humanae Vitae*. The Pope had been expected to reverse the Church's previous condemnation of birth control and it came as a shock – as much to the clergy as to the ordinary Catholic – when he did not.

Archbishop Roberts of Bombay started the debate in England in an article in *Search* at the beginning of the decade. Cardinal Heenan subsequently softened his public position on the issue, hinting that a lifting of the ban was not far off. Due to what amounts to an obsession with the Catholic position on birth control in the secular media, *Humanae Vitae* has become a large part of what defines the public's perception of Catholics. Yet it is something that the average contemporary Catholic rarely thinks about at all. It would be rare today to find even a regularly practising Catholic between the ages of twenty and forty, perhaps even fifty, who has not at some time used contraceptives. Market research undertaken by condom manufacturers has shown that Catholics are no less likely to be found among their customers than members of other denominations.

The situation appears to be much the same throughout Europe. Indeed, Spain and Italy, both countries generally perceived as Catholic in religion and culture, display zero or negative population growth. Either Italians and Spaniards are capable of prodigious feats of sexual continence – an idea that poses a radical challenge to the national stereotype in both countries; or one must conclude that they have been using contraceptives for decades. Although the Church has always condemned contraception, it has only empha- sized this aspect of its teaching since the 1920s, when reproductive issues were highlighted by its campaign against eugenics.

The conviction that the Church is wrong about contraception has led the younger generation to question other aspects of moral teaching. What has emerged is sometimes termed a 'pick and mix' Catholicism. Many Catholics now accept what is consonant with their own analysis or experience and reject whatever strikes them as unnecessary, hidebound or just plain silly. This is not quite the same thing as adopting the Protestant habit of relying on private conscience. These Catholics do accept, theoretically at least, that the Church has a teaching authority. However, they believe that the way the Church defines what is right or wrong is presently inadequate – too closely focused on particular acts and insensitive to the significance of differing situations.

Yet these Catholics are not moral relativists either. Indeed moral relativism, though the official house morality of secular humanism, turns out to be something of an Aunt Sally. The notion that something may be right for me and wrong for you or right today and wrong tomorrow may sound plausible in theory. But one American academic has stress-tested the idea to destruction by asking a class of self-declared relativists whether it was *ever* permissible to rape a woman, be anti-Semitic, call a black man the n-word or leave your car in a disabled parking slot without a permit. Suddenly the class turned into absolutists.

Yet for moral absolutes to be convincing depends upon applying a high degree of precision to the definition of 'sins'. The commandment 'Thou shalt not kill' is not taken literally in a way that would prohibit killing in self-defence or fighting as a soldier in a just war. It is refined and re-expressed as 'Thou shalt do no murder'. Yet the description 'adultery' is attributed by the Church not only to the wrong inflicted by a man who betrays and deceives his wife when he conducts an illicit affair with his secretary; but also to the woman, cruelly deserted by her spouse a decade previously, who seeks comfort in the arms of a new lover. Anyone with any instinctive feel for Natural Law knows these 'sins' to be of a different order from one another. But by applying the same label, the Catholic Church can give the impression that it draws no such distinction.

Those who adopt the 'pick and mix' approach would probably agree that it is *always and everywhere* wrong cynically to exploit another person for the gratification of selfish and egotistical sexual urges. They would readily recognize this as a moral absolute. But if you tell them 'Fornication is wrong', they will demand further and better particulars. The demand, therefore, is not for a complex theory of situational ethics so much as for a fresh moral vocabulary together with clearer explanations of why certain acts are held to be intrinsically evil. Pope John Paul II went some way to meet this demand in his encyclical *Veritatis Splendor*, explaining morality in the context of the nature of the human person and his or her relationship with God. Nevertheless, this will require much greater elaboration if the Church wishes her pronouncements on sexual morality to be taken seriously by younger Catholics. At the moment she is regarded as a lovable but batty old aunt, no doubt with a heart of gold, whose occasional censorious outbursts can be safely ignored.

One group who have been more or less forced to adopt this outlook are Catholic homosexuals. The Church unambiguously condemns unfair discrimination and unkindness towards gays, but holds that homosexual acts are themselves seriously disordered, even 'intrinsically disordered'. Most homosexuals, however, nowadays regard their orientation as a morally neutral fact, rather like being left-handed. Some become so affronted by the Church's attitude that they stalk off in a huff. But this is not an option for true believers. Richard Coles is a gay man who was once a pop star with the Communards and is today a BBC Radio 3 arts presenter. 'I believe in God, I believe in the Incarnation, I believe in almost all the dogmas of the Church,' he says. 'These things are true. How can I walk away?'[16] Nor is he the reluctant captive of a Catholic upbringing. He became a convert after studying theology, knowing precisely what the Church's attitude to him would be. His solution is to live as a Catholic and worship as a Catholic, but at the same time to simply ignore the Church's proscription of homosexual acts.

All this, of course, is grist to the mill of the fundamentalists who believe that hell is overflowing with lost souls. Those who subscribe to the post-Vatican II orthodoxy do not think of hell as a place so much as a state of separation from a loving God. Equally, purgatory is conceived no longer as a place of imprisonment, but more as a state of personal inadequacy and shame, the condition of being aware that one has failed to do one's best.

These radically different perceptions of what is true, what is right and what it is to be a Catholic contribute to an atmosphere of anticipation, a pervading sense that there is unfinished business waiting to be attended to. Some see that as the full implementation of Vatican II; some as its eventual repudiation. Others are hoping for a synthesis – not a *via media*, not 'common ground' or a compromise, but something quite different in itself.

In many ways the latter stages of the Pontificate of John Paul II have seen a sifting of the legacy of the Council, discarding innovations that have failed, restoring old things that have been carelessly misplaced. That process continues. The signs are that the squabbles about the liturgy will be resolved by allowing a greater pluralism of liturgical forms. Those who are wedded to the Tridentine Rite are now allowed it in small doses and can expect more generous provision. The banality of the vernacular and the sloppy way the Mass is celebrated in most parishes will probably be corrected. There may well be a reintroduction of some Latin prayers into otherwise vernacular services. Plainchant and other traditional forms of church music may even displace the trite and meaningless modern hymns. Dignity, an austere beauty and a numinous quality will consequently be brought back into the Mass. The significance of the Real Presence still needs to be unambiguously reasserted.

After that, it will all depend on the papal succession. Perhaps the idea of the 'people of God' will re-acquire its intended theological purpose, rather than being a charter for busybodies to usurp hieratic functions or demand to be consulted whenever a priest wants to change the position of a plaster saint. Maybe the active laity will discover that there are better things to do to 'prepare the Kingdom' than sit on committees to set performance indicators for bishops. It could be that the 'ecumaniacs' will be rescued from the brink of religious relativism and syncretism and a non-boastful, but distinctive Catholic identity will be respectable again.

Perhaps a church whose doctrines are immutable, but whose understanding and presentation of those doctrines does develop, will even acquire an understanding that accommodates homosexuals. Or ask itself if its God really is an inveterate practical joker who plants the seed of a priestly vocation in a woman's heart so that he can laugh like anything when she is turned away from the seminary door. Anything could happen. All sides could win. There might even be another council.

One evening at the beginning of March 1998, Tony Blair was spotted in a pew at Westminster Cathedral. It had been known for some time that the Prime Minister liked to accompany his Catholic wife and children to Mass. Two years earlier he had been caught receiving Holy Communion at the Catholic Church of St Joan of Arc in Highbury, and Ann Widdecombe had roundly ticked him off for doing so. But this time Blair was worshipping alone. The word went round that he was soon to become a Catholic.

It was an awkward time for such a story to break. In Northern Ireland the countdown to the Good Friday agreement had begun, but following a sudden surge in violence the talks were even more edgy than usual. When journalists began calling Number 10 to ask about Blair's presence in the cathedral, his press secretary, Alastair Campbell, acted decisively. Moderate opinion in the province understood that for an Englishman to be a Catholic did not prevent him from understanding the Unionist position. They had seen Chris Patten and Michael Ancram come and go as Northern Ireland ministers. But whenever talks with Republicans were in progress, the mood of Loyalists always became more febrile. In the hands of someone such as Dr Ian Paisley, a rumour like this could have the destructive power of Semtex.

Downing Street promptly issued an unequivocal denial that Blair was planning to convert. Briefing the lobby correspondents, the Prime Minister's official spokesman went further. Blair's religious practices, he insisted, were completely off limits to the press. There might be a 'minor element of legitimate public interest' if, and only if, Blair did decide to become Britain's first Catholic prime minister. But no such thing was in prospect, so any discussion of the PM's churchgoing habits was 'an intrusion too far'.[1]

The swiftness and clarity of Number 10's response succeeded in defusing the issue in Northern Ireland. The denial was given prominence in the *Belfast Newsletter*, the newspaper serving the province's Unionist majority. But despite the press office's stiff admonishment, London editors were determined to keep the story running. It soon emerged that this was not the only occasion Blair had heard Mass at the cathedral. He had been there several times since Christmas. Columnists and leader writers consulted their cribs on constitutional dilemmas. Was there any legislation debarring a Catholic from becoming Prime Minister? No, there was not. Could a Catholic appoint bishops of the Church of England? Theoretically, one could. But there was more to say on this issue, as Blair had taken a more interventionist line on ecclesiastical appointments than any of his recent predecessors. Soon after coming into office he had refused both candidates submitted by the Church of England to fill the vacant see of Liverpool.

The press kept on finding new angles. Labour spin doctors had laid on a photocall the previous autumn when the Blairs went to church during the party's Brighton conference. How did that square with the doctrine that the Prime Minister's religion is nobody's business?

A good deal of the reporting was downright sceptical. If Blair was not thinking of becoming a Catholic, why was he in the habit of visiting the cathedral? Both Westminster Abbey and Parliament's own parish church, St Margaret's, were a shorter walk from Downing Street. Fr. John Caden, a Catholic parish priest from Blair's Sedgefield constituency, sent a letter to a national newspaper reinforcing the government's official denial. Since he was not only Cherie Blair's spiritual pastor but also the Prime Minister's frequent tennis partner, Fr. Caden was certainly qualified to settle the matter.

Nevertheless, conjecture grew an angel's wings and would not be summoned back to earth. A few days later an article appeared on the features page of *The Times* under the byline of the Right Reverend Michael Nazir-Ali, the Bishop of Rochester. It was a strongly worded warning to the Prime Minister not to join the Catholic Church. Nazir-Ali had already made a name for himself as one of the Church of England's most media-savvy bishops. Newspaper reporters knew that he was a discreet, behind-the-scenes adviser to the Prince of Wales. He could correctly name all five Spice Girls and was the Church's foremost expert on New Age cults.

The Bishop's case, in a nutshell, was that Tony Blair could not be a Catholic and New Labour too. 'New Labour says it is committed to greater democracy, but this sits very oddly with membership of a Church in which government by counsel and consent remains very undeveloped,' Nazir-Ali wrote. 'Can a modern, democratic leader really declare that he orders his spiritual life within such a dogmatic framework?'[2]

The Bishop had clearly not troubled to ask himself how Chancellor Helmut Kohl, or the then Italian prime minister Romano Prodi, or various Catholic presidents, premiers or party leaders in France, Spain, Portugal, Belgium, Luxembourg, Holland, Ireland, Malta, Poland, Switzerland, Slovenia, Slovakia and Austria, in the predominantly Catholic republics of South and Central America, in Zimbabwe, Tanzania, and much of Francophone Africa, in the Philippines and South Korea – not to mention John F. Kennedy himself, had managed to resolve this supposed difficulty.

The Bishop was particularly exercised about the Catholic Church's adherence to the doctrine of papal infallibility, which he said evinced 'a harking-back to the ultramontane days of the First Vatican Council'.[3] By Catholic standards, the Council of 1870 was a relatively recent event. The idea of papal infallibility has been around a good deal longer. St Thomas Aquinas discussed it in the thirteenth century. But in 1870, it was proclaimed a dogma of the Church. There was some resistance to this move. The historian Lord Acton went round the Council trying to persuade delegates that the levels of anti-Catholic agitation in so many European countries at that time counselled caution. Proclaiming the dogma, he thought, would be misconstrued as a vainglorious boast. Many Catholics, including Newman, shared Acton's qualms about the timing, but few disagreed with the substance of the proposition and the vote was carried. Vatican II reaffirmed the dogma, with clarifications, in 1964; but that has not stopped people consistently misrepresenting it, occasionally through ignorance, but more often for propaganda purposes.

Infallibility does not mean that the Pope claims to be positively inspired by God in everything he says as a private individual; rather, that a guarantee is in place that the Holy Spirit will protect the Church from serious error in certain areas of its teaching. The word 'infallible' has a Latin root meaning 'incapable of deceiving'. Strict conditions need to be met for a papal statement to be infallible. The matter at issue must be a question of faith or morals; the Pope must explicitly state that he is speaking *ex cathedra* (from the chair of St Peter); also, he must make clear that the doctrine he is proclaiming is absolutely binding on the Church throughout the world. Successive popes have shown admirable restraint in using this gift. In fact, the procedure has been employed only twice in modern times: once by Pius IX in 1854 affirming the doctrine of the Immaculate Conception and again by Pius XII in 1950 defining the Church's teaching on the Assumption of the Blessed Virgin.

Since both these exercises of the prerogative related to esoteric aspects of Marian theology, towards which one might expect a Church of England bishop to be indifferent, it is hard to see why Nazir-Ali thought the issue worth bringing to the attention of the Prime Minister. But the Bishop gave the impression that he believed that Pope John Paul II was in the habit of speaking *ex cathedra* almost every time he sat down to dinner. A number of the issues that troubled the Bishop of Rochester – the Church's teaching on contraception and women's ordination, for example – remain controversial within the Catholic community. Others, such as those on divorce and abortion, enjoy almost universal assent. Yet the Bishop came close to suggesting that all these matters had been peremptorily settled at the capricious whim of an ageing Polish pope.

The Catholic hierarchy answered back. Bishop Vincent Nichols wrote a letter tartly commending to Nazir-Ali the example of an earlier Bishop of Rochester, the martyr St John Fisher, who had preferred to be guided 'not by what might win him popular support', but by 'the imperative of Truth'.[4]

There were other lessons in the public reaction to the rumours of Blair's imminent conversion for those who looked for them. It was significant that outside Scotland and Northern Ireland no Protestant voices were raised in protest. Bishop Nazir-Ali's objections were not, at root, sectarian. He wanted the Church to conform to the norms of secular liberalism. The idea of England as an essentially Protestant nation – the unifying myth that had sustained centuries of persecution of the Catholic minority – had completely evaporated. 'A Protestant crown for a Protestant country' had once been a powerful rallying cry; even an important element in an Englishman's self-definition. Its unspoken corollary had always been a Protestant prime minister too. But in 1998, no one was prepared to stand up and say such a thing, and anyone who had done so would surely have been regarded as a buffoon. Public opinion was indifferent whether Blair remained a member of the Established Church or became a Catholic. This did not mean, however, that Catholicism was no longer seen as something alien, exotic and culturally distinct. The old Protestant hostility had been replaced by a form of secular incomprehension, shading into suspicion, irritation and a new form of antagonism.

Blair's presence in the cathedral was variously interpreted by the pundits. For some it was part of the semaphore diplomacy of the Northern Ireland peace process. Ireland's Catholic president, Mary McAleese, had made a display of attending a Protestant service; maybe Blair was signalling back? For other commentators it was proof that the burdens of political office were weighing heavily upon the Prime Minister. Perhaps he had something on his conscience, or the strain was getting too much for him? Either way, religion was seen chiefly as a form of therapy. Few could imagine that a modern man like Tony Blair might simply want to participate in the celebration of the Eucharist.

There was little speculation about the impact Catholicism might have on Blair's political outlook or on his government's policy. This was odd because the Catholic Church during the course of the century had developed its social teaching into a coherent set of principles that could be applied to practical political problems. The Church still maintained a critical distance from political culture, but its teaching had developed a sharper edge. Much of this work had been carried out during the papacy of John Paul II, a pope whose doctrinal conservatism has led many to label him a political conservative. In fact, John Paul's criticism of 'savage capitalism' and the 'idolatry of the market' and his championing of human rights have a decidedly radical tone. He has written more encyclicals on political and social affairs than any previous pope, always placing the plight of the poor and the marginalized at the centre of his concerns.

Much of the media comment about Blair's taste for Catholicism rested upon unwarranted assumptions about the conservative character of the Church. Some writers drew parallels between New Labour's insistence on discipline and centralized control and the Catholic Church's supposed authoritarianism. It was pointed out that the Conservative politicians Ann Widdecombe and John Gummer had recently become Catholics; and the reactionary Alan Clark was known to be receiving instruction. Any move towards Catholicism on Blair's part, it was said, implied a continuing shift to the right in his political outlook.

Even as they freely traded the terms 'left' and 'right', these self-same commentators were confessing that they did not know what the words meant any more. A new world order, economic globalization and renewed enthusiasm for finding a Third Way called for a new and more sophisticated political taxonomy. Such a thing is only likely to emerge from a comprehensive reappraisal of political values. And if the place of religion in political culture is to be properly understood, the baby-boomer generation will need to question its own assumption that religion is limiting rather than liberating.

Perhaps nowhere more than in the old, unmodernized Labour Party did religious faith engender so much cultural suspicion. Certainly since the late 1960s, and probably long before, ambitious politicians were encouraged to secularize religious values to avoid appearing credulous. This was particularly ironic given the party's roots in Nonconformist Christianity. For Keir Hardie, socialism represented the embodiment of Christianity in our industrial system. But once the balance between Marxism and Methodism in Labour's thinking began to tilt towards the former, such sentiments came to betoken a flabby impressionability, a lack of ideological rigour.

Christian Socialism was banished to its own ghetto, surviving for years as little more than a series of ill-attended meetings in draughty halls and a bookstall at the Burston Fair. But John Smith changed all that. Under his patronage and the leadership of Chris Bryant, a young C. of E. vicar with parliamentary ambitions of his own, the Christian Socialist Movement (CSM) in the early-to-mid-1990s underwent a complete transformation. Its traditional themes of pacifism and common ownership were downplayed or ditched. Out too went the beards and the sandals, the teetotalism and the worthy-but-dull nonconformist rhetoric. In came new ways of thinking about social justice, the occasional bottle of Chardonnay and a Catholic priest as full-time administrator. It would be an exaggeration to say that the CSM was the vanguard of the New Labour project, but it did supply the proto-modernizers with a valuable claim to authenticity. Severing themselves from Labour's years of stagnation did not have to involve a repudiation of all of Labour's past. New Labour could say it was reconnecting with the party's founding fathers and founding – Christian – principles.

When, after John Smith's death, Tony Blair made his pitch for the leadership, he presented Labour's Marxist phase as a regrettable detour. The conceptual framework of 'scientific socialism' was to be abandoned. An old/new 'ethical socialism' would take its place, in which shared values would replace policy prescriptions as the operative criteria. From that moment Clause Four was a dead letter.

But some of Blair's advisers – apparently oblivious to the attendant irony – considered the word 'Christian' too problematic to use in an 'inclusive' party. Even the leader had to be cautious about defining what he believed for fear of causing offence to Muslims, Jews or – far more likely – the atheists who made up most of his members. But at Easter 1996, Blair gave an interview to the *Sunday Telegraph*'s Matthew D'Ancona, in which he spoke at length about the influence of religion in shaping his politics.

The venue was well chosen. Research had shown that the paper had a higher proportion of churchgoers among its readership than any other. On the face of it, the *Sunday Telegraph* offered an environment in which Blair could be frank, and not so acutely conscious of the pressure to defer to secular proprieties. Blair revealed himself as someone who took religious ideas very seriously; his conversation was peppered with references to Kierkegaard, Jung, Kant and the Scottish philosopher John Macmurray. Faced with this kind of interview, most politicians confine themselves to vague allusions to a belief in 'Christian values', by which they really mean no more than ethical principles. Blair was more specific. He said he recognized a moral purpose in human affairs that expressed itself in a duty to serve the common good: 'Christianity is more than a one-to-one relationship between the individual and God, important as that is. The relationship also has to be with the outside world . . . For a politician this idea has important consequences. It means that you see the need for change around you and accept your duty to do something.'[5]

Unusually for a politician, Blair did not emphasize the utilitarian arguments for religion, saying nothing whatsoever about how inculcating a sense of shame keeps the car-crime statistics down. Instead he was keen to stress the re-moralizing potential of his politics. 'I believe that people are more likely to act well and improve themselves in a society where opportunities are offered to them to do so; which strives to be cohesive and treats people as of equal worth.'[6]

Even at Easter such self-exposure carried risks. A politician does not need to wear his religion on his sleeve to attract sneering laughter, or give a hostage to the tabloids. The mere profession of faith can often be enough to be branded sanctimonious. Blair was careful to issue a string of caveats – 'I do not pretend to be better or less selfish than anybody else . . . I do not believe that Christians should only vote Labour' – and more in the same vein.[7] But a

Sunday newspaper is not a controlled environment. Other papers are bound to pick up the story and invite opportunistic reaction from political opponents. Blair had explained that his view of Christianity had steered him away from joining the Conservatives, whose outlook he thought too narrowly individualistic. With a little added topspin his adversaries were easily able to paraphrase that as 'No Christian can be a Tory, says Blair'— even though he neither meant nor said anything so crass.

These misrepresentations confirmed the instinctual fears of a number of Blair's team that religion was too perilous a territory to be ventured into ahead of the election. During the following twelve months the party preferred to shift the focus of its historical reconnections away from Keir Hardie and Labour's Christian founders to Clement Attlee and the delivery of social reform by the 1945 Labour government. But Tony Blair's Easter message – as it became known – was not the fiasco that the party's initial damage assessments described. He had admitted a place for religion in the shaping of his political thinking and – by implication – a place in the new political coalition he was forging for people who were similarly motivated and inspired. Blair had also declared himself 'an ecumenical Christian'[8] and frankly baffled by many disputes between Catholic and Protestant. He would reap enormous political benefits, as one by one all the mainstream Christian churches – Anglican, Nonconformist and Catholic – began to adopt New Labour as their own. They did not give public endorsements or issue instructions on how to vote from the pulpit, but leading churchmen made no secret of where their political hopes now reposed.

In the case of the Catholic Church this tendency was revealed at its most blatant by the publication, in October 1996, by the Catholic Bishops' Conference of *The Common Good*. 'Catholic Church says Vote Labour' and 'The Bishops' Guide on How to Vote' were typical of the headlines that greeted this document. The Church's spokesmen made earnest attempts to deny the thrust of that interpretation, pointing out that *The Common Good* was merely a pulling-together of all the various strands of Catholic social teaching as expressed in more than a dozen papal encyclicals over the previous hundred years. That much was true; but David Konstant, the Bishop of Leeds, did not seek to deny that the Church was trying to stimulate debate in the run-up to the election. The document was circulated to parish priests with instructions to use it as a basis for their sermons in the weeks prior to polling day. Many parishes set up study groups and the Church circulated information packs to aid analysis and discussion. The decision not to maintain a discreet silence during the election period was in itself a political gesture of some significance.

Little in *The Common Good* could be described as new. Rather, the wraps were belatedly being removed from Catholic social teaching, which in Britain has long been dubbed Catholicism's 'best-kept secret'. The bishops reasserted Pope Leo XIII's 1891 insistence on the primacy of Labour over capitalism and considered the implications of this principle at a time when many companies were 'downsizing' merely to achieve short-term increases in their share prices. The kind of discussion the bishops wanted to promote in the parishes would question the morality of large-scale redundancies. Do years of loyal service count for nothing? Shouldn't companies regard themselves as social institutions as well as economic ones, with staff as much 'stakeholders' in the business as shareholders? Catholic social philosophy goes further than vaguely pondering such moral dilemmas; it asserts a role for moral discrimination where Marxism and *laissez-faire* capitalism recognize only amoral abstractions. To the Catholic there is little to choose between Marxist economic determinism and the Thatcherite slogan 'There is no alternative.' Moral choices can and sometimes *must* be asserted in the face of economic forces, however overwhelming they may seem.

The document condemned a pure market philosophy (Adam Smith's invisible hand was declared a 'superstition') and stressed the importance of human dignity in employment. The implications of this emphasis could be very far-reaching, but remain hotly contested. The key text here is Pope John Paul II's 1981 encyclical *Laborem Exercens* which characterizes work as something that not only *expresses* human dignity but also *increases* it. On the face of it that means that there is something inherently wrong with economic strategies that deliberately use unemployment as a tool to achieve economic benefits like structural modernization or lower inflation – Norman Lamont's 'price worth paying', for instance. But can we extrapolate from this that there is something sinful about putting up interest rates when the economy begins to overheat? This argument has been made by at least one Catholic writer, who proposes that interest rate rises compensate for excessive consumer spending in the rich south-east by putting people out of work in the less prosperous north and are therefore unfair and exploitative.[9]

It was precisely to contain such tricky questions that the Catholic bishops took care to preserve a distinction between moral precepts and practical policies in *The Common Good*. They could confidently assert the former only by separating off the latter as a set of musings or conjectures about which they disarmingly admitted they might be wrong. They also took the precaution of securing the services of Clifford Longley as a consultant. The former *Times* and *Telegraph* leader writer could be relied on to challenge any unthinking calls for higher taxes and public spending or expressions of a reflexive distaste for the grubby business of wealth creation – the kind of thing that had vitiated the Church of England's 1985 document, *Faith in the City*. And right through every state of drafting, the bishops scrupulously examined the text for signs of anything that betrayed a lack of political even-handedness.

Thus, while the document could be read as endorsing Labour's then controversial policy of a minimum wage, it could be said to do so in a specifically Catholic way. It placed a clear moral responsibility upon employers to pay a decent living wage, but was only prepared to legitimize statutory intervention as a last resort if the bosses refused to pay up. This deftly reconciled a traditionally anti-statist instinct with the requirements of social justice. In other areas the report was more directly consonant with New Labour thinking. It questioned the need for internal markets in health and education; raised the problem of social exclusion; and flirted with the idea of forcing employers to negotiate with trade unions – thus actually anticipating Labour policy.

Tony Blair was so pleased with *The Common Good* that he wrote a warm letter to Cardinal Hume acknowledging the similarities between the New Labour and the Catholic approach to politics. In particular, he was struck by the way the Church talked about combining social solidarity and individual responsibility, with the government playing an enabling role. He was gratified too to note that the bishops had rejected the idea of 'trickle down', recognized that market forces could have harmful consequences and had warned that excessive economic individualism could undermine social values. The idea of bringing the social and the individual together in a new way, he thought, 'seems right'. Understandably, the Cardinal thought it best to tuck the letter away in a locked drawer.[10]

By the beginning of election year – 1997 – many Catholics who had previously voted Conservative were beginning to switch their allegiance to New Labour. If Tony Blair's rhetoric could be believed, for the first time since Chesterton and Belloc had tried to articulate their Third Way, here was a political party whose policies appeared to reflect a good deal of Catholic social philosophy. Things could only get better – they thought.

The romantic radicalism of the Distributists did not survive the Second World War and the Catholic community found it harder than most to share in the popular idealistic enthusiasm for Clement Attlee's 1945 Labour government. The celebrations at the close of hostilities were clouded by feelings of disillusion. Britain had originally entered the conflict to defend the integrity of Catholic Poland, but in victory had cynically abandoned the Polish people to the atheistic Reds. Catholics had accepted Britain's wartime alliance with Stalin only with serious misgivings. There is a scene in Evelyn Waugh's novel *Sword of Honour* in which Guy Crouchback's Uncle Peregrine – a Catholic of recusant stock – is horrified by the latest news from the Eastern front. 'The Bolshevists are advancing again. Germans don't seem able to stop them,' he laments. '. . . If one believes the papers, we are actually *helping* the Bolshevists.'[11] It is a comic scene, but it expresses a melancholy truth. Uncle Peregrine finds it impossible to understand the expediency demanded by total war. The writer's satire is restrained by a genuine sympathy. Waugh had himself shared some of that puzzled indignation when he tried unsuccessfully to prevent the Allies delivering Catholic Croatia into the hands of Tito.

The perception that war aims had been betrayed made Catholics all the more wary of the promises of peace. Catholics were, in any case, inclined to a theoretical scepticism about the welfare state. It sounded uncannily like the 'servile state' against which Belloc had warned for so long. Today it is fashionable to point up the demoralizing effects of a dependency culture on the poor; but little thought is given to how welfarism fosters irresponsibility among the better off. The Beveridge Report prompted Catholic alarm on both counts. 'It will be a sad day for England,' said Cardinal Griffin, 'when charity becomes an affair of the state.'[12]

Griffin was above all anxious to preserve separate Catholic institutions from the well-intentioned universalism of the 1945 Labour Government. Indeed, he was prepared to act ruthlessly to do so. After a row with the Health Minister Nye Bevan over the independence of seventy Catholic hospitals, the Cardinal threatened to scupper the National Health Service by forbidding thousands of Irish nurses to work for it. Bevan had to give way.

Catholics had also won a reasonably good deal under Rab Butler's 1944 Education Act. Whitehall would meet the day-to-day running costs of Catholic schools and provide half the capital investment. The Church would have to find the other 50 per cent of the capital costs, but would retain control over management and the curriculum. Nevertheless, Griffin condemned the arrangements, warning that they would bring about the death of Catholic education. In part this was tactical – he was holding out for 85 per cent of the capital monies – but it also reflected an anxiety that the state was essentially a secularizing force, and the less say it had in schooling, the better.

A by-product of the battle for Catholic schools was the establishment of the Association of Catholic Trade Unionists (ACTU) in 1947. A running battle had been taking place within the Labour movement for more than thirty-five years over the issue of secular education. In 1918, thanks to Arthur Henderson, the Labour Party had adopted the principle as official policy. Catholics, from within and without the Labour movement, were determined to resist. At one point there was an abortive attempt to set up a breakaway Centre Labour Party, and year after year a caucus of Catholic trade unionists would mobilize within the TUC to head off motions calling for the abolition of Catholic schools. Once those schools were secure, ACTU increasingly became involved in fighting Communism on the shop floor.

In retrospect, Cardinal Griffin's narrow focus on preserving specifically Catholic institutions can be seen as a failure to rise to a heaven-sent opportunity. He could have shown greater generosity of spirit, more optimism, a readiness to share in an enterprise that would ensure that never again did Britons have to endure the appalling poverty of the Depression years. But Griffin was no social visionary; he was a clerical administrator who set himself a restricted brief as guardian of Catholic institutional interests. As the leader of a ghetto church and an immigrant community he felt no great responsibility for the wider society. Protestant England was another country, sometimes indifferent, sometimes hostile to the Catholic community. Catholics had to look after their own. This mindset would not change until after the Second Vatican Council shifted the rhetorical emphasis from the defence of Catholic interests to a concern for the welfare of the wider world.

But even before this change the laity had to live and work in that alien territory beyond the ghetto. Most found themselves joining the consensus around the welfare state and many became active in the Labour Party. Glasgow, Liverpool, Tyneside and the East End of London were already Catholic Labour heartlands. The archetypal Catholic Labour MP of the post-war period was Bob Mellish. The son of a docker, Mellish was the thirteenth of fourteen children, eight of whom died of scarlet fever or meningitis. His father had taken part in the 1889 dock strike that Cardinal Manning helped bring to a negotiated settlement. In 1946, Mellish was elected MP for Rotherhithe, an area he would represent for the next thirty-seven years.

It was said of Mellish that his loyalties were to the Catholic Church, the docks community and the Labour Party – in that order. He had been in the House less than three years when he was sacked from the position of Parliamentary Private Secretary to the First Lord of the Admiralty for voting against a bill curbing the rights of Irish citizens in Britain. Mellish considered it a blatant piece of anti-Catholic discrimination.

When Harold Wilson brought Labour back into office in 1964, Mellish was sent to work for Dick Crossman, a man he had publicly insulted. But Mellish believed in hierarchy and discipline. At Housing and Local Government, Crossman was the bishop and Bob Mellish was not too proud to kiss his ring. He subsequently became Minister of Public Building and Works, where he fulfilled his two main ambitions – to floodlight Trafalgar Square and found a wild-flower sanctuary in Hyde Park. It is difficult to think of any politician before or since who ever did such little harm in a spending department.

In 1969, to the horror of many Labour backbenchers, Bob Mellish was made Chief Whip. They thought he would be an insufferable bully; but he turned out to be a thug with a heart of gold. Sitting behind Disraeli's old desk, he would listen sensitively to the secret griefs and scandalous admissions of Labour MPs like a kind old priest in the confessional. Yet in political matters Mellish remained ever the burly stevedore. In those days, supporters of trade union power were described as being on the right of the Labour Party, while those who manoeuvred to curb it – like Barbara Castle and Harold Wilson – considered themselves on the left. Mellish was a union man through and through, and bluntly told Wilson that he would never get his plan to tame the unions, *In Place of Strife*, through the House of Commons.

Mellish was pro-European and so fervently anti-Communist that he even supported Ronald Reagan's policy in Nicaragua – an issue on which Catholics divided, though most tended to be sympathetic to the Sandinistas. In Bermondsey (as his constituency was renamed) Mellish worked hard to deliver tangible benefits to his constituents. Critics saw him as a Tammany Hall political boss at the centre of a docklands Catholic clique. There was a good deal of truth in that, but the voters did not mind a bit. In the docks, ghetto-Catholicism was not just a metaphor. Mellish would not merely sympathize with their problems – damp housing, poor healthcare and educational facilities; he used his political muscle to get something done about them. He was the local boy made good, a docklands champion, a Millwall supporter whose life was centred at the heart of his own community. He lived in Bermondsey all his life, fathering five children – all of whom became policemen. The Pope made him a Knight of the Order of St Gregory the Great for his work on behalf of local Catholic schools.

In the late seventies, Mellish fought a rancorous battle against Trotskyite entryists in his local party organization. To the former altar boy these people were scum. They had long hair, dirty shoes and, despite all their middle-class advantages, they chose to live in disgusting squats. The aversion was as much aesthetic as political. What Bob Mellish liked to see were kids from families who barely had two pennies to rub together turning out well scrubbed in pristine cream shirts to crown the Queen of the May.

Despite a broad streak of political ruthlessness he lost control of the local party apparatus once he signalled his intention to retire. He was so furious that the gay Australian Marxist Peter Tatchell was nominated to succeed him that he decided to back a 'Real Labour' alternative. The Labour vote split, opening the way for the Liberal Democrat Simon Hughes, who has held the seat ever since. Mellish quit the Labour Party in 1982 after fifty-five years as a member. 'This is not the Labour Party I joined and worked for,' he wrote in a bitter valedictory to Michael Foot. 'Today it has a hit list of decent men and women. The left-wing Mafia do not give a damn for the electorate.'[13] When he went on television to explain his resignation, tears poured down his cheeks as he spoke. Denis Healey would later call him 'the essence of Old Labour'.[14]

Another Labour politician with a reputation as a bruiser, and who also ended up detached from his party, was Michael O'Halloran, MP for Islington North between 1969 and 1983. Just as Bob Mellish was the dockers' MP, O'Halloran spoke for railwaymen. 'Spoke' is perhaps not quite the apt word. O'Halloran made little impact in parliamentary debates, largely because he was – in the words of his colleague Tam Dalyell – 'the least coherent man ever to come to the House of Commons'.[15] He recognized his intellectual limitations and had never intended to become an MP, but was put up for the vacancy, rather to his surprise, by a scratch alliance of Irish Labour activists and the National Union of Railwaymen.

During the 1970s, Islington was changing fast. It was too early for gentrification, as we understand that term today, but white-collar workers – local council officers, social workers and so on – were steadily displacing the old Catholic working class. Many of these members of the public-sector salariat were Marxists who wanted to take an active part in Labour politics but found themselves shut out by Commie-hating Irish Catholics. In 1976, a party member reported to Labour's National Executive Committee that he had been unfairly expelled after complaining of excessive Catholic influence in the local party's affairs. Shortly afterwards, the complainant's wife was attacked on her doorstep and a broken bottle pushed into her face. She claimed that her assailant told her in a broad Irish brogue, 'That's for Michael O'Halloran.' The NEC sent a troubleshooter to chair Islington North's committee meetings to stop them degenerating into brawls.

But when further violence broke out the following year, it came from an unexpected quarter. A group of eighty Islington women from a pro-abortion group, some armed with wooden staves, broke into O'Halloran's office and beat the MP unconscious. Squabbling between the Irish Catholics and what O'Halloran called the 'trendy middle-class lefties' became so bad that the NEC eventually decided to suspend the local party. In 1981, O'Halloran together with sixteen local councillors defected to the SDP.

Michael O'Halloran said he had high hopes for the new Social Democratic Party because one of its leaders, Shirley Williams, was a Catholic. But he did not really fit in with the SDP's founding

Gang of Four. And what were they to make of this highly partisan Irishman (he even held an Irish passport) who insisted on voting against the renewal of the Prevention of Terrorism Act, a piece of legislation originally introduced by the SDP's leader Roy Jenkins when he was a Labour Home Secretary?

Violence continued to stalk the MP. In 1982, an angry constituent wielding a butcher's knife stabbed him through the chest, almost killing him. This incident upset the delicate sensibilities of the SDP. Although O'Halloran was the victim of a vicious and unprovoked attack, he was made to feel he had committed a social solecism, like passing the port the wrong way at dinner. A year later he resigned from the party, accusing the leadership of having a lofty and élitist attitude towards working-class members. The party, he said, was much more social than democratic. O'Halloran fought the 1983 election as an Independent Labour candidate, and lost.

Bob Mellish, Shirley Williams, Michael O'Halloran and the former Liverpool MP Eric Ogden – four Catholics who left the Labour Party, three of them for the SDP. They all said it was the party that had changed and not they. In each case there was a straightforward political explanation for whatever crisis precipitated their departure. (In Ogden's case his constituency had disappeared under boundary changes.) But perhaps their common Catholicism was not just a coincidence. Shirley Williams was a much more complex and evolved politician than the others and her religion cannot be so clearly isolated as a factor. But for Mellish and O'Halloran, Catholicism was an enormous part of their political identity. They saw themselves as Catholic politicians serving Catholic communities. Each interpreted his clash with Labour as a conflict of values that transcended the merely political and called into play a quite different order of obligation and fidelity. It has frequently been remarked that Catholics are natural political misfits; but most establish some working arrangement with their party. During the last twenty-five years of the twentieth century, however, quite a number of Catholics found such accommodations very hard to negotiate inside the Labour Party.

The Blyth Valley MP, Ronnie Campbell, has been one of only

a few Labour members to discuss openly the kinds of bullying meted out to Catholic MPs who adopt an openly pro-life stance. In theory, MPs are free to act on morally sensitive subjects as conscience dictates; such votes are not formally whipped. But Campbell says it is not like that in practice. 'To say Labour MPs have a free-conscience vote on abortion is an absolute lie,' he insists.[16] Campbell claims he has faced determined attempts to deselect him and been threatened with loss of union sponsorship because of his anti-abortion stand. More subtle pressures have also been applied. Senior frontbenchers have taken him aside and warned of the damage he could be doing to his career prospects; and before one crucial vote he received a letter from the party's General Secretary reminding him that support for abortion was party policy.

In Scotland, Labour officials twice banned the campaigning group 'Labour for Life' from taking a stall at the party's annual conference. 'This is not an issue about abortion but about freedom of speech – about democracy itself,' said the Catholic MP George Galloway after the second ban in 1995. 'Scotland's 800,000 Catholics have provided a rock-solid base for the Labour Party . . . for a Labour committee to pick a bloody fight with a core section of its own supporters verges upon insanity.'[17]

Galloway was right. It is difficult to understand why a Labour Party that preaches tolerance and pluralism is so often unwilling to embrace Catholics in that same spirit. Candidates for parliamentary seats are forced into casuistic contortions over the abortion issue if they hope to have any chance of selection. There is no logical reason why this should be the case. It is not as if there was any realistic prospect of repealing an abortion act that, according to the opinion polls, enjoys the support of something like 85 per cent of the public. There is a solid and unshakable majority in the Commons in favour of allowing abortion; and there probably always will be. But for some in the party, just to wish things otherwise is an unforgivable thought-crime.

Most Catholic MPs understand the political arithmetic. Ruth Kelly, a former *Guardian* financial journalist and Bank of England economist, is one of the brightest of Labour's 1997 intake. She is a practising Catholic who prays every day, and says unequivocally that abortion is wrong. 'That doesn't mean that as a politician I'm going to start campaigning to stop all abortions,' she says. 'I would prefer to see resources put into supporting people who have children. It's often very difficult for people who are abandoned by their partners, who have been kicked out of home, who are so financially impoverished they think they cannot afford to bring the child up. That's how public policy can help.'[18]

If Ruth Kelly's view represents that of the mainstream of Catholic Labour MPs (and it does), it is hard to see why Catholics in the Labour Party come under such pressure on this issue, or why voicing pro-life opinions should put their careers at risk.

Catholics may themselves understand that the issue is a political Aunt Sally, but the antipathy it engenders is an expression of a more deep-rooted suspicion of religious belief (especially of the Catholic variety) among their secular colleagues. The Lewisham MP Bridget Prentice was born and brought up in the west of Scotland but moved south to become a teacher at the London Oratory School before entering Parliament in 1992. She has heard anti-Catholic sentiments voiced at Labour Party meetings, but she thinks it may be a metropolitan phenomenon. 'In Glasgow it was normal to be a Catholic,' she says. 'In London I feel I'm being intimidated.'[19]

From time to time the Catholic Church strikes back, hinting darkly that there may be a political price to pay by pro-abortion candidates. A few months after the publication of *The Common Good*, and as if trying to correct the perception that the Catholic Church had wholly signed up to New Labour, Cardinal Hume ventured such a statement. 'If Catholics come across a candidate who is strongly pro-abortion, then they would not vote for them,' he told a journalist.[20] It is significant that he said 'would' rather than 'should' – descriptive not imperative, or at least maintaining a studied ambiguity about his intended meaning. Nor did the Cardinal explain how the strength of a candidate's pro-choice commitment was to be assessed. For example, is someone prepared to countenance abortion for rape victims to be considered 'mildly' pro-abortion? These hardly seem the terms in which to address moral absolutes. Most likely Hume was taking the opportunity to signal that he was no softer on the abortion issue than Scotland's Cardinal Winning, and at the same time to place himself at a respectable distance from New Labour. What he was careful not to do was forbid Catholics to vote for a pro-choice candidate, something that would have left them effectively disenfranchised in many constituencies.

Nevertheless, the secular response was as swift as it was predictable. Ann Furedi, the director of the Birth Control Trust, said the Cardinal's intervention 'seems guaranteed to increase women's suffering'.[21] Furedi must have had an extraordinarily high estimation of Hume's powers of persuasion if she really believed that with one elliptical remark the Cardinal was likely to upset the pro-choice apple cart. But it is characteristic of secular intolerance to hold that the mere expression of Catholic opinion causes devastating harm. Catholics are similarly blamed for the global population crisis, as if the Vatican's prohibition of contraception was dutifully respected by the Muslims of Bangladesh, the Hindus of India or the Confucian Chinese. (In any case, the introduction of contraceptives has proved ineffective in limiting population growth in countries where there remains an economic imperative to have a large number of children.)

In Scotland, attempts to silence Catholic objections to abortion certainly fuelled the dispute between Cardinal Winning and Tony Blair in the months leading up to the 1997 general election. Fr. Noel Barry, the Cardinal's press secretary, said that the row would never have assumed the proportions it did 'if Mr Blair had been willing simply to say that pro-life members of his party would be given the same latitude to fight their beliefs within the party as their opponents'.[22]

Scotland's 'Red Cardinal' had initially attacked New Labour on economic and social issues from the left. He felt the party was not only in danger of abandoning the poor, but was promoting 'a narrow ideology that presents the poor themselves, rather than poverty, as the real problem'.[23] He thought New Labour placed too strong an emphasis on cracking down on benefit fraud – a message calculated to appeal to the more mean-spirited sections of society, to whom, the Cardinal believed, too much consideration was already paid. When he was a trainee priest attending classes at the Gregorian University in Rome, Winning and his fellow students were asked whether cheating the welfare system was ever justified. He was the only one to give the correct answer – that yes, in circumstances of extreme poverty it *is* allowable not only to cheat, but even to steal. The Church does not condemn a man who pilfers a loaf of bread from the baker to feed his starving family.

Winning really knew what it was to be poor. His father, a former miner turned steelworker, lost his job in the Depression and took up manufacturing confectionery in the family's two-room-and-kitchen home in Craigneuk. When the time came for Winning to travel to Rome to prepare for his ordination, the equipment was sold to pay his fare. As an auxiliary bishop in the 1970s Winning was active in the campaign to save Upper Clyde shipbuilders, and the former Communist union organizer Jimmy Reid was a 'comrade' and an admirer. But there was never anything Marxist about Winning's politics; his critique of consumer capitalism was always based on Catholic principles. He was sensitive to the spiritual as well as the material disadvantages that poverty imposes. One of the things that concerned him most about the condition of the poor was that their daily struggle to make ends meet left too little time for the cultivation of values within the family, let alone for forming a personal relationship with Christ.

When Winning clashed with Tony Blair, it came as no surprise to his flock. The Cardinal was not in the habit of kow-towing to secular authority. He had frequently criticized Margaret Thatcher and once even rebuked the Prince of Wales for his 'woolly theology'.[24] Winning had also demonstrated an instinctual aversion to whatever happened to be vogue. 'If you are wedded to the fashions of the time, you'll be widowed before long' was one of his ever-handy aphorisms. And while Blair is prone to an airy, abstract form of discourse, the demotic Winning preferred plain speech. Yet the Cardinal's first encounter with the Labour leader, at a Scottish Press

Fund lunch in 1994, left him with favourable impressions of Blair's intelligence, confidence and moral seriousness. Despite their political differences, it seemed the two men would be able to work together without rancour. But the relationship began to sour when Blair proved less openly co-operative than the Cardinal had hoped during the row over the Labour for Life stall at the Scottish Labour conference in 1995. In fact, Blair quietly sorted the problem in the end, but the Cardinal was not aware of his intervention.

Early the following year, they met again over tea with the then Shadow Scottish Secretary George Robertson. It was at the time of the publication of the Scott Report into the arms for Iraq scandal and questions of ethics in public life were at the forefront of the Cardinal's mind. Throughout the affair a number of Conservative ministers had shown themselves disconcertingly prone to sophistry in their dealings with Parliament, the press and the inquiry itself. As their conversation turned to abortion, the Cardinal thought he detected in Blair a similar kind of double-speak.

The Labour leader was already on record as saying, 'Any sensible person is against abortion. The real question is whether the law should make criminal those who face the acute moral and personal dilemma of carrying an unwanted child and decide to abort; in other words, to force where we have failed to persuade.'[25] He reiterated this view in his discussion with the Cardinal, but made his point rather less precisely. The impression of one witness to the conversation was that Blair had said that though he was 'personally opposed to abortion' he did not want to 'impose that view on others'.[26]

To the Cardinal, this made no sense at all. The only reason to be personally opposed to abortion was because it was wrong. If so, it should be treated — as Winning liked to say, somewhat provocatively — 'like any other form of murder'. The Cardinal looked the politician square in the eye. 'On what other policies do you apply such a logic?', he demanded sharply. Blair froze for a moment, genuinely startled that what he considered his own eminently reasonable position should be so peremptorily challenged by a prince of the Church. He began to elaborate his argument once again, this time at considerable length, making frequent open-palmed appeals for some sign of concurrence. But Winning withheld his blessing, sitting through the whole performance wearing an expression of disdain.[27]

Blair's argument was the same one he had advanced in 1988 for voting against David Alton's proposal to restrict abortion to the first eighteen weeks of pregnancy. 'The inescapable consequence of the Alton bill is that a woman will be made, under threat of criminal penalties, to carry and give birth to a child, perhaps severely disabled, that she does not want. I do not say she is right, in those circumstances, to have an abortion. But I cannot, in conscience, as a legislator, say that I can make that decision for her.'[28] When the issue came up again in April 1990, Blair voted against lowering the limit to twenty-two weeks, but supported a compromise move to fix it at twenty-four weeks. To Winning this voting record was baffling. If Blair could not 'in conscience' make the decision for a woman at twenty-two weeks, how come he felt able to do so at twenty-four?

By now the Cardinal thought Blair a trimmer and quite possibly a phoney. This was a view arrived at in private and was not voiced outside the Cardinal's immediate circle. The following October, Winning recorded an interview for the BBC series *Everyman*. The memory of the 1994 pro-life stall ban and of the attempted ban the following year still rankled. In the course of the programme the Cardinal described Labour's actions at that time as 'near Fascist'. He also said that Labour's failure to condemn abortion belied its claim to be a party that espoused Christian values. Either a degree of imprecision on the Cardinal's part or the way in which the film was edited – most probably a combination of the two – left Winning's message open to misinterpretation. In retrospect it seems likely that what the Cardinal intended to do was call on Tony Blair to exercise moral leadership and openly and unequivocally condemn abortion. But that is not the way the story was spun.

The Cardinal, who had gone off on a trip to Rome over the weekend the programme was broadcast, returned to find himself at the centre of a political firestorm. He was accused of branding

Tony Blair a Fascist and a sham. Blair himself seems to have taken the Cardinal's words as a call for Labour to end the convention of 'free votes' on abortion and to enforce a pro-life policy through the party whip – something he immediately pledged never to do. He also pledged not to allow abortion to become 'a party political issue'.[29] Meanwhile, a group of Scottish Catholic MPs, including John McFall, Helen Liddell and Tom Clarke, popped up in the media making statements critical of the Cardinal. Winning believed that the campaign of criticism had been orchestrated by Blair's press secretary Alastair Campbell, and determined to have it out with the Prime Minister man to man.

At first Labour spokesmen hinted that the Cardinal would need to apologize if he wanted to meet Blair again. But George Galloway MP offered himself as an honest broker. 'It's time the man in the red hat met the man with the red rose,' he told the press. Galloway also sought to reassure the Church hierarchy that Alastair Campbell was not responsible for the furore, fingering BBC publicity officers – keen to generate a newsline from Winning's *Everyman* interview – as the true culprits. In an article for the *Daily Express* the MP defended Winning's right to speak out: 'You could argue that he has a responsibility, to make it clear that the rights of unborn children are an article of faith in the Catholic Church. That is a Clause Four that will never be ditched.'[30] Jimmy Reid also came out in support of the Cardinal. 'When party leaders are promoting themselves as paragons of religious conviction, people who are certainly religious are entitled to say What about this? and What about that?'[31]

Peace was soon restored – for a while at least – and Cardinal Winning was quick to praise Tony Blair's 'inspirational leadership' in negotiating Northern Ireland's Good Friday agreement. But the Cardinal's part in the campaign to stop the scrapping of Clause 28 would later occasion yet another spat with the Labour Party.

When Michael Martin was elected in October 2000, he became the first Catholic Speaker of the House of Commons since the Reformation. It was appropriate that he should have come from the

Labour benches – Labour has long supplied by far the largest number of Catholic MPs. But in the early 1970s, a Tory Catholic, Sir Robert Grant Ferris, sat in the high chair as Deputy Speaker. That was not the only dignified office he held. The future Lord Harvington had been a chamberlain to two popes – Pius XII and John XXIII. He was a dedicated foxhunter, who in his youth had been an activist in the pro-Franco Friends of National Spain, and who used to take Margaret and Dennis Thatcher on sailing holidays on his yacht. Grant Ferris was not, however, particularly right-wing by the standards of other prominent Catholic Tories during the 1960s and '70s.

Patrick Wall, a former Royal Marine, exemplified the type. As chairman of the Monday Club he was entirely focused on the Red Menace. He had early concluded that White Supremacy in southern Africa was vital to keeping Communism at bay and he spent much of his political career drumming up support for the apartheid regime in South Africa and Ian Smith in Rhodesia. He claimed to have been encouraged in this view by a Black African statesman who had told him, 'We don't trust you British because you don't support your own tribe.'[32] Anthony Fell MP, another Catholic member of the Monday Club, also took an energetic part in the Rhodesia campaigns.

Wall's international interests were boundless. He was a good friend of Chiang Kai-shek and loyally insisted on calling Taiwan 'the Republic of China'. He always took a very firm line against the Russians, once suggesting that NATO should mine the Baltic Sea to confine the Soviet Navy to its ports. One of his cold warrior organizations, Western Goals UK, caused a scandal by inviting a German neo-Fascist to address a fringe meeting at the Conservative Party conference. His anxiety about the Communist threat was genuine, as was his profound concern about the changes taking place in the Catholic Church after Vatican II. He believed that there was a tendency in the Church to reject authority in favour of 'self-interest disguised as conscience' and helped set up the organization Pro Fide to fight it. Anthony Fell, by contrast, was liberal in his religion and became actively ecumenical.

Also in the Monday Club was the Epping Forest MP, John

Biggs-Davison. Unusually for a Catholic, his particular hobby-horse was support for the Ulster Unionists. He ferociously opposed the Anglo-Irish agreement, yet campaigned for the release of Annie Maguire and her family when they were wrongly convicted of preparing the explosives for the Guildford pub bombings.

Unlike the Catholic MPs in the Labour Party who tended to represent constituencies with a substantial Catholic population, and whose self-identification as Catholics was consequently more pronounced, these right-wing Conservatives appeared to the outsider to be first and foremost members of the Tory tribe. In Patrick Wall's case his faith to an extent fuelled his antagonism to atheistic Communism. But these MPs' common political obsessions – Suez, Rhodesia, the twilight of Empire and the Union – had nothing to do with their Catholicism.

Standing quite apart from this group was the Catholic convert Humphry Berkeley. He had a mischievous sense of humour and had been sent down from Cambridge for writing a series of letters to the headmasters of top English public schools under the pseudonym Rochester Sneath. This invented persona posed as the head of an invented school and carried on a hilarious correspondence with his 'colleagues', forewarning them of the moral shortcomings of masters who might be applying to them for a job and inviting their advice on similar headmasterly topics.

Berkeley was very much on the liberal wing of the party, opposing capital punishment and apartheid and in 1966 introducing a Private Member's Bill aimed at legalizing homosexuality. He also took a relaxed view of soft pornography, which he felt was quite healthy in small doses.

Berkeley turned out to be yet another example of a Catholic political misfit who crosses the floor. In fact he made quite a habit of changing his party allegiance. He sat as Conservative MP for Lancaster from 1959 to 1966, when he lost his seat. He resigned from the party in 1968 but rejoined the following year. A year later, he quit again to join the Labour Party, switched to the SDP in 1981 and returned to Labour seven years afterwards. His serial resignations were not prompted by opportunism but tended to reflect some clash of principle. His initial split with the Tories was over the party's attitude to race relations.

On one occasion Berkeley's faith saved his life. In the late 1970s, he worked as an adviser to the Prime Minister of Transkei. One night a group of local policemen (probably acting under orders of the South African security service) seized him, beat him almost unconscious, bundled him into the boot of a car and drove to a lonely spot, where they made ready to shoot him. Berkeley prepared himself for death, making the sign of the cross and saying, 'May God forgive you.' This so spooked his would-be assassins that they ran away in terror.

Over the years Catholics came to the fore representing all strands of political opinion in the Conservative Party. Their religion was not an obstacle to advancement. Peter Rawlinson was Attorney-General in Edward Heath's 1970–74 administration. Norman St John-Stevas became Leader of the House of Commons under Margaret Thatcher. Chris Patten, Michael Ancram, John Patten and Barney Hayhoe all progressed through the ministerial ranks and became Privy Councillors. Many others, though less successful, are well known to the public. Bill Cash was the unofficial leader of the Maastricht rebels (and more recently has been active in the Jubilee 2000 campaign to cancel Third World debt). David Amess speaks for Essex, and Julian Brazier for the family (and a tax on childless couples), Edward Leigh for foxhunting, handguns and keeping the Thatcher flame alive.

Nevertheless, an opinion poll reported in the *Guardian* in June 2000 showed only 17 per cent of Catholic voters expressing support for the Conservatives.[33] This did not represent a sudden conversion to New Labour so much as the result of a long period of growing disaffection with the Tories. During Margaret Thatcher's premiership Catholic spokesmen were less inclined than those of other denominations to blame her personally for fostering materialism and greed. They saw the Prime Minister not so much as a cause but a symptom of these social ills. They knew it was not enough to re-moralize the political leadership; the point was to re-moralize the electorate. However, as Mrs Thatcher once told Liverpool's

Archbishop Worlock, she had a problem with the idea of compassion.[34] She would equally have recoiled from Continental-sounding notions like 'solidarity'. Not only was she not speaking the same language of social justice and responsibility as the Catholic hierarchy, her idiosyncratic reading of the parable of the Good Samaritan, delivered to the Kirk's General Assembly in May 1988, sounded very like a repudiation of Catholic social teaching. In the gospel according to Thatcher, the most significant fact about the Samaritan was that he had the money to pay the bill at the inn: wealth-creation being necessarily antecedent to philanthropy. From this she went on to argue that altruism was an essentially private matter, not the business of governments or society. Yet, in the original story, society (as represented by a succession of Establishment figures) is put to shame by a foreigner for shirking its own obligations and passing by on the other side of the road.

The political mood of Catholic communities at the parish level is informed by reports from numerous Catholic organizations. The Catholic Housing Aid Society, founded by Maisie Ward in 1956, was one of the charities that co-founded Shelter a decade later, and subsequently London's housing advice centre SHAC. There are a number of Catholic guilds representing doctors, nurses, teachers and social workers. The Catholic Fund for Overseas Development (CAFOD), is one of the leading non-governmental organizations operating from England. It engages in advocacy programmes on behalf of the world's poor as well as supplying development and emergency aid. Christopher Dawson's Sword of the Spirit, renamed the Catholic Institute for International Relations (CIIR) in 1965 and enjoying consultative status at the United Nations, takes a moral position on advocacy issues and analyses the prosperous North's relations with the developing South not only in economic terms, but also in the light of theological reflection. Throughout the Thatcher and Major governments the messages coming back from these front-line organizations was one of growing exasperation.

Ever since Indonesia's illegal annexation of East Timor in the mid-1970s, Britain's Catholics were exhorted from the pulpit to write to their Members of Parliament and lobby for an end to the occupation and a ban on arms sales to Indonesia. Yet the Conservative government continued to supply guns and vehicles to the Jakarta regime, including twenty-four Hawk jets. In 1993, Douglas Hurd spoke dismissively of those organizations in the West that raised moral objections to the occupation. Although something like a quarter of a million Catholic East Timorese were killed by the occupying forces and torture was common, the story was barely reported in the British media, with only a handful of journalists – notably, Hugh O'Shaughnessy, Hugo Young, John Pilger and the film-maker Chris Wenner – taking a sustained interest. One Catholic cabinet minister tried hard to change his colleagues' minds, handing out as Christmas presents copies of Timothy Mo's novel *The Redundancy of Courage*, a fictionalized account of East Timor's liberation struggle. But not even Wenner's film of the 1991 Santa Cruz graveyard massacre prompted much soul-searching among politicians. Meanwhile, however, East Timor support groups had sprung up all over the country, a number of them developing out of justice and peace groups attached to Catholic parishes. Catholic priests, together with respectable middle-aged parishioners (some of them erstwhile Tory voters), found themselves risking arrest as they demonstrated outside British Aerospace's factory at Warton, where the Hawk jets were manufactured. In 1996, a Liverpool jury acquitted four women, three of whom had broken into the facility and caused £1.5 million worth of damage to a Hawk awaiting shipment to Indonesia. Throughout all this, says the institute's director Ian Linden, the CIIR was 'locked out of the Foreign Office'.[35]

Another area of conflict between Catholic political activists and the government during the 1980s centred on the activities of the Catholic peace movement. Pax Christi became well known for its 'peace liturgies' enacted at nuclear submarine facilities in Scotland and each Ash Wednesday on the steps of the Ministry of Defence in Whitehall. Monsignor Bruce Kent was given leave of absence from his diocesan responsibilities to play a leading role in the Campaign for Nuclear Disarmament (CND). Kent invited Catholics to consider an awkward moral dilemma: if it would be wrong to unleash nuclear weapons against civilian targets such as cities (as nearly all Catholics would agree it would be), is it not also immoral to threaten to do so? This became the subject of a lively debate in Catholic circles, though many found themselves able to accept the principle of deterrence.

Although Kent received quiet encouragement in his activities from Cardinal Hume, he did not enjoy the support of Rome. Pope John Paul II had been briefed by the Reagan administration on its strategy to exhaust the Soviet economy by raising the stakes in the arms race. The Vatican's rhetoric on this issue was duly toned down in the run-up to the deployment of Cruise and Pershing missiles in Europe, and there were attempts to rein in the peace movement. Monsignor Bruno Heim, the Pope's diplomatic representative in Britain, issued a statement in May 1983 describing advocates of unilateral disarmament as 'blinkered idiots'.[36]

But even as John Paul II was co-operating with the United States in plotting the downfall of Soviet Communism, he was adapting ideas from liberation theology that have proved unsettling to political conservatives. The notion that economic and social structures can themselves be described as intrinsically sinful is one that causes conservatives predictable anxiety. Moreover, in 1984, the Pope unequivocally condemned those 'who are in a position to avoid, eliminate or at least limit certain social evils, but who fail to do so out of laziness, fear, . . . secret complicity or indifference, and those who take refuge in the supposed impossibility of changing the world . . .'[37] Since the collapse of Communism, Rome has moved the focus of its political activities towards the shortcomings of un-restrained markets and the unjust burdens placed upon developing countries. In global terms, this can be seen as shifting the Catholic Church's political centre of gravity some distance to the left.

In Britain, however, it has been the Church's policy since the time of Cardinal Manning to encourage Catholics to join all mainstream political parties and act as a 'leaven' within them. British Catholics did not form a Catholic party of their own, such as the Popular Party in Italy or the Centre Party in Germany, and have kept any engagement with European Christian Democracy a cross-party affair. On a visit to Parliament in 1965, Cardinal Heenan explicitly warned against the formation of a 'Catholic bloc', where Catholics from different parties would act in concert. The Cardinal's address reflected a move away from the model of Catholic action established under Pius XI and Pius XII, where the laity operated under the direction of the bishops to pursue Catholic institutional interests. The new form of lay Catholic activity, ushered in after Vatican II, was founded on the idea of individual 'service' to the wider community, aimed at building a more perfect world. So long as Catholics can square their party's programme with the key principles of Catholic social teaching – solidarity, subsidiarity and a preferential option for the poor – there is no reason why they should not be active in the Conservative Party, Labour or the Liberal Democrats, or any other party for that matter.

Not that religious belief always sits easily with political engagement. In August 1995, David Alton stood down after sixteen years as an MP, partly out of irritation at a perceived increase in secular intolerance within his party. On the other hand, his former colleague Charles Kennedy became the first Catholic to lead any of the three main parties, tilting it towards a more vigorous social justice agenda. In the Conservative Party, Catholics can expect a sympathetic hearing of their views on the family, the sacramental nature of Christian marriage and the importance of individual responsibility. But they can sometimes encounter blank incomprehension and even scorn when they start to talk about 'justice'. Contemporary Conservatism is highly suspicious of this word, which it has come to associate with the shrill assertion of 'rights' of dubious provenance. For the Catholic, however, it is inextricably bound up with the dignity of the human person, created in the image and likeness of God.

At the leadership election following the Tories' election defeat in 2001, three of the five contenders – Michael Portillo, Michael Ancram and the eventual winner, Iain Duncan Smith – were Catholic. Two further Catholics, Damian Green and Liam Fox, were appointed to senior positions in Duncan Smith's shadow cabinet. In his column in the *Guardian*, Labour's former deputy leader Roy Hattersley, himself the son of a defrocked Catholic priest, rang an alarm bell. Two out of three of the major parties, he said, were now led by 'official' Catholics; the third by Tony Blair, who might as well be one. Surely this must have some political consequences? Other commentators took up the theme. After much head-scratching a consensus emerged: yes, consequences there would certainly be, but what they were no one could tell – beyond the obvious fact that faith-based schools would prosper and multiply.

Labour continues to be unsympathetic over pro-life issues and is reluctant to give official recognition to the merits of marriage or the conventional nuclear family for fear of making the children of other kinds of household feel second-rate. It has also refused to make the repeal of the discriminatory 1701 Act of Settlement of (which prevents a Catholic succeeding to the throne) a legislative priority, though few Catholics are too concerned about that.

On the whole, the Catholic organizations gave the first four years of Tony Blair's government good reviews. CAFOD was encouraged by the International Development Secretary Clare Short's enthusiasm for debt relief and by her understanding that the demands of justice can sometimes require sacrifices, a recognition made real in the scrapping of the link between aid and trade. (Catholics are far less upset by Short's calls for condoms to be as available as Coca-Cola than the newspapers think they are. And many were sympathetic when she compared the Orange Order with the Ku-Klux-Klan, an offence for which some of her Cabinet colleagues thought she should be sacked.)

CAFOD was also delighted by Cherie Blair's involvement in launching its landmines campaign, distributing balloons on the steps of Westminster Cathedral. (There were even rumours of a papal damehood in the offing.) And the CIIR no longer found the doors of the Foreign Office barred. Instead, it was invited inside for frequent consultations. This may owe something to the fact that four Catholics – Keith Vaz, John Battle, Baroness Scotland and Tony Lloyd – have been appointed at various times as ministers in that department.

A source of further cheer at the end of June 2000 was Tony

Blair's decision to address Hans Kung's Global Ethics Foundation in Tübingen. As one sharp-eyed journalist noted, there is a consonance between some of the Catholic theologian's writings and New Labour rhetoric.[38] A different translator of *On Being a Christian* might well have rendered Kung's slogan 'not for the élite, but for all' as 'for the many, not just the few'. But the occasion sparked another fit of secularist angst in Downing Street. Press briefings heavily underscored the point that though Blair might talk about his 'values', 'vision' or 'philosophy', he was certainly not going to talk about religion.

The Prime Minister's conference with liberal-minded Kung sent out quite a different political message from that of William Hague's meeting with the American fundamentalist preacher Marvin Olasky, who has called for the winding-up of the welfare state. Nevertheless, there remains a strong tendency, fed by the media, generally to identify Catholicism with the political right. For many people the recent convert Ann Widdecombe is the only Catholic politician they could name. Yet there are numerous others who are far more representative of the Catholic mainstream. One might choose Patricia Scotland, who is just as devout a Catholic, and the first black woman to become either a Queen's Counsel or a government minister; or Peter Kilfoyle, who resigned from the front bench in January 2000 to express his own 'option for the poor' in his Liverpool constituency; or John Battle, who trained to be a priest before entering politics and knows more about theology than anyone in the House of Commons, including Tony Blair. The long tradition of Catholic working-class affiliation with the Labour Party is often overlooked today. No doubt some Labour MPs find it expedient to maintain a degree of reticence about their faith, at least at Westminster. But there have always been some, like the late Derek Enright, MP for Hemsworth until 1995, who have remained unashamed in their allegiance. 'I am part of the Catholic community,' Enright once told the House. 'I speak as a Catholic under the direction of the hierarchy and the splendid guidance of Bishop David Konstant.'[39] Any truly pluralistic politics must be able to accommodate that, without cavil.

Malcolm Muggeridge likened his strategy as a Christian in the media to that of the piano player in a brothel who includes 'Abide with Me' in his repertoire for the edification of both staff and clientèle. Many other Catholic journalists have done exactly the same thing: thumping out the secular tune most of the time, slipping in the subtly Catholic piece every now and again. The approach is sensible, moderate and very English in its Catholicism. Despite Bishop Vincent Nichols' pre-millennial exhortation to 'go out and tell everyone they meet' about their faith, most English Catholics would really rather not.[1] Breathless proselytizing and public displays of piety are alien to their tradition. Besides, secular morality now requires religious people to be saints and not sinners. Journalists who fail to practise in their personal lives what they preach in print risk savage punishment at the hands of their Fleet Street colleagues. Hypocrisy, once viewed pragmatically as 'the tribute vice pays to virtue', had by the late twentieth century become one of the most vile transgressions imaginable: a sin crying out to the tabloids for vengeance.

St Mugg avoided this difficulty by getting his sinning in first. His drinking, his womanizing and his open marriage to Kitty Dobbs, niece of Beatrice Webb: all the elements of the Muggeridge legend duly became part of his 'conversion story' too. Though some commentators tartly observed that Muggeridge had conveniently arrived at religion at an age when the tumults of the flesh had subsided, nobody who knew him well ever doubted his sincerity. Through all those years of dissipation, Muggeridge said he had always heard 'God padding after [him] like a Hound of Heaven'.[2]

Malcolm and Kitty Muggeridge were received into the Catholic Church on 27 November 1982 at the Chapel of Our Lady Help of Christians in Hurst Green, not far from their home at Robertsbridge in Sussex. Bishop Cormac Murphy-O'Connor presided, assisted by the parish priest and by Father Paul Bidone, an Italian who had founded a home for mentally handicapped children near Hampton Court. Lord and Lady Longford were present as sponsors – the equivalent of godparents for grown-up converts.

It was a media event. Reports and photographs of the occasion appeared on the front page of every Sunday broadsheet the next morning. As if performing one of his trademark pieces to camera – tortured grimaces, expressive hand gestures, long periodic sentences – Muggeridge spoke of 'a sense of homecoming, of picking up the threads of a lost life, of responding to a bell that has long been ringing, of finding a place at a table that has long been left vacant'.[3] Father Bidone told reporters that Malcolm and Kitty 'exuded happiness as if it were bursting from their hearts'.[4] The colour writers found both novelty and pathos in the presence of a coachload of Bidone's young charges, whose inarticulate cries and murmuring enlivened the liturgy. One report portrayed the Down's Syndrome children as living gargoyles.

Musing on Muggeridge's reception in the following week's *Spectator*, Auberon Waugh was mock-wistful, recalling that 'there was no chorus of mentally handicapped children to welcome my reception into the Church with whistles, hoots or shrieks . . . Perhaps they are produced only on solemn pontifical occasions, as the *castrati* used to be in earlier times.' For Waugh, their presence at Hurst Green harked right back to the communal spirit of the early church – just the kind of attitude that led to the amendment of the Creed, post-Vatican II, to begin 'We believe' rather than 'I believe'. The new convert, he feared, had fallen in with the wrong lot. 'Whatever Mr Muggeridge may say to the contrary,' Waugh concluded, 'I suspect that he is a modern (i.e. early) Christian rather than a traditional (or evolved) one. He writes of his joy in the Christian fellowship exactly as if religious belief were some form of high-minded football supporters' club.'[5]

Yet Muggeridge was hardly a liberal in the usual sense of the word. Shortly after the promulgation of *Humanae Vitae* in 1968, he wrote a letter to *The Times* paying tribute 'to the Pope's noble statement on birth control'. He was one of the first to denounce what he called 'the sexual vomitorium' of the permissive society and was convinced that ecumenism could only lead the Catholic Church, like the C. of E., straight into oblivion.[6] Indeed, for most people the idea of Malcolm Muggeridge as a clap-happy trendy was so counter-intuitive that only the mischievous Waugh could have conceived it.

Muggeridge's prompt support for the papal stand on contraception suggests that his Catholic sympathies long predated his conversion. This is confirmed by his discovery – in media terms, at least – of Mother Teresa of Calcutta. It was Muggeridge's BBC interview in 1968, swiftly followed by a book and a film (both entitled *Something Beautiful for God*) that launched the obscure Albanian nun as an icon of contemporary Catholicism, a world figure whose moral authority soon commanded the deference of statesmen. In return, she played an important part in bringing about Muggeridge's conversion – though not quite as important as the medium of television itself.

Muggeridge was in Calcutta filming *Something Beautiful for God* when he witnessed a rare miracle of modern technology. It was so dark inside Mother Teresa's Home for Dying Destitutes that the cameraman, Ken Macmillan, wanted to abandon the shoot. Inspired by an irrational faith, the presenter demanded that he keep the cameras rolling. Muggeridge recalled:

When the film came to be processed, the inside shots were bathed in a wonderful soft light, which, as Ken Macmillan agreed, could not be accounted for in earthly terms. I have no doubt whatever as to what the explanation is: holiness, an expression of love, is luminous. The camera had caught this luminosity, without which the film would have come out quite black, as Ken Macmillan proved to himself when he used the same stock in similar circumstances and got no picture at all.[7]

Muggeridge made his name in journalism as a professional sceptic. As a leader writer on the *Manchester Guardian*, deputy editor of the *Daily Telegraph*, editor of *Punch* and a radio and television panellist, he specialized in skewering the bogus and the self-deluded. In the Soviet Union in the early 1930s, unlike many of his fellow Fabian Socialists, he quickly rumbled Stalin and his commissars. That such a journalist should so readily accept the very aspects of faith that cradle Catholics find hardest to believe is, even more than the manifestation of divine light, a thing to wonder at.

Muggeridge was one of only a very few print journalists of his generation to recognize early on the enormous potential of television. His career as a television personality spanned more than thirty years. But the most extraordinary film he ever took part in never reached an audience, despite its unbeatable ingredients: a beautiful princess, two Hollywood matinée idols and a spectacular location.

In February 1980, a shadowy multimillionaire approached William F. Buckley, host of the US current affairs show *Firing Line*, with a curious proposal. Buckley and his crew would be given the run of the Sistine Chapel for forty-eight hours, starting at midnight on a date only weeks off. The backer would meet all the production costs; Buckley and his director had only to emerge with two half-hour documentaries. There was one further condition. The mysterious millionaire insisted on 'glamour'.

As a member of the Gstaad set, Buckley had no trouble casting his show, even at such short notice. A few telephone calls secured Charlton Heston, David Niven and Princess Grace of Monaco. But one more presence was needed to lend gravitas to the programmes. Muggeridge had already appeared on *Firing Line* to discuss 'the culture of the left' after Buckley had read *Winter in Moscow*, the journalist's indictment of Stalinism. The two had a common background in intelligence work: Buckley with the CIA in Mexico, Muggeridge with MI6 in Mozambique during the Second World War. Despite their political differences (Muggeridge still considered himself on the left), they got on so well that Muggeridge was invited to complete the line-up.

Princess Grace opened the first programme, reading the story of the Good Samaritan. Muggeridge, pacing up and down in his overcoat, then provided an explanation of the text; the movie stars chipping in with their occasional thoughts. These were not always spiritually uplifting. David Niven, for example, grouched about the excessively litigious climate in America, warning that anyone minded to play the Good Samaritan these days would do well to take out indemnity insurance first. Programme two continued in a similar vein, exploring the theme of the Prodigal Son. But Muggeridge stole the show with a parable of his own devising, featuring a caterpillar who has a vision of the afterlife. Rushing out to tell his fellows the good news that one day they will all become beautiful butterflies and fly away, the caterpillar encounters only cynicism and disbelief. 'You poor fool,' the other caterpillars say, 'you are just afraid of death and have invented this story to comfort yourself.'[8]

The day after the shoot, Buckley and Muggeridge were summoned to an audience with Pope John Paul II. When it was Muggeridge's turn to be presented, the Pope fixed him with a piercing look and asked, 'You . . . you are radio?' Muggeridge, completely nonplussed, could only stammer something in the affirmative. Apparently satisfied, his Holiness moved on.[9]

Was the Vatican behind this scheme all along? Who authorised the closing of the Sistine Chapel for forty-eight hours for the benefit of this bizarre cast and its mysterious backer? And why the insistence on Hollywood glamour? Perhaps someone in the Curia was inspired by Hilaire Belloc's idea of casting Catholics as the bosses and the chic and hoped to apply it on a global scale. If so, the ambition failed. Despite the exclusive footage and the star-studded cast, none of the television networks would touch the project.

The Pope and the public may have seen Muggeridge primarily as a broadcaster, but he also made a lasting impact on Britain's press. Ever since the Second World War, newspaper discussion of politics and public policy had developed a progressively secular tone. Religion was sidelined. Initially, it shrank into a specialist topic. Then it became too negligible for a whole job on a Fleet Street payroll. When William Rees-Mogg became editor of *The Times* in 1967, there was only one journalist covering religious affairs and he was billed as the paper's Ecclesiastical and Naval Correspondent.

It was around this time that Muggeridge first added his Christian hymn to the bordello songbook. He reintroduced an unashamedly religious angle to the consideration of national and international events and in so doing revived a sub-genre that thrives to this day.

At first, his colleagues behaved like the cynical caterpillars – Mugg, they sneered, had caught religion in his dotage. But the readers liked what he wrote. God, ethics and morality were back on the agenda – first as a response to the 'sexual vomitorium', but gradually as legitimate subjects in their own right. The comment pages of the British press would never be the same again.

Catholics, who had lacked a strong voice in the op-ed pages since the days of Chesterton and Belloc, queued to enlist in the ranks of the higher punditry. Thirty years later, almost every newspaper in Britain would have a columnist who ranged broadly across topical issues from an identifiably Catholic perspective. A snapshot taken to coincide with the Church's World Communications Day in April 1998 included no fewer than sixteen Catholics with bylined columns in national newspapers.

Not all of them would immediately be recognized as 'Catholic journalists'. The spirit of Vatican II encouraged lay Catholics to pursue a broader range of truths and to put their talents at the service of humanity rather than badger people into becoming converts. But at a time when society tends to banish religious ideas and concerns to the margins of public space (this is especially apparent in academia, party politics and commercial life) newspapers continue to offer Catholics a crucial opportunity to take part in the national conversation.

As media power has grown and social deference dwindled, journalists have increasingly come to represent the Catholic laity in the public mind. Asked by some polling organization to name Britain's most prominent Catholics during the last quarter of the twentieth century, at least as many respondents might have listed Paul Johnson, William Rees-Mogg, Hugo Young or Auberon Waugh as the Duke of Norfolk or any Catholic MP. And where the BBC might once have consulted a priest such as Ronald Knox or Martin D'Arcy for a Catholic take on breaking news, in the 1990s producers preferred to approach journalists such as Joanna Bogle and Cristina Odone.

This has not always proved popular with the bishops. Paul Johnson's status as one of Britain's most visible Catholics – perhaps the *most* visible to Middle England – was particularly vexatious to Cardinal Hume. Johnson knew it. 'They hate me down there,' he would say, gesturing in the direction of Archbishop's House. 'They think I'm a terrible embarrassment.'[10] As, indeed, he was.

Even the meekest monsignor on the diocesan staff could become shockingly acerbic at the mention of Johnson's name. Though denigrated with the kind of toxic scorn the Church once reserved for heretics, Johnson regards himself as a bastion of orthodoxy. That is only the slightest of contradictions in the life of this most contradictory man.

Johnson is a cradle Catholic. His mother was of Irish extraction; his father was descended from one of those Lancashire families that stuck fast to their faith throughout the Reformation. He likes to point out that he has 'not a single drop of Protestant blood' in his veins, an observation that irritates his wife Marigold, who thinks it needlessly sectarian. But Johnson likes to express his loyalties with emphasis. On the wall above his writing desk is a postcard of Stonyhurst College, which he has labelled 'the best school in the world'. Catholicism matters to Johnson. He describes it as the most important thing in his life. Consequently, he is never happier than when 'biffing' in print those who do not share Mother Church's values.

On the wall opposite the photo of his Alma Mater, Johnson keeps an eighteenth-century Spanish crucifix looted from a convent during the Civil War. It is an extremely realistic image of Christ's agony – the pain-wracked body seems to writhe and twist against the restraining nails – and it is liberally spattered with blood. Johnson kisses the feet of this dying Saviour every morning before sitting down to write his 'essay' for the *Daily Mail*.

When he bought the crucifix, Johnson did not intend it to be locked away in his study. He had planned to display the gruesome thing in his hall to gratify Catholic visitors and administer a salutary shock to Protestants and agnostics. As usual, Marigold exercised a restraining influence.

Johnson began his career in journalism on the political left. He wrote for the *New Statesman* between 1955 and 1970 and was the magazine's editor for the last five of those years. His appointment to the editorship was controversial. Could a Catholic ever be trusted to uphold the progressive traditions established by Shaw and the Webbs and maintained by Clifford Sharp and Kingsley Martin? Leonard Woolf thought not. Woolf, literary editor of the *Nation* until its merger with the *New Statesman* in 1930, was still a member of the magazine's board. Paul Johnson, he warned, would 'receive secret orders over Vatican Radio' dictating the line for the weekly leaders.[11] Bloomsbury's anti-Catholic prejudice was as vital as ever; Johnson had to spend six months on probation and provide written guarantees of the magazine's future direction before he was confirmed in the role of editor.

In the early period of Johnson's editorship the *New Statesman* achieved a record circulation of 93,000 copies. But sales soon declined and the verdicts on Johnson's tenure are somewhat varied. One former *New Statesman* writer, Alan Watkins, describes a kindly editor who allowed members of staff who disagreed with him to have their full say in the paper.[12] Another, Christopher Hitchens, accuses Johnson of using the *Statesman* as 'a platform for some extremely idiosyncratic opinions of a chauvinist nature' and recalls 'vicious articles calling for martial law in Ulster, a firm hand with African rebels in Rhodesia and the restoration of capital punishment'.[13]

Articles like these point to a greater degree of consistency in Johnson's political opinions over the years than most people, including Johnson himself, are inclined to admit. The authorized version has him as a leftist firebrand who, like his patron saint, underwent a conversion on the road to Damascus when he heard the voice of Margaret Thatcher. Hitchens dismisses this as a cynical fabrication. Johnson, he says, 'constructed the myth of a radical past, the better to betray this same illusion for the grimy shillings of the tabloids'.[14]

Certainly Johnson's membership of the Savile and Beefsteak clubs does not suggest a particularly anti-Establishment outlook. Labour was in office during his editorship and Johnson at times came to regard himself as an honorary member of the kitchen cabinet. When Harold Wilson and Barbara Castle ran into trouble with *In Place of Strife* – their scheme to limit trade union power – Johnson vowed that 'Harold, Barbara and I are going to see this through together.'[15]

Johnson's despatches from Paris in May 1968, however, crackled with revolutionary fervour. They could almost have been written by a Situationist. 'Debate and formulation are inseparable from action – and action in the street,' he sloganized excitedly from the barricades, as he watched the students discover *sous les paviers, le plage*.[16]

But that was the last time Johnson would side with the insurgents for many long years. Once he had made the transition from Labour to Conservative, from the *New Statesman* to the *Spectator* and the *Mail*, he became a staunch upholder of the law. If there were any heads to be cracked, they would be cracked by the legally constituted authority. Only in 1994, afraid that Britain's craven rulers were ready to capitulate to Brussels, would Johnson once again toy with the idea of insurrection. But by then he had dallied so long in reactionary company that the vocabulary of rebellion had deserted him. Calling for 'cold steel, hot blood, a whiff of grapeshot' he sounded not so much the *soixante-huitard* as one of Gordon's colonels forming a square against the dervishes.[17]

Johnson started out in left-wing journalism as a protégé of Nye Bevan. He later attached himself to Harold Wilson before leaving the Labour Party in the late seventies, ostensibly in protest against the illiberalism of the compulsory closed shop. Once identified as a Conservative, he quickly became one of Margaret Thatcher's most ardent champions. He never had much time for John Major, whom he thought weak, dim-witted and altogether common. When Johnson switched allegiance once again in the mid-nineties, bestowing his blessing upon Tony Blair, his enemies on the left began to cite these serial turns of coat as evidence of a compulsive infidelity, amounting to a character defect or a moral failing.

To the Catholic mind, as so many Catholic politicians have demonstrated, however, political apostasy is perfectly acceptable. As Johnson liked to point out, politics set itself up during the twentieth century as a rival to religion, offering an alternative scheme of salvation. Ideology posed as faith; policy prescriptions were purveyed as principles. Besides, the Catholic would expect any secular design eventually to unravel, it being founded, by definition, on a partial or distorted comprehension of the human condition. One political system might grotesquely exaggerate the collective at the expense of the individual; another place an inordinate emphasis on race or nation. Most would attribute quasi-magical powers to mundane institutions – monarchy, markets, 'This Great Movement of Ours'. For someone of Paul Johnson's background, abandoning his comrades for personal gain might be wrong, but ditching one clapped-out ideology in the hope that another might be more successful would be quite in order.

Not that Johnson felt much need for pleas in mitigation. He preferred to carry the battle to the enemy. He delighted in being the scourge of the left, resolutely refusing to recognize any ethical dimension in his adversaries' arguments. Naturally combative, he liked not just to confound, but to humiliate opponents. His red hair and florid face, combined with an explosive temper, made him an intimidating figure in debate, whether on television or across some metropolitan dinner table. Stone-cold sober, confronting a blank page in the isolation of his study, Johnson would exercise even less restraint.

As the Cold War gave way to a growing consensus about the role of free markets, the battleground changed. Johnson's targets became more widely dispersed. Sexual politics, identity issues, the 'culture wars', moral decline – all seemed to make him furious. Johnson had never held himself on a tight stylistic rein; he always liked to exaggerate for effect. But this broader agenda imposed even fewer restraints than conventional political journalism had done and Johnson indulged his taste for hyperbole – on one occasion calling for a neutron bomb to be dropped on Los Angeles in retaliation for Neil Jordan's film *Michael Collins*. He became the *Daily Mail*'s resident moralist, delivering tirades against single mums and homosexuals. He branded Channel 4's boss, Michael Grade, 'Britain's pornographer in chief'.[18]

On religious topics he can be just as forthright. The Christian outlook Johnson promotes does not bend the rules. It knows the difference between right and wrong and, unlike the Church of England, it makes no accommodations with transient fashion. A principle is a principle and that is that. Its moral code appeals to a readership that relishes seeing transgressors punished and is adamant that individuals should take responsibility for their own actions rather than call on 'society' or the taxpayer to bail them out. Nothing could be better crafted to please doing-quite-nicely-thank-you Middle England than this assurance that in addition to their unit trusts, they are also accumulating riches in heaven. But within the Catholic community Johnson's appeal has been somewhat broader. For sure, he speaks chiefly for an authoritarian group that thinks the modern world is going to hell in a hand basket. But even those who consider Johnson's theology a little under-developed and some of his attitudes distasteful credit him with defending Catholicism against blasphemy and insult.

Johnson's reputation does not rest on pound-a-word tabloid journalism alone. He is a prolific author of history books that have sold very well, particularly in the United States. He has chosen big subjects of global significance – histories of the Jews, Christianity, the modern world and the American people – and looked at them in the round, examining culture as well as politics, individual human actors as well as economic forces and social classes. He says he does not give a hoot when academic reviewers complain he relies too much on secondary sources; but he is sensitive to criticism of inaccuracy. It is for this reason that he deflects comparisons with Belloc (whom he resembles in both partisan belligerence and didacticism), preferring to nominate G. K. Chesterton as his muse. But Chesterton never made a lasting enemy.

The sport of Johnson-baiting has provided much pleasure to liberal journalists throughout the last decade. In *Private Eye*, Johnson is known as 'Loony-Bins'; in the *Guardian* Diary, Matthew Norman refers to him as 'my sane and rational friend'. Johnson has only himself to blame. Though he gave up drinking in 1993, goes every morning to church (St Mary and the Angels – Cardinal Manning's former headquarters in Bayswater) and is widely rumoured to have mellowed, his columns have become noticeably dottier. He admires Swedish meter maids for their beauty and their rigour. He wonders whether he has chosen the wrong career, saying that he should have been a portrait painter, given his habit of spending afternoons on the London Underground staring into strangers' faces. Soon after he became unofficial adviser to Tony Blair, he ruined a perfectly coherent article on abortion by urging the Prime Minister to pledge that '. . . my Government will make nubile women of all age groups aware of their responsibilities'.[19] It never made the Queen's Speech. Blair had earlier taken a pass on another well-meant tip from his mentor: that he should forget about devolution as it would take up too much parliamentary time.

Francis Wheen, in his *Guardian* column, has made a running gag of Johnson's multiplying inconsistencies. Most jobbing journalists, faced with another column on the same old subject, tend to recycle vintage copy. Johnson flatly contradicts his earlier columns, frequently with as much vehemence as when he first advanced the opposite opinion. Wheen, it has become clear, maintains a more meticulous archive of Johnson's work than the 'essayist' himself.

Sometimes the contradictions are merely social. For instance, Johnson will one day condemn the vice of shameless name-dropping and the next make such a feature of his friendship with some highland grandee in his column that he looks like a castle-creeper and a snob himself. On other occasions his inconsistency evinces a moral confusion. Johnson can seem to condone, even admire, adultery when it is committed by someone rich, important or successful – Charles II, say, or Alan Clark. Yet he can be unequivocally censorious if the sinner is someone like David Mellor, whom he finds unattractive. A section of the Conservative

Party has not forgiven Johnson for, as they saw it, demanding the sacking of the disgraced Tim Yeo in 1994, saying that the MP should 'expect no mercy ... adultery is wrong and must be punished.'[20] In fact Johnson did not so much call for condign punishment on that occasion as acknowledge its inevitability.

Though he claims to ration his writing on religious topics to four occasions per year, in fact, Johnson rather more frequently addresses subjects of concern to the Church. The senior Catholic clergy charged with the Church's central administration have long been among his most severe critics. Johnson's suggestion that AIDS research should not be given a high priority on the grounds that its chief beneficiaries are promiscuous homosexuals was thought particularly disgusting. When he writes about ecclesiastical affairs Johnson can cause even more acute embarrassment. Cardinal Hume was determined to hold Britain's Catholic community together, to prevent it splitting into mutually recriminatory camps of 'traditionalists' and 'progressives'. He was appalled by the vicious faction-fighting among Catholics in the United States and was determined to stop it happening here. He almost despaired at Johnson's leaden-footed interventions into a whole range of sensitive issues. But exasperation turned to fury when, right in the middle of delicate negotiations with the Anglicans – many of whose clergy had converted to Rome over the issue of women priests – Johnson blasted out a triumphal fanfare announcing that the conversion of England was at hand, and dismissing the rump Church of England as the Church of Sodom.

Leading Anglicans began to petition the Cardinal. Was there nothing he could do to silence Johnson? There was not. Johnson thought Hume a kindly man, but believed he was the prisoner of his advisers – particularly of a clique associated with the *Tablet*, a journal Johnson says 'always seeks to undermine and belittle Catholic orthodoxy'.[21]

Early in 1994, Dr Timothy Bradshaw, Dean of Regent's Park College, Oxford, wrote an article for *The Times* complaining that there was a 'powerful corps of Roman Catholic journalists' writing 'corrosive articles' about the C. of E. Bradshaw's copy was fairly tame, but the paper decided to make a splash of it, using all the tricks of the sub-editor's trade. Taken together with headlines and captions the piece appeared to suggest that there was a 'papist plot' to undermine the Church of England and to replace it as the Established church with the Catholic Church.[22]

Perhaps those responsible were thinking of Auberon Waugh, who had asked whether the Archbishop of Canterbury really had the power to turn women into priests. If such a power existed – and no one had thought so for 2,000 years – it remained untested. Waugh proposed that an Australian archbishop try it out on kangaroos first, and only if it worked should it be licensed for use on human beings.

And certainly Johnson was in the frame. But if there was a plot, who else was among the conspirators? Absurdly, the newspaper fingered Clifford Longley, the religious affairs commentator of the *Daily Telegraph*, who – though indeed a Catholic – had probably done more than any journalist to foster cordial relations between the two churches over the previous twenty-five years. Longley sued for libel, collecting an unqualified apology and damages.

'I have become broadminded,' Johnson announced to a sceptical world in 1996, 'but I am less tolerant than I was towards those who, themselves without faith or reverence, use the media to sneer at and defile the things that others hold dear . . . I feel myself increasingly militant towards these mockers and polluters, not at all inclined to turn the other cheek.'[23] The Church was certainly much happier when Johnson left ecumenical matters alone and turned his fire on secular targets. This he did to tremendous effect, 'getting up' science in a matter of weeks so he could see off New Darwinists such as Richard Dawkins. It may sound unlikely, but Johnson became really quite an expert on the perils of 'germ-line engineering.' Even with lots of sinister new technologies to rail against, he still refused to adopt a softer line on the C. of E. Only eight months after announcing his new broadmindedness he declared Anglicanism to be 'now so damaged and corrupt, so obviously morally diseased . . . as to constitute a leprous liability to other churches'.[24]

Johnson once admitted that whenever he was thriving,

particularly when he felt himself to be enjoying some *undeserved* success, he was always troubled by a nagging and irrational fear that God would step in and floor him with what he called a 'divine biff'.[25] According to Catholic theology, God does not behave like that. But in May 1998, the Almighty seems to have stepped out of character. Perhaps he was answering the stream of prayers that had been sent up over the years from Westminster Cathedral. Quite suddenly Paul Johnson found himself at the centre of a sex scandal. He was discovered to have a mistress whom he frequently persuaded to spank him. The *Daily Express* screeched that 'the man who preaches morality is a hypocrite'.[26]

More illuminating than the details of this affair was Johnson's statement to the journalists who doorstepped him on the morning of his disgrace. 'I am a sinner,' he told them. 'That is why I go to Church every day.'[27] Re-reading Johnson's religious writings in the light of that revealing remark – in particular his work of Catholic apologetics *The Quest for God* – is not so much to find oneself in the company of a humbug as to witness a confession by other means. 'I am a chaotic person, a wild person and I need discipline,' Johnson admits in the context of explaining why he finds the authority of the Catholic Church so attractive.[28] He is clearly a man with no illusions about his own propensity to sin, and who welcomes strict rules – the stricter the better – to keep himself in check.

This would also explain Johnson's obsession with punishment. He clearly feared – and yet, in an odd way almost relished – its inevitability. Contemplating the Last Judgement, he seems almost more fascinated by the sorting of the sheep from the goats than by the spectacle of Christ's Coming in splendour. After the death of Sir James Goldsmith from cancer Johnson tried to calculate how many days the late industrialist would get off purgatory in consideration of the painfulness of his death. All this suggests a preoccupation with justice at the expense of mercy, and with the letter of the law instead of its spirit. Not that there is anything especially unorthodox here. Johnson knew enough scripture and theology to back up whatever he believed. But the emphasis is telling.

An idea that recurs time and again in Johnson's writing is that of a person 'making a mess of his life': going off the rails, becoming bankrupt, getting divorced. This was the fate that befell several of the subjects in his notorious book *The Intellectuals*, in which he catalogued the private vices of the intelligentsia from Rousseau to Fassbinder. Johnson himself has been married for over forty years, brought up four children and produced a substantial body of work to survive him. Yet he seems to have lived in acute fear of making a mess of his own life. The more unruly his passions became, the more he required the Catholic Church to maintain the very austerity and authoritarianism that it yearned to shrug off. Inevitably, Johnson has projected his private anxieties on to the wider society. That is evident from his practice of justifying religion not by its own precepts but in instrumental or utilitarian terms – as a mechanism for social control, good for keeping the crime rates down, and so forth. He may be remembered as a Catholic champion, perhaps even as a Defender of the Faith in the Chestertonian tradition. But Chesterton's vision of the 'Catholic thing' will for ever remain bright, generous-spirited and inspiring. Whereas the pernickety, rule-obsessed Catholicism Johnson clings to is already looking somewhat rancid.

Take the single sentence: 'God is love; and he that dwelleth in love dwelleth in God, and God in him.' Apply that to all cases of morality, apply it with intelligence and realism, and it both enlarges and illuminates the moral code. Remember that God's love is not selfish in the way that human love tends to be; then ask what love suggests in this case or that, and the moral answer often stands out quite clearly. The codes are necessary . . . but they are attempts to codify rules for loving conduct and owe their authority to that.[29]

This approach to Christian morality could not be more different from that of Paul Johnson. But these sentences were not written by a subversive modernist or a leprous Anglican. They are the words of William Rees-Mogg, editor of *The Times* from 1967 to 1981, columnist, antiquarian bookseller and Tory peer.

As his readers are well aware, there are few subjects on which Rees-Mogg does not feel able to offer a confident and well-informed opinion. (Pressed by an interviewer to name one topic on which he could not pontificate, Rees-Mogg thought long and hard before replying, 'Well, I wouldn't write an article about mountain climbing.')[30] But while the evolution of his ideas about economics – from loose Keynsianism to monetarism under the tutelage of Peter Jay – or about Europe – from Heathite enthusiasm to litigious scepticism (he tried to challenge the ratification of the Maastricht treaty in the courts) – have excited a great deal of controversy, the development of Rees-Mogg's theology has passed almost unnoticed. Which is odd, since it is so startlingly radical.

Under the influence of the German idealist philosophers Rosenzweig and Schelling, Rees-Mogg has tried to chart the way to a free, undogmatic Christianity. At the centre of this project stands St John, whom Rees-Mogg sees as 'the Apostle of divine love'. Johannine Christianity is can-do Christianity. Its emphasis, Rees-Mogg says, 'is on the positive, on affirmation, on saying yes'. So what are its implications for sexual morality? 'A God of love cannot be hostile to the expression of love in a sexual relationship, so long as it *is* an expression of love and not of power, hatred or exploitation.'[31]

Rees-Mogg claims that his ideas are wholly compatible with Catholic orthodoxy. And in case anyone gets the impression that he might be a touch susceptible to ecumenical drift, he is reassuringly tough on the Protestant tradition. 'Any doctrine which deprives Christian life of joy and hope, *anathema sit*. Any cutting down of maypoles, or destruction of ordinary pleasures, let it be condemned . . . Any doctrine that God so hates men as to predestine them to eternal damnation is an abomination.'[32]

In his early years, Rees-Mogg's Catholicism was so discreet as to be almost invisible. 'Rees-Mogg was a bit of a disappointment,' remembers the CND campaigner Bruce Kent, who ran the Newman Society at Oxford when they were undergraduates. 'He was known to be a Catholic, but had not gone to a Catholic school and did not attend the Chaplaincy. One had to wonder, therefore, whether he was really one of us.'[33]

Rees-Mogg's Catholicism came from his Irish-American mother. His father was Church of England. Although Downside was only a few miles from the family home in Somerset, his father preferred to send the young William to Charterhouse. The novelist Simon Raven, a fellow Carthusian, claims that Rees-Mogg was a rather priggish Catholic who, as head boy, ran a campaign against masturbation, spreading the false story that it was a major cause of syphilis. Sadly, such colourful stories about Rees-Mogg often turn out to be untrue – he does not, for instance, regularly play tennis in a double-breasted, pin-striped suit; and he did not spend his undergraduate years lying in bed on the phone to his stockbroker after inheriting a bundle from a great-aunt.

It was after coming down from Oxford that Rees-Mogg discovered the intellectually elevated sermons of Canon Alphonso de Zulueta at the Church of the Holy Redeemer in Cheyne Row. He became a regular churchgoer. He also began to encounter a series of psychic phenomena. Early in 1962, he had a clear premonitory dream of his father's death, which was fulfilled in an uncannily exact manner later that year. 'By the time my father died, I had been in mourning for more than nine months.'[34]

Then, in the middle of a fitful afternoon nap, he experienced something halfway between a vision and a dream. He saw himself as a pallbearer at a funeral. He recognized the setting as Camley Church, a place he knew well, but was puzzled by the fact that rushes were spread all over the floor. Subsequently he researched some of the detail he had so vividly observed, discovering that in the eighteenth century it had been customary to litter the church with rushes. Since he had not known that fact at the time of his experience, the event took on a peculiar significance, leading him to believe in the possibility of telepathic communication with the dead. Rees-Mogg also claimed to have been visited on three occasions by a family banshee, a footloose, Atlantic-hopping spirit who also haunted his American cousins. Wisely, he took these curious events as an encouragement not to dabble in the occult but to deepen his Catholic faith.

Rees-Mogg was one of the first Catholics to appear comfortably at home in the Establishment. Despite Norman Fowler's jibe that he spoke 'with the authentic voice of the patrician tendency', Rees-Mogg did not owe his position to patrimony or caste.[35] His forebears were middling Somerset landowners, more squires than grandees. He married his secretary, Gillian, whose father was Mayor of St Pancras. He was simply gifted, self-confident and fortunate enough to be very successful in journalism at an early age.

He began at the *Financial Times* where, as a leader writer, he was as much a player in the political game as a commentator. On the day in 1963 that Alec Douglas-Home became Prime Minister, Rees-Mogg was at the Carlton Club urging Rab Butler to refuse to serve. Two years later, by now at the *Sunday Times*, he wrote an article entitled 'The Right Moment to Change' that forced Home to give up the Tory leadership. (Years later, when Rees-Mogg launched an assault on a vulnerable John Major, saying that 'his ideal level of political competence would be Deputy Chief Whip, or something of that standing', he was accused of hunting for a second scalp.)[36] As for the string of directorships and public appointments that followed his fourteen-year stint as editor of *The Times*, Rees-Mogg ascribes them to the laws of career-dynamics – 'Once in orbit, you stay in orbit.'[37]

Rees-Mogg does not often use his column as a pulpit. He thinks proselytizing is a waste of time. But his habit of drawing general lessons from the detail of his own life means that he is widely recognized as writing from a Catholic point of view. He vigorously opposes abortion, which he calls 'killing for convenience' and has even argued that the US Supreme Court is guilty of genocide, pointing out that 'five times as many American babies have died as a result of Roe vs. Wade as Jews were killed in the Holocaust'.[38] He opposes relaxation of the divorce laws, supports measures to strengthen the family and opposes euthanasia. Rees-Mogg does not believe that sexual behaviour is the main criterion of personal morality, but regards promiscuity as psychologically damaging to everyone, gay or straight. Cardinal Hume would have put his imprimatur on most of that.

But there is one area in which Rees-Mogg disagrees with the

Catholic bishops. He thinks they have no business meddling in political matters, particularly in economic questions. He insists that they can hardly offer informed moral judgements about policies where politicians or experts disagree on the likely outcomes. When, in 1996, the bishops released their pre-general election document *The Common Good*, Rees-Mogg savaged it in *The Times*. 'The bishops are avowed dirigistes,' he complained. 'This is not even New Labour doctrine . . . The bishops want to go back to the regulatory systems Britain struggled to throw off in the 1980s.'[39] This earned him a cheer from the Catholic Viscountess Sidmouth, who declared she would 'sooner consult the Governor of the Bank of England on the mystery of the Incarnation than seek the advice of bishops on economics'.[40] But Rees-Mogg received a rap across the knuckles from David Konstant, Bishop of Leeds. *The Common Good*, Konstant told him pointedly, was 'a presentation of the social teaching of the Catholic Church . . . drawn almost exclusively from the teaching of successive popes'. Political and economic life, the bishop went on 'are never value-free zones' and the Catholic faith has 'an inescapable, though sometimes neglected, social dimension'.[41]

Had he not by then already departed to Buckinghamshire to enjoy a mellow semi-retirement, a spat between the Bishop of Leeds and Lord Rees-Mogg might have stimulated an interesting reaction from another of Fleet Street's Catholic eccentrics, Sir Peregrine Worsthorne. There is no telling what he might have said: which is largely the point. He has such a quirky mind that even those who feel they share his general political outlook can never be certain what line he will take on any issue.

At the height of Margaret Thatcher's success, which he had done a great deal to promote, it was Worsthorne who coined the phrase 'bourgeois triumphalism'. His own conservatism was anything but populist. The suburbs held little fascination for him. He liked to think of himself as a high-table Tory, more Oakeshott than Oxshott.

Worsthorne attended a Catholic prep school for a short time, but spent most of his schooldays at Stowe, a non-Catholic insti-tution. There he taunted his history master with Hilaire Belloc's provocative assertion that Elizabeth I, the Virgin Queen, died of a sexually transmitted disease. After the army and Cambridge, he became a journalist, working first on the Glasgow *Herald*, and later for *The Times* and the *Daily Telegraph*.

In his memoirs he details a series of exotic sexual escapades, including the seduction of a baroness in the ruins of Hamburg. His first wife was French. Before their marriage, the couple 'lived in sin'. Claudie became pregnant and had a backstreet abortion, so clumsily carried out that she nearly died. Worsthorne described this as 'a deeply shame-making and horrifying episode that rocked me to the very roots of my being'.[42]

Worsthorne makes occasional references to his Catholic faith in his columns but seldom displays a sophisticated grasp of theology. On one occasion, he mused aloud on the similarities between cannibalism and the doctrine of Transubstantiation, concluding that they had more in common than we might have thought. But like Katie Grant, the Glasgow *Herald* columnist, Worsthorne is related to an old recusant family, the Towneleys of Towneley Hall in Lancashire. Worsthorne's brother became so interested in this connection that he changed his name to Towneley and lived the life of a Catholic country gentleman. Each year on All Souls' Day the Towneley clan are allowed back into the chapel of their ancestral home to pray for the souls of the Towneley martyrs who were killed during the persecution. A Benedictine prior performs the Mass, dressed in pre-Reformation vestments. Worsthorne himself was named after a nineteenth-century Towneley eccentric, 'Owd Peregrine', who used to dress so scruffily that he once was mistaken by his own gamekeeper for a poacher and locked up for the night. By contrast, young Peregrine was something of a dandy.

Like Paul Johnson, Worsthorne claimed to be an unashamed reactionary. Like Auberon Waugh, he initially adopted this position in defiance of the priggish tone of the progressive consensus. The trio would sometimes hail one another in their columns ('As the estimable Paul Johnson . . .') like mastodons booming across the primeval swamp. Worsthorne believed that the permissive attitudes of the 1960s were responsible for many of the social problems afflicting Britain during the subsequent twenty-five years.

Worsthorne was long expected to become editor of the *Daily Telegraph*, but in 1973, he blew it by becoming the second person ever to use the 'f-word' on live television. The first was, of course, Kenneth Tynan. The audience may have expected it of Tynan, but no one ever thought to hear it from a *Telegraph* journalist on the early evening current affairs programme *Nationwide*. His proprietor felt he had brought the newspaper into disrepute and made it clear that he would never entrust Worsthorne with the editorship. Many years later Lord Hartwell was forced to cede control of the title to the Canadian entrepreneur Conrad Black, a Catholic convert. Once again Worsthorne acted rashly, criticizing Black in the *Spectator*.

Nevertheless, in 1986, Black made Worsthorne editor of the *Sunday Telegraph*. The most successful Sunday broadsheet then, as now, was the *Sunday Times*, edited by Andrew Neil. Neil ran his paper like a supermarket. It was divided into a large number of sections and each section was stocked with articles to suit every conceivable taste and interest. His supporters claimed this was democratic – handing power over to the readers. Instead of consuming whatever some journalist deemed suitable, you could pick and choose as you wished. Nobody was expected to get through the whole paper, except perhaps its workaholic editor.

Worsthorne took the opposite view. He saw it as the editor's job to edit – to sift through all the possible stories and select those he thought it was important for his readers to see, together with some they would find entertaining or amusing. What was left out of the paper was as important as what went in. Consequently, he produced a very thin paper with only a few sections. Worsthorne's *Sunday Telegraph* was a *succès d'estime* – for all those involved in politics and political journalism it was a mandatory read. It had character. It understood its readers as part of a community of interest, taste and outlook. It had coherence and elegance. It sold comparatively few copies whereas Andrew Neil's *Sunday Times* was tremendously successful.

Worsthorne's failure might have been a metaphor for something taking place in the wider culture. In his retirement he realized that the moral counter-revolution for which he said he had 'long prayed' was not going to happen. At least, not in his lifetime. 'The old socialist-liberal enemy has unexpectedly found new reinforcements in consumer capitalism,' he concluded sorrowfully.[43] It was now the pursuit of profit rather than some misconceived notion of personal freedom that caused the continuing erosion of moral standards.

Chesterton and Belloc were in no doubt that unrestrained capitalism acts as a solvent of morality, culture and religion. It is amazing that it took the Cold War generation of Catholic journalists so long to reach a similar conclusion. In the mid-nineties, Worsthorne announced that he had stopped reading Johnson's *Daily Mail* columns. He felt that the right had already won all the intellectual arguments against what he persisted in calling 'Roy Jenkins's permissive society'; but winning the argument had not, and would never, change a thing. Despite Johnson's philippics, 'divorce, single-mums and homosexuals continue to flourish'.[44] It was time for all good reactionaries to bow out.

But there were still surprises to come. As the millennium approached, Worsthorne, like the Catholic Church, decided it was time to atone for past wrongs. He wrote articles admitting that for much of his career he had traduced homosexuals unfairly and had made cheap racist remarks – largely to needle sensitive liberals. He recanted his homophobia, unequivocally condemned racism and apologized to anyone he had ever offended. That will probably prove to be another hopelessly romantic gesture. The idea that true contrition is automatically followed by a grant of absolution may be axiomatic to Catholics, but hardly anyone else thinks the same way.

From the moment Cristina Odone entered a broadcasting studio for the first time it was clear that the new editor of the *Catholic Herald* was determined to challenge the prevailing orthodoxy. But to the bafflement, perhaps even chagrin, of the producers who thought they had discovered her, the dogmatism she was out to refute was not the Pope's but their own secular certainties.

They did not know what to make of her. Surely the young American in the short skirt had come to debunk 2,000 years of fuddy-duddy history? Surely she was not going to stand up for those patriarchs who wished to deny women their fundamental right to abortion on demand? Yet here she was – long before New Labour came up with the tag – placing traditional ideas in a modern setting. Nor did anyone expect a single Catholic woman to confess to a sexual appetite while defending moral absolutes. She must be either hypocritical or strangely confused.

Odone soon found herself dealing with people who made no distinction between the Catholic and the puritan. When someone suggested that the slightest moral lapse would be incompatible with her status, she snapped back that if she were editing a motorcycle magazine she would be allowed the occasional speeding ticket. And, no, that did not mean she thought there should be no speed limit. It was an old argument – years before, Arnold Lunn had done his best to explain that when Catholics cease to behave, they do not cease to believe.

The *Catholic Herald* itself was hardly a modern setting. Housed in scruffy offices near the Barbican, it was one of the last places in London where you could hear the click-clack of manual typewriters or find box files from the 1950s still in use. Odone's office was decorated with plaster saints and a picture of Basil Hume asleep on a ski lift. The place looked as if it had not been decorated since the days when the *Herald* was tinged with anti-Semitic innuendo.

Odone's predecessor, Peter Stanford, had struggled hard to boost the circulation sufficiently to persuade extra investment out of the paper's owners. The title had to perform two apparently incompatible roles. Every parish that had the bishop along for a First Holy Communion ceremony wanted a picture in the *Herald*. But few readers were interested in parochial twaddle; they wanted features, columns, reviews, ideas, controversies and international scope. Stanford gave them lashings of liberation theology and all the news from Nicaragua – so much so that critics re-christened it the

Sandalista Herald. But the paper was sold through parish churches and if the local priest did not care for the tone of that week's editorial, or could not find the picture he wanted, he could always 'forget' to leave his pile by the church door. Stanford quit, exhausted. It was the right moment to go. Shortly afterwards, a book he co-authored about Catholics and sex hit the bookshops. Its opening line was: 'Every Catholic knows that they are just a screw away from perdition.'[45] Paul Johnson called for all copies to be pulped.

Odone's first move was to get the *Herald* into the newsagents. Next she lectured the clergy on the need to refine their spin. She told them they had allowed perceptions of the Catholic Church to decline to the level of 'a B-movie starring Victoria Gillick'.[46] Then she decided to broaden the appeal of the paper with articles by Paul Johnson, Auberon Waugh and Piers Paul Read – each writing for a fraction of his usual rate.

But the Cardinal was not happy. Odone was given a stern talk on the dangers of factionalism and urged to rein in her more conservative columnists. Yet in June 1993, the Manchester-based publishers of the downmarket *Universe* announced they were planning to launch a new broadsheet – the *Catholic Times* – that would be 'less left-wing than the *Herald*'. Clearly they were going flat out for conservative and traditionalist readers. What is more, it was hinted that the new project had the support of the Bishops' Conference of England and Wales, who just happened to own a sizeable stake in the company. It was a murky and complex affair, which even the Church's official spokesman confessed he could not fully explain. Odone promptly threw a party, stuffed with Catholic and media celebrities, to re-launch the *Catholic Herald*.

With two business tycoons – Conrad Black and Rocco Forte – now on its board, prospects for the *Catholic Herald* began to brighten. The paper was attracting new and younger readers. Significantly, these readers tended to prefer a broadly traditional style of religion. But they were not necessarily conservative in outlook. Most probably took a more relaxed view of sexual morality than the Church prescribed, but the idea of moral absolutes *per se* did not repel them. They did, however, recoil at what Damian Thompson (now the *Catholic Herald*'s literary editor) has called 'the liberals' grisly enthusiasm for inclusive language, pottery chalices and folk masses'.[47]

Odone's departure from the *Catholic Herald* in May 1996 coincided – but was not directly connected – with a major public row. She had published a first novel and taken sabbatical leave to complete another. Deciding not to return, she sent a letter of resignation to the chairman. It arrived just as the paper ran an article by one of her star writers, the novelist Alice Thomas Ellis, criticizing the record of Archbishop Derek Worlock, who had recently died. The uncritical tone of the 'tributes' and obituaries had riled her. In particular, Worlock's ecumenical double act with his Anglican opposite number, David Sheppard, was being lauded as an unqualified success. Thomas Ellis pointed out that there had been a virtual collapse of religious observance in Liverpool during Worlock's watch. The *Herald* received dozens of complaints from priests, some threatening to stop stocking the paper. Despite protests from staff and contributors, it printed an apology in its next issue and announced that the controversial columnist had been sacked.

Alice Thomas Ellis had been deliberately provocative. She wanted to force into the open arguments that she believed to be stifled by the authorities. These were not simply about ecumenical relations, but covered the decline in the teaching of Catholic doctrine in schools, the anodyne liturgy and the Church's continuing failure to inspire large numbers of members. Many of her supporters had serious doubts about Cardinal Hume's judgement. They felt that even as he was cracking down on inflammatory statements by traditionalists, he was allowing an 'ultra-liberal' agenda to advance by stealth.

Some time after quitting the *Herald*, Odone received a summons from the Vatican. She was asked to prepare a paper on 'writing as a vehicle of Christian values' to be read aloud to the Pope in January 1999 as part of the Church's preparation for the millennium. When Cardinal Hume got wind of the plan he telephoned the Curia, urgently – but unsuccessfully – attempting to have the invitation rescinded. Then one of his aides faxed the Curia a cutting of an article Odone had contributed to the *Erotic Review*, in which she fantasized about spending time on a desert island in the company of the Labour politician Peter Mandelson. This too failed to scandalize the Vatican. Hume never got the point of Odone. He called her the Odd One, and was always anxious that she would bring the Church into disrepute. She did make some bizarre statements – 'Catholicism is like spaghetti, you have to eat up all the strands' – but this media-savvy Italian-American was much more typical of the Catholic mainstream than the Cardinal ever realized.[48]

The *Catholic Herald* is now edited by Dr William Oddie, a former Anglican priest, who was also invited to 'discuss the tone of his journalism' with the late Cardinal in the summer of 1996. The summons was issued even before Oddie filed a provocative piece arguing that the Queen had lost any claim on the loyalty of her Catholic subjects by encouraging the Prince and Princess of Wales to obtain a 'quickie divorce'. This further riled the Cardinal, who had only just previously mounted a *démarche* towards Buckingham Palace, inviting the Queen to Vespers, dining at Windsor Castle and so on.

Oddie is a former *Mail on Sunday* controversialist and he knows what makes a good story. Consequently, the news pages of the *Catholic Herald* have largely lost the dreary parish-magazine look they once had. Alice Thomas Ellis is back, writing a cookery column. Other regulars include Lord Longford, John Gummer, Mary Kenny and the thoughtful Father Ronald Rolheiser. The leader line is scrupulously orthodox, but room is always provided for dissenting opinion. Perforce the paper has to concentrate on news about the Catholic Church, which these days often means yet another rush of allegations of priestly paedophilia in Cardiff or Sheffield or an ill-mannered spat between conservative and progressive women's groups.

Parochialism is even less evident at the *Tablet*. There the reader will find a collection of Catholic journalists including Libby Purves of *The Times*, the *Evening Standard*'s Melanie McDonagh, the

Financial Times's Jimmy Burns, Paul Vallely of the *Independent on Sunday*, Clifford Longley, Hugo Young, and the broadcasters Margaret Howard and Denis Tuohy. The *Sunday Times*'s polymathic cultural commentator Brian Appleyard used to be a regular contributor to the magazine's arts pages.

The *Tablet* offers its writers the chance to discuss the spiritual side of life without self-consciousness. In the secular media there is a palpable pressure always to gloss or qualify words such as the 'soul' or the 'transcendent'. Beyond the well-known journalists mentioned above, the editor, John Wilkins, can draw upon an impressive list of Catholics from the academic world as well as retired diplomats and senior civil servants, including Sir Michael Palliser, Sir Michael Quinlan and the former Cabinet Secretary, Lord Hunt of Tanworth. Wilkins is renowned for having one of the finest private intelligence services going, which surpasses even the KGB in its successful penetration of the secret world of the Roman Curia. He owes this in part to the efforts of one of the *Tablet*'s most well-connected patrons, the late Frank Doria Pamphilij – a British naval officer called Frank Pogson who, when he married into one of the grandest Roman families in 1953, agreed to adopt their name. Until his death in 1998, Doria Pamphilij lived in the enormous 1,000-room palazzo on the Via del Corso, which houses, among its many art treasures, Velázquez's magnificent portrait of Giovanni Battista Pamphilij, Pope Innocent X.

The magazine also benefits from a capacious institutional memory. Launched in 1840 by the convert Frederick Lucas, it is the oldest Catholic publication still in circulation. After it was bought by the future Cardinal Vaughan in 1868, it remained in the hands of the hierarchy until 1936. For the next thirty-one years its editor was Douglas Woodruff, a former *Times* journalist. Woodruff was married to Mia Acton, a granddaughter of the historian, a woman of extraordinary talents and energy who became the undisputed *grande dame* of English Catholic society. The Woodruffs were close with two popes – John XXIII and Paul VI – and made the *Tablet* the centre of an intellectual circle that included, at various times, Hilaire Belloc, Graham Greene, Evelyn Waugh, Martin

D'Arcy and Christopher Dawson. According to Auberon Waugh, the Woodruffs' social pyramid had the Pope at the top, followed by cardinals, bishops, priests and laymen and laywomen in strict order of rank. The choice of wine served at meals depended upon the seniority of the clergyman present.

Under Woodruff's successor, Tom Burns, the *Tablet* opposed Pope Paul's encyclical *Humanae Vitae* (which Burns early on declared a dead letter) and welcomed most of the changes instituted by Vatican II. Today the magazine is critical of the over-centralization of power in the Church and of the Vatican's attempts to have done with discussion in areas such as women's ordination, and of attempts to prohibit certain theologians from publishing. Its outlook is more liberal than radical; nevertheless Paul Johnson says the *Tablet* 'has no right to call itself a Catholic magazine' and will not have it in the house.[49]

The Catholic Church is fond of publishing documents and holding seminars on the importance of the media. There is even something called World Communications Sunday and each diocese is supposed to set aside one day a year to think media thoughts. The key text is 'The Decree on the Means of Social Communication', promulgated by Vatican II in December 1963. This contains an instruction for all Catholics working in the secular media as journalists, radio or television producers: 'It will be for them to regulate economic, political or artistic values in a way that will not conflict with the common good.'

The tone is pure Vatican. Non-Catholics have every right to be startled at the huge assumptions implied by the word 'regulate', but should not be too alarmed. These documents are drafted in Latin, a language that tends to exaggerate the Church's *imperium*. And though there is a group of Catholic writers and journalists – the Keys – that meets in the crypt of a Holborn church, it is a small social and study circle and not the core of a sinister freemasonry.

The decree can be read as imposing a serious obligation on Catholic journalists to approach their work with a sense of moral purpose. But the instruction is so broadly drawn that it makes any form of concerted action impossible. Catholics are bound to squabble amongst themselves about how 'the common good' should be defined.

So how much does their religion shape the work of Catholic journalists today? Few would say that it has no impact whatsoever. Most would allow that as one of the factors shaping identity it is bound to colour the way they look at the world – in much the same way, perhaps, as being born a Yorkshireman might. For a small number, it is privately a much more significant influence than they care to own in a secular workplace.

The *Guardian*'s Hugo Young says that he does not see himself as a Catholic journalist, so much as a journalist who happens to be a Catholic.

I suppose I do write to promote an idea of the common good, though my conception of it is more conditioned by secular and political factors than by religious ones. I do involve myself in Catholic organizations [Young is a director of the *Tablet* and a former chairman of the Catholic Institute for International Relations] and my enthusiasm for Europe may owe something to Catholicism. But it would be wrong to make too many assumptions on that score. My old friend Bill Cash is a Catholic but an ardent Eurosceptic too.

But Young acknowledges that his Catholic education was an important influence. 'The monks at Ampleforth planted a seed of idealism that interested me in the idea of a better and fairer world. But once you get into the question of how you bring about a better and fairer world, then you're into a secular argument – at least for 90 per cent of the time.'[50]

Mark Lawson, *Guardian* columnist, novelist and presenter of *Front Row* on BBC Radio 4 and *Review* on BBC 2, occasionally makes a stab at regulating cultural values. 'The main Catholic idea I try to promote is that things happen because people make choices. There is a creeping determinism in literature and the arts. Events are said to be determined by psychology, cultural factors, or just occur randomly and arbitrarily. I try to challenge that and point up the importance of human beings making real choices and decisions.'[51]

The *Guardian* has a decidedly secular feel. Some of its columnists regard religion as complete baloney or actively pernicious; nevertheless the paper finds a surprising amount of room, both in its news and features pages, for coverage of religious (and indeed Catholic) subjects. It accommodates quite a range of Catholic voices. As well as Young and Lawson, Madeleine Bunting has moved on from the religious affairs slot to address broader social and cultural themes, writing generally with the grain of the paper's liberal outlook. By contrast, Leanda de Lisle, a Tory countrywoman, offers a counterpoint to the leader line.

Charles Moore, editor of the *Daily Telegraph*, became a Catholic in 1994. 'Religious truths have primacy over political principles,' he says. 'If the two were ever in conflict, I would always choose faith over party.' Moore is probably unique among London's daily newspaper editors in being able to say that it is the declared policy of his paper 'to hold that the Christian story is true'. This is 'a working assumption' on which staff and readers can rely.[52] According to his mailbag, Jewish readers keenly approve.

Consequently Catholic writers enjoy more latitude at the *Telegraph* than elsewhere. Daniel Johnson brings a combination of earnestness and impressive scholarship to his consideration of ideas and events that is in many ways reminiscent of Christopher Dawson. Clifford Longley is unquestionably the doyen of religious affairs writers. Christopher Howse even instructs the paper's readers about the lives of the saints.

The late Auberon Waugh, who wrote for both the *Daily Telegraph* and its Sunday stablemate, always claimed to regard journalism as essentially a part of the entertainment industry. He thought that those who believed their copy was likely to influence political or public opinion were almost always deceiving themselves. He once tried to take a moral stand on an important policy issue himself, but failed to make any impact. That was during the Nigerian Civil War, when Waugh was one of only a handful of journalists who campaigned against the then Labour administration's complicity with the Nigerian federal government in the starvation and slaughter of millions of (Catholic) Ibos in Biafra.

In matters of religion he could swing from pessimistic atheism to Catholic orthodoxy within the same conversation, usually settling in the end for Pascal's wager.

Like many Catholics, he advocated shorter prison sentences for criminals and he admired Lord Longford's public stand on behalf of Myra Hindley. Unusually for a right-winger, he was completely opposed to capital punishment.

Waugh's true vocation lay in persecuting conceited politicians and cultural grandees, ruthlessly holding them up to public ridicule. Much satirical writing is impelled by a vigorous moral indignation. If that was true of Waugh, he disguised it behind a surface cynicism. He enjoyed his journalism but did not think it had any ameliorating effect.

Waugh understood that the only reason he was dubbed 'a prominent Catholic layman' and invited to pontificate about ecclesiastical affairs was because he was his father's son. At first he found the role preposterous, but he soon grew into it, reading up on theology and church history. Before long he was volunteering to review books on religious subjects and persecuting recalcitrant bishops in his columns. But he was always careful to avoid moralizing and detested what he called the 'punishment freaks' who lacked a proper Catholic sympathy for the sinner. He may, however, have seriously underestimated the efficacy of his prose. Liverpool's Archbishop Derek Worlock believed that a series of critical articles that Waugh wrote about him in *Private Eye* mysteriously found their way to the Vatican and cost him a cardinal's hat. Waugh downplayed his role in this matter, saying that it was outrageoulsy conceited of Worlock to think he was in line for preferment in the first place.

At the Journalists Jubilee in Rome at the beginning of June 2000, Pope John Paul II made clear that however sceptical the professionals themselves may be, he still had faith in the power of newspapers to bring about real changes in society. Seven thousand of the world's press had congregated for the event and thousands more participated via live video links with Washington, Manila, Johannesburg and Mexico City. After praying in the Sistine Chapel and visiting the tombs of St Paul and St Peter, the pilgrims gathered for the papal address. After a few introductory remarks about the Internet, globalization and so on, the Pope invited all Catholic journalists to re-examine the meaning of their vocations:

This is the crux of the ethical question, which is inseparable from your work. Journalism, with its immense and direct influence on public opinion, cannot be guided by economic forces, profit and partisan interests alone. Instead, it must be regarded in a certain sense as a 'sacred' task, to be carried out with the awareness that the powerful means of communication are entrusted to you for the common good and, in particular, for the good of society's weakest groups: from children to the poor, from the sick to those who are marginalized or discriminated against.[53]

The Pope went on to discuss the importance of the 'dignity of the human-person' and commended a new publication drawn up by the Vatican, entitled *Ethics in Communication*. The Church's code of practice on media self-regulation has long been somewhat tougher than anything put out by the Press Complaints Commission. It lays down its own rules on privacy and sensitivity to the feelings of the vulnerable, and its restrictions on defamation are far tougher even than the English libel laws. The Catechism forbids not only calumny – spreading false stories about people, but also detraction – saying disparaging things about someone, even though they are true. Copies of the new guidelines have been made available to Catholic journalists everywhere. So now, you might say, they have their orders and there can be no more excuses.

It would certainly be fascinating to be a fly-on the wall when the Catholic editor of a red-top tabloid (Piers Morgan of the *Mirror*, say) explains to his proprietor that he is no longer going to be guided by considerations of circulation or profit and that henceforth the paper's focus will shift from the private lives of celebrities towards doing something for the marginalized.

G. K. Chesterton understood the relationship between journalist and proprietor. On his return to Fleet Street after some years away, he noted that 'the men in debt that drank of old, drink in debt today, chained to the rich by ruin'.[54] Little changed during Chesterton's time and little has changed since. The salaries are better these days but the chains are still there, in the form of mortgages and short-term contracts. The newspapers have dispersed to Canary Wharf, Derry Street and Wapping, but in their hearts most journalists know they are still prisoners of the Fleet.

One who certainly felt that way was Noel Whitcomb. After attending a Catholic school, his first taste of journalism was a spell on *G. K.'s Weekly* in the 1930s. He began as a tea boy but was soon promoted to 'Staff Poet'. After the war he joined the *Daily Mirror* and was given a job that many hacks of his generation would have died for. The *Mirror* paid him to hang around London pubs and fall into conversation with interesting people. In the late morning he would begin his daily crawl at the George in Mortimer Street, before making an unsteady progress through Fitzrovia and Soho, and collapsing into El Vino some time in the late afternoon.

As the *Mirror* provided generous expenses, Whitcomb quickly became one of the most popular men in London. Louis MacNeice would slip out of the BBC to meet him; and sometimes Dylan Thomas or Augustus John would join them. Whitcomb even enjoyed convivial pints with the Devil's Disciple, Aleister Crowley.

But he soon tired of this cushy number. At *G. K.'s Weekly* there had been passion, energy and a sense of purpose. Whitcomb had once taken Mr Belloc his tea. He knew there must be more to journalism than propping up the bar. But how could he break out and make his name? One day in 1947, he found the answer. Years before anyone had heard of Kelvin MacKenzie, Whitcomb recognized that readers knew that most of what appeared in the papers was not in any real sense 'true'. What they wanted was sensation; what the bosses wanted was circulation – so why not make everybody happy?

Whitcomb found a terrier that could talk. He interviewed the dog, taking down every word in his notebook. A photographer was summoned to take its picture and the story of the talking Jack Russell was the next morning's front-page splash. For this seminal piece of journalism Whitcomb was rewarded with his own showbiz column. He stayed at the *Mirror* until the early eighties, writing entertainingly, but deriving no sense of fulfilment from his job. But he kept his disappointment private. To the outside world he was the jaunty fellow in the trilby, always the happy luncher. In fact, he was so much the *bon viveur* that Robert Maxwell took one look at his expenses and fired him. Later, of course, the crooked proprietor would run off with his pension.

Noel Whitcomb was Fleet Street's last direct link with the Chesterbelloc. He started out in a newspaper office buzzing with Catholic idealism. But across the span of his career the old things did not hold; they ceased to matter any more. Whitcomb liked to console himself with Evelyn Waugh's dictum that any fool can publish a book, but 'it takes a particular kind of fool to hold down a job on a daily newspaper'.[55]

Karen Armstrong, former nun and biographer of God, reported that when she gave up the Catholic faith the world stopped being 'fraught with significance'.[1] For Armstrong, the semiotic hush descended as a merciful relief. By contrast, the poet Gerard Manley Hopkins always delighted in experiencing a creation shot through with mystery and meaning. Paul Claudel too found pleasure in a world that was 'every inch a text, announcing humbly its own nothingness, but also the eternal presence of the absolute'.[2]

'Catholics imagine both God and the world somewhat differently from others,' explains the American sociologist Andrew Greeley. 'They tend to see the Ultimate lurking in the commonplace. They are inclined to view the objects, events, persons and relationships of ordinary life as metaphors for, or sacraments of, the Ultimate.'[3]

This sacramental principle – the idea that nature, objects, created things can have a mediating quality – presents the Catholic artist, writer and craftsman with a particular challenge. For David Jones, *homo faber* was *homo significatur*, with an ambition to make signs that did not merely signify in the usual sense, but could serve as a channel of divine grace.

This is not to say that Catholic art is better than other art, or that the Catholic aesthetic is itself necessarily superior. The Protestant idea of the absent God has inspired many austere masterpieces; and the atheist can often express a quintessence out of nothingness. Besides, the sacramental principle operates independently of authorial intention. Whether they like it or not, downright anti-religious artists may find their work commandeered by the Holy Spirit. Error has no copyright.

The theologian David Tracy has christened this propensity of the Catholic mind 'the analogical imagination'.[4] The concept has implications that go far beyond questions of taste and style – the alleged Catholic preference for lush, sensual imagery and so on.

A 1993 survey conducted in the United States included questions specifically designed to quantify the impact of the analogical imagination on Catholic involvement in the fine arts.

America's cultural élite at that time, says Andrew Greeley, thought the Catholic community irrelevant: 'Catholics are not interested in fine arts and fine arts are not interested in Catholics.'[5]

The survey's findings delivered an unambiguous challenge to this preconception. Catholics turned out to be significantly *more* likely to visit art galleries, go to the opera, ballet and classical music concerts than Protestants, even after age, gender, race, postcode, education and income variables had been equalled out. But the real surprise came when Greeley tested the data against two additional factors: the frequency of church attendance and grace-scale score. (The grace scale is a measurement of the respondent's image of God. At one end is a severe, vengeful and regal God, at the other a loving and merciful God.)

The results demonstrated that:

- Catholics who attend Mass frequently are much more likely to take an active interest in the arts than those who go to church less often. (Among Protestants it makes no difference.)
- Catholics who perceive God as loving are more likely to take an active interest in the arts than those who see Him as a stickler for discipline. (Again, among Protestants it makes no difference.)

Intrigued by his findings, Greeley decided to check if there was any correlation between grace-scale scores and church attendance. Again, the results were instructive:

- Catholics are more likely to be frequent churchgoers if they picture the Almighty as a God of love.
- Protestants are more likely to be frequent churchgoers if they picture Him as a God of wrath.

The lesson Greeley draws for Catholic bishops is that if they wish to fill up their pews, they should continue to promote the post-Vatican II model of a God of love. But they should also reverse the trend towards adopting the Protestant aesthetic in liturgy and church décor. For the 'Catholic mind' and the 'analogical imagination' are not woolly metaphors; they really do exist and have a bearing upon behaviour. And that is where Greeley leaves it. But this research may have further implications for the ecumenical project. If Catholic and Protestant brains are hard-wired in different configurations, any unity will have to be based upon an acceptance of diversity. The survey begs many more intriguing questions about the minds of Muslims, Jews, agnostics and atheists. Pedants will doubtless scoff, and demand confirmatory double-blind crossover studies before they will believe a word of it. But for many Catholics, and many Protestants too, the research merely provides a patina of – albeit cod-scientific – respectability to a truth they have always quietly known.

Mr Caraman was a Smyrna merchant with a pocket full of currants (c.i.f. London). He made a packet shipping dried fruit from the Levant and bought a large house in Hertfordshire, complete with a private chapel. There he and his Italian wife raised nine children. The two boys were sent to Stonyhurst, and both joined the Society of Jesus. John went out to the missions in Rhodesia; Philip became a protégé of Fr. Martin D'Arcy at Campion Hall.

After his ordination in 1945, Philip Caraman joined the Writers' House, attached to the Jesuit headquarters in Farm Street. His first job was to edit the Society's journal, *Letters & Notices*. This was dull work, and not at all likely to stretch his talents. At last, after two long years, D'Arcy told Caraman that he wanted him to reinvigorate the literary magazine the *Month*, and win it a national reputation.

Instead, he won it an international reputation. Thomas Merton sent his copy from America; François Mauriac filed from France. John Rothenstein, the director of the Tate Gallery, was the magazine's art critic. Evelyn Waugh agreed to write book reviews, and in return Caraman not only helped him with the research for his book *Helena*, but also became his confessor. Soon afterwards he signed up Graham Greene. And, ever on the look-out for fresh talent, he recruited Vincent Cronin and a clever young woman from Edinburgh who was still finding her confidence and style. Caraman gave Muriel Spark encouragement with both, before receiving her into the Catholic Church.

Edith Sitwell would be another of Caraman's converts, but Rosamond Lehmann was the one that got away. After the death of her daughter, Lehmann found it impossible to cope with bereavement. Her friend Edward Sackville-West, motivated by the best of intentions, but without great sensitivity, tried to press her into becoming a Catholic. Fr. Caraman was invited to visit. Lehmann was determined to persist in trying to contact her daughter through a medium and the priest had to tell her in as kindly a manner as possible that that sort of thing was forbidden.

Caraman became editor of the *Month* in the year Greene published *The End of the Affair*. Waugh had already published *Brideshead Revisited* and was at work on his *Sword of Honour* trilogy. The church was showing a serious interest in the novel, and the novel was showing a serious interest in the Church.

Catholicism and fiction had been entwined since the middle of the previous century. Both Cardinals Wiseman and Newman wrote novels and, in choosing martyrdom and conversion as their themes, provided an example of the use of fiction to expound the truths of the faith. This propagandist approach was taken up by R. H. Benson, and to an extent by Hilaire Belloc and even G. K. Chesterton. But many Catholic writers eschewed dogmatizing, preferring to impart a Catholic flavour to their work in terms of setting, or by bringing a Catholic moral and literary sensibility to bear. The 'Catholic novel' is, therefore, something that requires a more expansive definition than popular usage allows.

The American writer Flannery O'Connor, for instance, set her stories in a Baptist landscape. Her southern Gothic swamps are as far from a Catholic milieu as you can get. There are hardly any Catholic characters in her books; and the fact that one volume of her stories, *Everything that Rises Must Converge*, takes its title from the writings of the theologian Teilhard de Chardin is something of a connoisseur's point. Unlike, say Georges Bernanos's *Diary of a Country Priest*, O'Connor's stories are not obviously Catholic, but reveal themselves as such through what the author called 'the action of grace in territory largely held by the Devil'.[6] O'Connor herself was certain that her faith was her muse. 'I write the way I do because and only because I am a Catholic,' she said. 'I feel that if I were not a Catholic I would have no reason to write, no reason to see, no reason to feel horrified or even to enjoy anything.'[7] And she was adamant that her religion posed no creative constraints. 'When people have told me that because I am a Catholic, I cannot be an artist, I have had to reply, ruefully, that because I am a Catholic, I cannot afford to be less than an artist.'[8]

When Catholic writers conspicuously introduce Catholic themes, they can often generate scepticism about their sincerity. Evelyn Waugh's *Brideshead Revisited*, for instance, can be read as a lament for a vanished social order – one that disappeared not within the timescale of the novel but immediately after the First World War. Those who comprehend the novel chiefly in these terms find the whiff of incense gratuitous, something the mischievous author laid on only to occasion further annoyance. But Waugh's decision to adopt a religious theme at the time was more than a grumpy outburst of reactionary defiance. It established a mark of difference, challenging the worth of a worldly conception of happiness by holding it up to comparison with a state of grace. The reductive social reading also misses the significance of the vulgar sanctuary lamp, put out when the chapel is closed up by the family, but ultimately restored for the benefit of the soldiery.

Graham Greene provokes a similar kind of scepticism about his motives. Norman Sherry's perhaps over-generous biography seeks to validate the downright incoherent moral theology of novels such as *Brighton Rock* and *The Heart of the Matter*, proposing a far-from-orthodox paradox in which the worst sinners emerge as the greatest saints. Set against this interpretation are the strictures of critics such as Michael Shelden whose *The Man Within* accuses Greene of a cynical use of Catholicism in his writing and diagnoses a pervasive morbidity in the author's interest in both murder and damnation. Shelden pursues his indictment with all the forensic determination of an American district attorney up for re-election, a fact that itself is enough to plant a seed of reasonable doubt. Yet, once a jury is provided with evidence of the mismatch between Greene's faith and his sexual dalliances, in particular his notorious affair with a fellow Catholic, Catherine Walston, the pendulum begins to swing the other way. A man who in real life is prepared to flirt with eternal damnation to spice up his adultery might be capable of anything in his fiction. On the other hand, it is not surprising that there should be some psychological traffic between the two domains. A writer whose characters are 'going to seed in outlandish places; unshaven; guilt-ridden; on the bottle' could plausibly pass off his own journey to the dangerous edge as a form of research.[9] Evelyn Waugh saw the illicit liaison as a sign of humility. Asked to explain how Greene could possibly square the Walston affair with his Catholicism, Waugh told the story of a medieval pope who used to dance through the streets of Rome wearing a clownish paper hat to remind his flock that he was only human and to deter them from venerating him as a saint. 'Mrs Walston,' Waugh said, 'is Graham's paper hat.'[10]

To the Oxford Dominican Herbert McCabe, Greene was a 'Catholic's Catholic'.[11] Certainly, Catholics have over the years been markedly less inclined to judge him severely, or to regard his religiosity as bogus. This is not simply an expression of confessional solidarity, but because they find that even the ambivalence and doubt in Greene's work chimes with their own experience. And as Piers Paul Read has observed, Greene's perception of the Church was entirely dynamic. He not only entered into the spirit of Vatican II, but explored the ideas of liberation theology. For Father Rivas in *The Honorary Consul* the Church is not a clerical and hierarchical institution but 'this *barrio*, this room'.[12] Moreover, the sterner aspects of the pre-conciliar church were as problematic in real life as they were in Greene's fiction. Many of those things that made non-Catholic readers uncomfortable with *The Heart of the Matter* are no longer emphasized by the Church today, and were absent from Greene's later writing. However, those who are discomforted by the very idea of God as an unseen actor in a realistic narrative are going to have a problem with Catholic fiction anyway.

In answer to the doubters, Graham Greene's confessor, Leopoldo Duran, has attested to the writer's utter religious seriousness. Greene's travelling companion for more than twenty years and the inspiration for *Monsignor Quixote*, Father Duran says Greene's 'obsessive faith', and the tension between theological curiosity and scepticism that it engendered, underpinned his fiction to the end.[13]

Moreover, Greene's genuinely pained reaction to having one of his novels placed on the Vatican's index of banned books offers a further proof of the authenticity of his Catholicism. The *Index Librorum Prohibitorum* dated from the middle of the sixteenth century and was not abolished until 1966. Curiously, it was *The Power and the Glory* that, in the autumn of 1953, upset the Holy Office of the Inquisition. Although the censors acknowledged that the novel sought 'to bring out the victory of the power and the glory of the Lord in spite of man's wretchedness', they nevertheless felt the author had failed to achieve his literary objective. Wretchedness, they felt, had carried the day. The Holy See demanded that changes be made in subsequent editions.[14]

Other British writers who, at one time or another, had found themselves on the Index included Milton, Hobbes, Locke, Hume, Defoe, Swift and Laurence Sterne. The French fared even worse with Rabelais, Montaigne, Pascal, Voltaire, Rousseau, Stendhal, Balzac, Victor Hugo and Emile Zola all on the list. Andre Gide had been added the previous year and the complete works of Jean-Paul Sartre would be similarly proscribed in 1959.

Evelyn Waugh was furious at Greene's treatment and offered to organize a campaign in his defence. Greene, however, chose to submit, writing a deferential letter to the Holy Office concluding 'I remain, with deep respect for the Sacred Purple, Yours Faithfully . . .'[15] This decision to contain his indignation and forgo an opportunity to have a public spat with Rome is not one that a mere religious poseur would be likely to make. Rather, it demonstrates a mature tolerance of the shortcomings of institutional authority that is the mark of a genuine fidelity.

No revisions were made in the end. Indeed, some years later, after the Index had been scrapped, Greene had an audience of Pope

Paul VI, who warmly praised his novels, particularly *The Power and the Glory*. Presumably, the Pontiff had first read and appreciated the book while the ban was still in force.

Although Catholics have never been out-and-out cultural separatists, there was a move in some Catholic schools even as late as the 1960s to establish a sort of Catholic canon. This would begin with Chaucer, and move on to Shakespeare (for whom an intriguing claim of Catholicity has been advanced by the Jesuit Peter Milward that does not wholly depend on the disputed historical question whether the bard was a secret Catholic). Alexander Pope would figure largely and perhaps even Dryden, who was a Catholic until it ceased to suit him politically. Ernest Dowson, Francis Thompson, Coventry Patmore and Gerard Manley Hopkins, R. H. Benson, the Chesterbelloc, Roy Campbell, Compton Mackenzie, Waugh and Greene would all have places in the Pantheon. Today extra seats would be provided for David Lodge, Piers Paul Read and George Mackay Brown, and perhaps for David McLaurin, a young writer who is in fact a priest, and whose novels of moral dilemmas played out against a backdrop of South American political intrigue acknowledge the influence of Greene without apparent anxiety. Strangely excluded, even at the height of his popularity, was J. R. R. Tolkien, probably the best-selling Catholic writer of the twentieth century. Tolkien's appeal has tended to be strongest among the spiritually inclined but unchurched: Californians, hippies and the sort of people who congregate at Glastonbury heedless of the fact that Satan is a 'spiritual' being too. Many Catholics fail to detect much religion in *The Hobbit* and *The Lord of the Rings* beyond a vague Manichaeanism, but Tolkien's most recent biographer Joseph Pearce has unearthed persuasive evidence that Tolkien himself regarded his Catholic faith as the most powerful influence on his writing.

David Lodge's first work, *About Catholic Authors*, was furnished with an *imprimatur* and a *nihil obstat* and was a pamphlet in the 'Tell Me Father . . .' series – just the kind of improving text that would have been handed out to pious youngster under the pre-conciliar dispensation. It records the correspondence between Fr. Aloysius, an English teacher, and one of his former pupils, now away doing National Service. The priest recommends suitable Catholic writers from Britain, Europe and the United States. While he was writing it, Lodge was also working on his first novel, *The Picturegoers*, which explores how young Catholics were coming to terms with new social and sexual mores. *About Catholic Authors* seems impossibly innocent and remote to us today. It is evocative of a period when the trendiest teenage hangout was a milk bar. Oddly, *The Picturegoers* feels far less dated. That is not because sexual guilt is still a significant factor in a Catholic upbringing, but rather because guilt remains a key motif in most representations of Catholicism, whether in novels or films.

Indeed most of the creative work featuring the Catholic faith over the past half century has been produced by 'recovering Catholics'. Antonia White and Michèle Roberts have both testified to the traumatizing effects of a convent education on thousands of Catholic women. The Liverpudlian film-maker Terence Davies, whose autobiographical sequence *Trilogy* prompted one American reviewer to say that he made Ingmar Bergman look like Jerry Lewis, brands Catholicism as pernicious. Davies's adolescent Catholic guilt was exacerbated by his homosexuality. There is a recriminatory streak too in much of the work of the screenwriter Jimmy McGovern – creator of *Cracker*, *The Lakes* and *Priest*. The latter, once again preoccupied with guilt and gay sex, was a film the Catholic bishops hated, but it did provide a cameo debut for the young Euan Blair. No doubt the underlying anger in these works stems from genuinely painful experiences, but it all seems very old-fashioned now that two generations of Catholics have grown up since the Second Vatican Council without ever having been made to feel guilty about anything.

Occasionally, a writer has surfaced who is more comfortable with his Catholicism. When Piers Paul Read started out, he gave the confident impression that he was the heir and successor of Graham Greene. But he never really gained the serious critical attention his early work deserved, something all the more odd given that, as the son of Herbert Read, he was born into the world of letters. He was among the first victims of a creeping secular fundamentalism among the wider intelligentsia and before long retreated from the field, declaring the death of the Catholic novel and taking up a safe niche writing thrillers. Often rumoured to be ready for a comeback, Read appears still to be sitting it out, waiting for the cloud to pass, too bruised by insult and neglect to do much to change the cultural weather himself.

Read, like Alice Thomas Ellis and David Lodge, has remained a 'Catholic novelist' in a fuller sense than simply being a writer who happened to be born a Catholic. The case of Anthony Burgess is more problematic. Extravagant claims are sometimes advanced regarding the catholicity of his work. Though there is clear reference to Catholic faith and thinking in works such as *A Clockwork Orange*, *Earthly Powers* and *The Kingdom of the Wicked*, Catholicism really represented little more than a small piece of territory in Burgess's vast cultural hinterland.

Indeed, as the century progressed the Catholic faith increasingly became more a matter of reference or allusion than thematic substance: one more heavily foxed page in post-modernism's dictionary of quotations. This phenomenon has been particularly evident in cinema. Alfred Hitchcock and Charles Laughton were two Jesuit-educated Britons who brought an identifiably Catholic sensibility to Hollywood. Laughton's *The Night of the Hunter* is made all the more Catholic (in the Flannery O'Connor sense) by its depiction of the action of grace in territory held in part by the Devil, and otherwise by Southern evangelicals. In the work of more recent Catholic film-makers such a quality, though arguably still present, is considerably more elusive. In 1995, to mark the hundredth anniversary of cinema, the Vatican awarded its own equivalent of the Oscars to forty-five feature films that it believed displayed 'particular religious merit'. The selection was made by the Pontifical Council on Social Communication and contained a surprise or two. Alongside Andrei Tarkovsky's *The Sacrifice*, Pier Paolo Pasolini's *The Gospel According to Matthew*, Roland Joffe's *The Mission* and Gabriel Axel's *Babette's Feast*, came Charlie Chaplin's *Modern Times* (a nod, no doubt, to Catholic Social Teaching) and to general media astonishment Charles Crichton's *The Lavender Hill Mob*. The chosen films were qualified for inclusion under one of three categories: Religion, Values and Art – distinctions that to the Curia of Pius XII would have been unthinkable.

But if Catholic writers and film-makers had a struggle negotiating their accommodations with secular values, pity the poor painter. Apart from Georges Rouault, there has scarcely been a religious artist of consequence or reputation anywhere during the period. When a grateful nun thanked Henri Matisse for his work in the Chapel of the Rosary at Vence, saying, 'It is wonderful, this gift you have given to God,' the artist is reputed to have snorted, 'God? I did it for myself.' And that, one way or another, became the orthodoxy of the twentieth century.

In Britain any catalogue of important Catholic art looks pretty thin after Eric Gill, David Jones and Gwen John. Damien Hirst was brought up a Catholic, but his chief memory of the experience is of feeling so bored in church that he would while away the time looking at gruesome pictures of Christ on the cross.

Chris Ofili too confessed to being a Catholic in *The New York Times*, but this looked like special pleading, since the Brooklyn Museum was being besieged at the time by an angry crowd, outraged at his portrait of the Virgin decorated with elephant dung.

Oddly, the twentieth century was *the* century of the Catholic curator. John Rothenstein became Director of the Tate, Michael Levey ran the National Gallery, and John Pope-Hennessy managed the triple: the V&A, the British Museum and the Metropolitan Museum in New York. But Pope-Hennessy played his Catholicism close to his chest. And Levey found that exposure to Fine Art and scholarship shrivelled his faith; unlike Bernard Berenson, who was charmed into becoming a Catholic by the frescos in the monastery at Monte Olivetto Maggiore. Only Rothenstein was a 'downright muscular and decided Catholic'; so much so that he once defended his critical judgement by knocking out a querulous dealer at a Tate reception. That judgement led him to spend the gallery's acquisitions budget on Eric Gill and Augustus John, passing up the offer of Matisse's *The Red Studio* for £800. He is nowadays blamed for the post-impressionist-shaped hole in the collection at Tate Modern.

The Catholic contribution to the world of music proved more impressive: Edward Elgar, Malcolm Williamson, Lennox Berkeley, Edmund Rubbra and James MacMillan. Elgar's *Dream of Gerontius* introduced Cardinal Newman's poem to a wider public, even if it was bowdlerized when played in an Anglican cathedral. Mac-Millan's beautiful *Corpus Christi* is sure to survive the third millennium. And BBC Radio 3 owes its existence to Harman Grisewood, friend of the Chesterbelloc, unofficial patron of David Jones, one-time director of the spoken word and controller of the Third Programme.

For many, the second half of the twentieth century seemed a lean time for Catholic culture in Britain. A section of the Catholic community experienced an acute anxiety, fearing that without its religious dimension the national culture would, as Christopher Dawson had warned, rapidly decay. Various projects were initiated to 're-evangelize' or 're-sacralize' the age. It is still too soon to say whether they will all prove abortive. There is by no means a consensus about the causes of the malaise – if, indeed, malaise there be. Certainly, 'secularization' has been a significant factor; but there are disagreements too about what that has entailed and even about when it occurred. Some regard the phenomenon as a long drawn-out process beginning at the Enlightenment – a progressive retreat of religion, first from the public domain into the private, followed by a gradual falling-off of observance. Those who take this view regard it as quantifiable – empty pews, crises of vocations and so on – and susceptible to the analytical methods of social science. Others, adopting techniques drawn from cultural theory, have constructed a revisionist position. They identify a prevalence of religious 'discourses' in society at large until some time around 1963, whereafter they quickly disappear. The tendency of both arguments is towards cultural determinism.

A more optimistic perspective apprehends the intellectual history of the period as a succession of short-winded enthusiasms, fads or fashions. Both individually and cumulatively these have generated a climate inimical to Catholicism but have not prevailed against it. Fascism and Communism have come and gone. Liberalism and Humanism have come and stayed, but today appear to be in crisis. Consumer capitalism, now in its globalized form, poses practical as well as theoretical challenges.

But by far the most intractable set of ideas are those bundled up in the portmanteau of post-modernist theory. They are responsible for ontological and epistemological chaos; the giddy instability of meaning and significance and a pervasive scepticism that there can be anything more to 'truth' than a variety of rival interpretations, each presumably as 'valid' as another. In Britain, the Catholic response to all this has been muted. There has certainly been nothing comparable to the Catholic intellectual revival before the Second World War.

There are a number of reasons for this reticence. There have been Catholic philosophers – good ones such as Wittgenstein's pupil Elizabeth Anscombe, and the moral philosopher Alasdair MacIntyre, who has revived the notion of virtue. But there was no 'Catholic philosophy' – at least, not a 'house philosophy', as Thomism had once been. Secularization has also forced a divergence between philosophy and theology, with the latter sometimes portrayed as not really a respectable discipline at all, but rather as a cranky and esoteric field of enquiry somewhat akin to astrology.

In fact, the schools of theology are thriving. They have even produced a new generation of thinkers who see in post-modernism not simply a crisis but an opportunity. It is in the Incarnate Christ – and only in the Incarnate Christ – they say, that order can be restored, meaning stabilized, truth grounded. Let all other grand narratives – whether of history, class or progress – dissolve, leaving only the grandest narrative of all, the action of Divine Providence in human affairs. This may have some way to go before achieving full intellectual coherence, let alone widespread cultural acceptance. But if and when such ideas do come to fruition they will need to be vigorously promulgated.

I have already remarked that an excess of ecumenical tact combined with a desire for social assimilation has led Britain's Catholic community quite literally to withdraw from the streets. The same factors have hushed the Catholic voice in the 'public square' – the domain of politics and public policy debates, of cultural activity and the clash of ideas.

In case anyone should mistakenly assume that I am advocating a return to crude Catholic triumphalism, let me make my position absolutely clear. After Vatican II 'Catholic culture', narrowly conceived, was no longer the point. Catholics were enjoined to prepare Christ's kingdom, not construct their own cultural fiefdom. Moreover, the Church no longer claimed that Catholics had a monopoly of a singular truth. Instead, it more modestly offered the fruits of its ruminations on what it is to be human, while encouraging its members to amplify their understanding through a humble interaction with members of other faiths and of none. Catholics would no longer go about as a gang; but, acting as individuals, would place themselves at the service of their fellow men, seeking to make societies and cultures sacred from within. Simultaneously, the Church began to shed its historic antagonism towards modernity and its emancipatory impulses. For sure, it declared some of the new freedoms worthless, but it embraced others and set out to evangelize them. All that was good.

Unfortunately, some Catholics have proved incapable of distinguishing between a healthy pluralism and what Timothy Radcliffe, a former Master of the Dominican Order, has described as 'a wishy-washy relativism'.[16] Mistakenly believing that disagreement is incompatible with the demands of unity, mutual respect and co-operation, they fail to strike an appropriate balance between humility and confidence. They act as though the teachings of the Catholic faith were no more preferable to Catholics than those of any other religion. So 'non-judgemental' have they become that even the mere suggestion that the tenets of another faith or denomination may be to any degree defective is held to show a 'lack of respect' and constitute some kind of offence. They even protest at any criticism of atheism. Atheism, they ask, isn't that something we're supposed to learn from? For such people 'Catholic identity' ceases to be the visible characteristics of a community; it becomes, rather, an intensely personal, even secretive affair, a badge discreetly worn on the inside of one's lapel. To the practitioners of this cultural cringe, any form of public dispute or debate is ecumenically incorrect. And since they can never disagree, they can never truly learn.

For Timothy Radcliffe, by contrast, Catholicism is a faith that yearns to be seen. 'We should take a greater part in the debates of our society. There are so many new ethical problems emerging, particularly with the development of biotechnology . . . we should roll up our sleeves and throw ourselves into public debate.'[17] Another liberal-minded churchman, Cardinal Martini, the Archbishop of Milan, has shown there is nothing shameful about an energetic affirmation of the Catholic case. Some years ago he instituted the 'Cattedra dei non credenti', a series of debates between Catholics and non-believers, moderated by the Cardinal in full fig, and held in a vast auditorium. Italians of all ages and backgrounds travel miles to take part and there are never enough tickets to satisfy demand. The events spark wider discussion throughout Italy, prompting television discussions and articles on the comment pages of the newspapers.

It is hardly possible to imagine such a thing happening in this country. Yet only a few decades ago it happened all the time. Huge crowds would turn out to hear G. K. Chesterton or Ronald Knox debating with their opponents. This book is subtitled 'Britain's Largest Minority', but over the past forty years Britain's Catholics have almost ceased to constitute an identifiable minority. Their recent past was repudiated as too defensive or triumphalist and they were encouraged to submerge their Catholic identity in an ecumenical anonymity, to become more a flavour than a brand. But if Catholics want to have a say in the national conversation, that will not do in the future. In the world of pluralism, with all its jostling minorities scrambling for places at the table, anonymity has no cultural purchase.

Bibliography

Allitt, Patrick, *Catholic Converts*, Cornell University Press, 1997

Arnstein, Walter L., *Protestant Versus Catholic in Mid-Victorian England*, University of Missouri Press, 1982

Beck, G. A., *The English Catholics 1850–1950*, Burns & Oates, 1950

Belloc, Hilaire, *Characters of the Reformation*, Tan Books, 1992

——*The Crisis of Civilisation*, Tan Books, 1992

——*Essays of a Catholic*, Sheed & Ward, 1931

——*The Great Heresies*, Tan Books, 1991

——*Survivals and New Arrivals*, Sheed & Ward, 1929

Bence-Jones, Mark, *The Catholic Families*, Constable, 1992

Benson, R. H., *Confessions of a Convert*, Fisher Press, 1991

Bovey, Nigel, *Christians in the House*, Egon, 1998

Boyle, Nicholas, *Who Are We Now?*, T. & T. Clark, 1998

Boyle, Raymond & Lynch, Peter (eds.), *Out of the Ghetto*, John Donald 1998

Buckley, William F., *Nearer My God*, Doubleday, 1997

Burns, Tom, *The Use of Memory*, Sheed & Ward, 1993

Butler, Carolyn (ed.), *Basil Hume: By His Friends*, Fount, 1999

Byrne, Lavinia, *Woman at the Altar*, Mowbray, 1994

Caldecott, Stratford (ed.), *Beyond the Prosaic: Renewing the Liturgical Movement*, T. & T. Clark, 1998

——*Eternity in Time*, T. & T. Clark, 1997

Chadwick, Owen, *The Christian Church in the Cold War*, Allen Lane, The Penguin Press, 1992

Chesterton, G. K., *A Short History of England*, Fisher Press, 1994

——*Autobiography*, Fisher Press, 1992

Collected Works, Vol., (Aidan Mackey, ed.), Ignatius Press, 1994

——*The Everlasting Man*, Ignatius Press, 1993

——*The Collected Poems of G. K. Chesterton*, Methuen, 1937

——*Orthodoxy*, The Bodley Head, 1943

Cozzens, Donald B., *The Changing Face of the Priesthood*, Liturgical Press, 2000

Dalrymple, Jock, *Jack Dominian – Lay Prophet?*, Geoffrey Chapman, 1995

Davie, Grace, *Religion in Britain Since 1945*, Blackwell, 1994

Dawson, Christopher, *Inquiries Into Religion and Culture*, Sheed & Ward, 1933

De Lisle, Leanda and Stanford, Peter, *The Catholics and their Houses*, HarperCollins, 1995

Donovan, Daniel, *Distinctively Catholic: An Exploration of Catholic Identity*, Paulist Press, 1977

Fernandez-Armesto, Felipe, *Truth: a History*, Bantam, 1997

Fernandez-Armesto, Felipe and Wilson, Derek, *Reformation: Christianity and the World 1500–2000*, Bantam, 1996

Fraser, Antonia, *The Gunpowder Plot*, Mandarin, 1997

Gallagher, Donat (ed.), *Essays, Articles and Reviews of Evelyn Waugh*, Penguin, 1986

Gilbey, Alfred, *The Commonplace Book of Monsignor A. N. Gilbey*, Bellew, 1995

Gill, Eric, *Autobiography*, Lund Humphries, 1992

Gillis, Chester, *Roman Catholicism in America*, Columbia University Press, 1999

Gorman, W. Gordon, *Converts to Rome: a Biographical List of the Most Notable Converts to the Catholic Church*, Sands, 1910

Gove, Michael, *Michael Portillo*, Fourth Estate, 1995

Greene, Graham, *Collected Essays*, Penguin, 1970

——*Brighton Rock*, Penguin, 1973

——*The Heart of the Matter*, Penguin, 1973

——*The Power and the Glory*, Penguin, 1973

——*The End of the Affair*, Penguin, 1973

Hastings, Adrian, *A History of English Christianity 1920–1990*, SCM, 1991

Holland, Bernard, *Memoir of Kenelm Digby*, Fisher Press, 1992

Hornsby-Smith, Michael (ed.), *Catholics in England 1950–2000*, Geoffrey Chapman, 1999

Horton, John and Mendus, Susan, *After MacIntyre*, Polity Press, 1994

Hume, Basil, *Towards a Civilisation of Love*, Hodder & Stoughton, 1988

Johnson, Paul, *The Quest for God – A Personal Pilgrimage*, Phoenix, 1997

——*Wake Up Britain!: A Latter-day Pamphlet*, Weidenfeld & Nicolson, 1994

——*The Intellectuals*, Phoenix, 1996

——*To Hell with Picasso*, Phoenix, 1997

Kenny, Anthony, *A Path From Rome*, Sidgwick & Jackson, 1985

Kent, Bruce, *Undiscovered Ends: An Autobiography*, Fount, 1994

Kilfoyle, Peter, *Left Behind: Lessons from Labour's Heartland*, Politico's, 2000

Knox, Ronald, *Barchester Pilgrimage*, Sheed & Ward, 1935

——*A Spiritual Aeneid*, Burns & Oates, 1950

——*Belief of Catholics*, Ernest Benn, 1928

Leslie, Shane, *Long Shadows*, John Murray, 1966

Levey, Michael, *The Chapel is on Fire*, Jonathan Cape, 2000

Lodge, David, *How Far Can You Go?*, Penguin, 1981

——*The Picturegoers*, Penguin, 1993

——*The British Museum is Falling Down*, Penguin, 1981

Longley, Clifford, *The Warlock Archive*, Geoffrey Chapman, 2000

——*The Times Book of Clifford Longley*, HarperCollins, 1991

MacIntyre, Alasdair, *After Virtue*, Duckworth, 1999

Martin, Malachi, *The Jesuits*, Simon & Schuster, 1987

Martindale SJ, C. C., *The Life of Monsignor Robert Hugh Benson*, Longmans Green, 1916

Maurin, Peter, *Catholic Radicalism*, Catholic Worker Books, 1949

McBrien, Richard, *Catholicism*, Geoffrey Chapman, 1994

McLaurin, David, *The Bishop of San Fernando*, Flamingo, 1995

——*Mortal Sins*, Flamingo, 1996

——*Tropical Darkness*, Flamingo, 1997

McClelland and Hodgett (eds.), *From Without the Flaminian Gate*, Darton Longman & Todd, 1999

Milward SJ, Peter, *The Catholicism of Shakespeare's Plays*, Saint Austin Press, 1997

Moloney, Thomas, *Westminster, Whitehall and the Vatican*, Burns & Oates, 1985

Morris, Kevin L., *Mgr Ronald Knox: A Great Teacher*, Catholic Truth Society, 1995

——*Hilaire Belloc: A Catholic Prophet*, Catholic Truth Society, 1993

Muggeridge, Malcolm, *Conversion*, Hodder & Stoughton, 1996

——*Confessions of a Twentieth-Century Pilgrim*, Harper & Row, 1988

Milibank, John; Pickstock, Catherine and War, Graham (eds.), *Radical Orthodoxy*, Routledge, 1999

Newman, J. H., *Apologia Pro Vita Sua*, Sheed and Ward, 1945

——*Present Position of Catholics in England*, Burns and Lambert, 1851

——*The Second Spring* (sermon preached in the Synod of Oscott, 13 July 1852), Thomas Richardson, 1852

Nichols OP, Aidan, *Catholic Thought Since the Enlightenment*, Gracewing 1998

——*Christendom Awake*, T. & T. Clark, 1999

Noel, Gerard and Stanford, Peter, *The Anatomy of the Catholic Church*, Michael Russell, 1994

Oddie, William, *The Roman Option*, HarperCollins, 1997

Parsons, Gerald (ed.), *Religion in Victorian Britain*, Manchester University Press, 1988

Pearce, Joseph, *Literary Converts: Spiritual Inspiration in an Age of Unbelief*, HarperCollins, 1999

——*Tolkien, Man and Myth*, HarperCollins, 1998

Purves, Libby, *Holy Smoke*, Hodder & Stoughton, 1998

Redford, John, *Catholicism: Hard Questions*, Geoffrey Chapman, 1997

Reid, Scott (ed.), *A Bitter Trial*, Saint Austin Press, 1996

Roberts, Michèle, *Impossible Saints*, Virago, 1998

Rees-Mogg, William, *An Humbler Heaven*, Hamish Hamilton, 1977

Schuster, George, *The Catholic Church and Current Literature*, Burns, Oates and Washbourne, 1930

Seward, Desmond, *The Monks of War*, Methuen, 1972

Sewell, Brocard, *The Habit of a Lifetime: An Autobiography*, Tabb House 1992

Sheed, F. J., *A Map of Life*, Sheed & Ward, 1933

Shelden, Michael, *Graham Greene: The Man Within*, Heinemann, 1994

Sherry, Norman, *A Life of Graham Greene, Vol. 2: 1939–55*, Jonathan Cape, 1994

Sire, H. J. A., *Father Martin D'Arcy – Philosopher of Christian Love*, Gracewing, 1997

Spark, Muriel, *Curriculum Vitae*, Constable, 1992

Speaight, Robert, *The Life of Hilaire Belloc*, Hollis & Carter, 1957

Stanford, Peter, *Cardinal Hume and the Changing Face of Catholicism*, Geoffrey Chapman, 1993

——*The Devil: A Biography*, Arrow, 1996

——*Lord Longford: a Life*, Mandarin, 1995

Sykes, Christopher, *Evelyn Waugh: a Biography*, Penguin, 1982

Vallely, Paul (ed.), *The New Politics: Catholic Social Teaching for the Twenty-first Century*, SCM, 1998

Vidler, Alec, *A Variety of Catholic Modernists* (the Sarum Lectures, University of Oxford (1968–9), Cambridge University Press, 1970

Walsh, John, *Growing up Catholic*, Macmillan, 1989

Ward, Maisie, *Gilbert Keith Chesterton*, Sheed and Ward, 1944

Watkin, E. I., *Roman Catholicism in England from the Reformation to 1950*, Oxford University Press, 1957

Watkins, Alan, *Brief Lives*, Hamish Hamilton, 1982

Waugh, Evelyn, *A Little Learning*, Penguin, 1983

——*Brideshead Revisited*, Penguin, 1962

——*Sword of Honour*, Eyre Methuen, 1980

Whitcomb, Noel, *A Particular Kind of Fool*, Quartet, 1990

Wilson, A. N., *God's Funeral*, John Murray, 1999

——*Hilaire Belloc*, Hamish Hamilton, 1984

Online sources for Church documents:

www.vatican.va

www.ewtn.com

www.tasc.ac.uk/cc/

Notes

Chapter 1

1. Conversation with the author.
2. Evelyn Waugh, *Brideshead Revisited*, Penguin, 1962, p. 87.
3. Cardinal Griffin in foreword to G. A. Beck, *The English Catholics 1850–1950*, Burns & Oates, 1950, p. iv.
4. Conversation with the author.
5. Conversation with the author.
6. Editorial in *The Free Presbyterian Magazine*, July 1999.

Chapter 2

1. J. H. Newman, *The Second Spring* (sermon preached in the Synod of Oscott, 13 July 1852), Thomas Richardson, 1852, p. 17.
2. *The Times*, 3 August 1847.
3. W. Gordon Gorman, *Converts to Rome: a Biographical List of the Most Notable Converts to the Catholic Church*, Sands, 1910. (First published in 1878 as *Rome's Recruits*, Gordon Gorman's list went into a number of revised editions. Consequently the figures quoted here, from 1910, will include some converts from the Edwardian period.)
4. *The Times*, September 1874, quoted in Michael J. Walsh, 'Catholics, Society and Popular Culture' in McClelland and Hodgett (eds.), *From Without the Flaminian Gate*, Darton, Longman & Todd, 1999, p. 355.
5. Nicholas Wiseman, Pastoral Letter: 'From Out the Flaminian Gate', 7 October 1850.
6. Walter L. Arnstein, *Protestant Versus Catholic in Mid-Victorian England*, University of Missouri Press, 1982, p. 46.
7. *The Times*, 19 October 1850.

8. *Punch*, No. 19, 1850, quoted in Arnstein, op. cit., p. 47.

9. *The Times*, 21 November 1850.

10. J. H. Newman, *Present Position of the Catholics in England*, Burns & Lambert, 1851, p. 249.

11. *The Times*, 9 April 1870.

12. Arnstein, op. cit., p. 107.

13. H. E. Manning, 'The Work and Wants of the Catholic Church in England', *Dublin Review*, New Series 1, 1863, p. 162.

14. *Tablet*, 21 August 1999.

15. Antonia Fraser, *The Gunpowder Plot*, Mandarin, 1997, p. 295.

16. Ronald Knox, *Barchester Pilgrimage*, Sheed & Ward, 1935, p. 82.

17. Robert Hitchens, quoted in Joseph Pearce, *Literary Converts*, Harper-Collins, 1999, p. 76; see also Brian Masters, *The Bensons*, 1993, pp. 206–7.

18. Shane Leslie, *Long Shadows*, John Murray, 1966, p. 106.

19. Letter from Hilaire Belloc to A. C. Benson, 1 August 1907, quoted in C. C. Martindale SJ, *The Life of Monsignor Robert Hugh Benson*, Vol. II, Longmans Green, 1916, p. 45.

20. Hilaire Belloc, *Characters of the Reformation*, Tan Books, 1992, p. 58.

21. Hilaire Belloc, op. cit., pp. 124–5.

22. Kevin L. Morris, *Hilaire Belloc – a Catholic Prophet*, Catholic Truth Society pamphlet, 1995, p. 11.

23. A. N. Wilson, *Hilaire Belloc*, Hamish Hamilton, 1984, p. 320, quoting H. R. Williamson, *Catholic Herald*, 24 July 1953.

24. Felipe Fernandez-Armesto and Derek Wilson, *Reformation: Christianity and the World 1500–2000*, Bantam, 1996.

25. John Morrill, introduction to Stratford Caldecott (ed.), *Eternity in Time*, T. & T. Clark, 1997, p. 5.

26. Francesca Murphy, 'Can There be a Catholic History today?', Caldecott, *Eternity in Time*, pp. 125–6.

27. Christopher Dawson, preface to *Inquiries Into Religion and Culture*, Sheed & Ward, 1933, p. vi.

Chapter 3

1. Hilaire Belloc, *Survivals and New Arrivals*, Sheed & Ward, 1929, p. 135.
2. Patrick Allitt, *Catholic Converts*, Cornell University Press, 1997, p. 80, quoting Brian Martin, *John Henry Newman: His Life and Work*, Chatto & Windus, 1982, p. 144.
3. Quoted in A. N. Wilson, *God's Funeral*, John Murray, 1999, p. 348.
4. Archives of the English Province of the Society of Jesus.
5. George Tyrrell, *The Church of the Future*, privately published in 1903 under the pseudonym Hilaire Bourdon; see also Allitt, op. cit., p. 122.
6. Letter from George Tyrrell to A. L. Lilley, 14 August 1908, quoted in Alec Vidler, *A Variety of Catholic Modernists* (the Sarum Lectures, University of Oxford, 1968–9), Cambridge University Press, 1970, pp. 117–8.
7. Malachi Martin, *The Jesuits*, Simon & Schuster, 1987, p. 262.
8. Ronald Knox, 'After 33 years – Preface to the new edition', *A Spiritual Aeneid*, Burns & Oates, 1950, p. xiv.
9. *The Times*, 29 December 1994.
10. Sermon at St Michael's College, 1986, and reiterated in 1994, on the occasion of the twentieth anniversary of *The Chesterton Review*, reported in *Wanderer*, 29 September 1994.
11. 'The Secret People', G. K. Chesterton, *Collected Works*, Vol. X, Ignatius Press, p. 408.
12. G. K. Chesterton, *Autobiography*, Fisher Press, 1992, pp. 111–12.
13. Robert Speaight, *The Life of Hilaire Belloc*, Hollis & Carter, 1957, p. 204.
14. Hilaire Belloc, *Cautionary Tales*, Everyman, 1997, pp. 47–58.
15. Maisie Ward, *Gilbert Keith Chesterton*, Sheed & Ward, 1944, p. 275.
16. A. N. Wilson, *Hilaire Belloc*, Hamish Hamilton, 1984, p. 181.
17. Peter Maurin, *Catholic Radicalism*, Catholic Worker Books, 1949, p. 132.
18. G. K. Chesterton, *Orthodoxy*, The Bodley Head, 1943, p. 70.
19. 'Medievalism', G. K. Chesterton, *Collected Works*, op. cit., p. 552.
20. G. K. Chesterton, *Autobiography*, p. 340.

21. Maisie Ward, op. cit., p. 417.

22. Maisie Ward, op. cit., p. 114.

23. Eric Gill, *Autobiography*, Lund Humphries, 1992, p. 155.

24. Patrick Allitt, op. cit., p. 179.

25. Eric Gill, *Autobiography*, p. 249.

26. Ibid.

27. Tom Burns, *The Use of Memory*, Sheed & Ward, 1993, p. 165.

28. Graham Greene, *Collected Essays*, Penguin, 1970, p. 282.

29. Ronald Knox, quoted in Kevin L. Morris, *Monsignor Ronald Knox: a Great Teacher*, CTS, 1995, pp. 8–17.

30. Letter from Belloc to J. S. Phillimore (1920), quoted in Robert Speaight, op. cit., p. 391; also A. N. Wilson, *Hilaire Belloc*, op. cit., p. 243.

31. A. N. Wilson, *Hilaire Belloc*, p. 240.

32. H. J. A. Sire, *Father Martin D'Arcy – Philosopher of Christian Love*, Gracewing, 1997, p. 71.

33. Maisie Ward, op. cit., p. 551.

34. Tom Burns, op. cit., p. 30.

35. Hilaire Belloc, *The Cruise of the Nona*, 1928, p. 164, quoted in A. N. Wilson, *Hilaire Belloc*, p. 290.

36. Rabbi Wise, quoted in Maisie Ward, op. cit., p. 228.

37. Thomas Moloney, *Westminster, Whitehall and the Vatican*, Burns & Oates, 1985, p. 55.

38. Letter from Joyce to Hinsley, 8 April 1936, archives of the Archdiocese of Westminster; quoted in Thomas Moloney, op. cit., p. 57.

39. Letter from Hinsley to Wegg-Prosser, 23 February 1936, archives of the Archdiocese of Westminster, quoted in Thomas Moloney, op. cit., p. 59.

40. Thomas Moloney, op. cit., p. 210.

Chapter 4

1. Graham Greene, *Collected Essays*, Penguin, 1970, pp. 260–62.

2. Conversation with the author.

3. Mark Bence-Jones, *The Catholic Families*, Constable, 1992, p. 118.

4. Quoted in Joseph Keating, 'Charles Waterton', *Catholic Encyclopaedia*, Vol. XV, *www.newadvent.org/cathen*.

5. Arthur Machen, *Things Near and Far* (1926), in Alfred Gilbey, *The Commonplace Book of Monsignor A. N. Gilbey*, Bellew, 1995, pp. 159–60.

6. Thomas Walker, *Aristology, or the Art of Dining* (1835) and Sanders, *The Holland House Circle*, quoted in Alfred Gilbey, op. cit., pp. 164–5.

7. Alfred Gilbey, op. cit., p. 117.

8. Alfred Gilbey, quoted in *Sunday Telegraph*, 21 November 1993.

9. *The Times*, 27 March 1998.

10. Alfred Gilbey, op. cit., dedication page.

11. *Sunday Telegraph*, 28 May 1995.

12. Libby Purves, *Holy Smoke*, Hodder & Stoughton, 1998, pp. 119–121.

13. *Daily Telegraph*, 28 November 1998.

14. *Catechism of the Catholic Church*, Veritas, 1994, § 1934.

15. *Catechism of the Catholic Church*, § 1931.

16. Conversation with the author.

17. *Washington Post*, 6 February 1978.

18. Desmond Seward, *The Monks of War*, Methuen, 1972, p. 292.

19. *The Times*, 14 January 1998.

20. Speech to the Catholic Teachers' Federation conference, 1984.

21. *Sunday Telegraph*, 11 August 1991.

22. Quoted by James Fox (author of *White Mischief* (1982)) *Sunday Times*, 13 June 1999.

23. Evelyn Waugh, quoted in Mark Bence-Jones, *The Catholic Families*, Constable, 1992, p. 282; see also Michael Davie (ed.), *The Diaries of Evelyn Waugh*, Phoenix Press, 1995.

Chapter 5

1. *Herald*, 11 September 1999.

2. *Scotland on Sunday*, 30 January 2000.

3. Quoted in Brian Wilson, *Celtic: a Century with Honour*, Collins, 1988;

see also Raymond Boyle and Peter Lynch (eds.), *Out of the Ghetto*, John Donald 1998, p. 100.

4. *Mirror*, 7 February 1997.

5. *Daily Record*, 31 May 1999.

6. Words and music of Rangers songs can be found at *http://home.wanadoo.nl/maarten.geluk/glasgow.html*.

7. *Scotsman*, 22 September 1999.

8. *Herald*, 13 June 1999.

9. Herbert Spencer Lecture, Oxford University, November 1963, published in *Harpers Magazine*, November 1964, pp. 77–86.

10. *Herald*, 29 September 1996.

11. *Herald*, 24 February 1995.

12. *Scotsman*, 9 June 1999.

13. James MacMillan, lecture at the Edinburgh Festival, 9 August 1999.

14. Quoted in ibid.

15. *Guardian*, 14 December 1996, quoting *Guerin Sportivo*.

16. James MacMillan, op. cit.

17. *Independent*, 12 January 1992.

18. Quoted in James MacMillan, op. cit.

19. *Sunday Herald*, 15 August 1999.

20. Donald Findlay, review of Tom Devine (ed.), *Scotland's Shame*, Mainstream, Edinburgh 2000 (a collection of responses to James MacMillan's lecture incorporating the original text), *Sunday Times*, 16 April 2000.

21. Ibid.

22. *http://www.swrb.com/newslett/actualnls/NatCov.htm*.

23. *Scotsman*, 19 January 1999.

24. *Scotland on Sunday*, 30 January 2000.

25. David Bryce, former Grand Secretary of the Orange Order, quoted in Joseph Bradley, 'Images, Perceptions and the Ghetto', Boyle & Lynch (eds.), *Out of the Ghetto*, John Donald, 1998, p. 102.

26. *Scotsman*, 22 May 1998.

27. James MacMillan, op. cit.

28. Quoted by J. Fraser Field, *The Pernicious Bias that Few Recognize*, Catholic Educator's Resource Centre at *http://catholiceducation.org/articles/media/me0001.html*.

29. Quoted in *Independent*, 27 May 1993.

30. Article in *Catholic Herald*, quoted in James MacMillan op. cit.

Chapter 6

1. Cardinal Heenan, quoted in Michael Hornsby-Smith (ed.), *Catholics in England 1950–2000*, Geoffrey Chapman, 1999, p. 55.

2. Anthony Kenny, *A Path From Rome*, Sidgwick & Jackson, 1985, p. 153.

3. *Spectator*, 23 November 1962.

4. *Tablet*, 19 June 1999.

5. See Grace Davie, *Religion in Britain Since 1945*, Blackwell, 1994, p. 58.

6. Conversation with the author. See Michael Hornsby-Smith, *Roman Catholics in England*, Cambridge University Press, 1987; 'Into the Mainstream: Recent Transformations in British Catholicism' in T. Gannon (ed.), *World Catholicism in Transition*, Macmillan, 1988, pp. 218–31; and 'Believing Without Belonging? The Case of Roman Catholics in England' in B. Wilson (ed.), *Religion: Contemporary Issues*, Bellew, 1992, pp. 125–34.

7. See Donald B. Cozzens, *The Changing Face of the Priesthood*, Liturgical Press, 2000, pp. 97–110.

8. *Tablet*, 24 July 1999.

9. Sermon preached by The Most Reverend Cormac Murphy-O'Connor on the occasion of his installation as Archbishop of Westminster, 22 March 2000, *www.tasc.ac.uk/cc/cn/00/000322a.htm*.

10. *Bull of Confirmation*, 26 January 1564.

11. Quoted by David Joyce, 'The Beauty and Spirituality of the Traditional Latin Mass', Latin Mass Society, *www.latin-mass-society.org/beaut.htm*.

12. Scott M. P. Reid (ed.), *A Bitter Trial*, The Saint Austin Press, 1996, pp. 43–5.

13. *The Times*, 6 July 1971.

14. *Christian Order* website at *www.christianorder.com*.

15. Ibid.

16. Conversation with the author.

Chapter 7

1. Lobby briefing and statement from 10 Downing Street press office, 4 March 1998.
2. *The Times*, 9 March 1998.
3. Ibid.
4. *The Times*, 12 March 1998.
5. *Sunday Telegraph*, 7 April 1996.
6. Ibid.
7. Ibid.
8. Ibid.
9. Paul Vallely, *New Statesman*, 27 November 1998.
10. Confidential source.
11. Evelyn Waugh, *Sword of Honour*, Eyre Methuen, 1980, p. 670.
12. J. Derek Holmes, 'English Catholicism from Hinsley to Heenan', *Clergy Review* (1977), p. 49, also quoted in Michael J. Walsh, 'Catholics, Society and Popular Culture', McClelland and Hodgetts (eds.), *From Without The Flaminian Gate*, Darton, Longman & Todd, 1999, p. 364.
13. *Daily Telegraph*, 11 May 1998.
14. *Guardian*, 11 May 1998.
15. *Independent*, 2 December 1999.
16. *Sunday Times*, 5 January 1997.
17. *Flourish*, March 1995.
18. Nigel Bovey, *Christians in the House*, Egon, 1998, p. 117.
19. Nigel Bovey, op. cit., p. 163.
20. *Daily Telegraph*, 30 December 1996.
21. Ibid.
22. *Herald*, 30 April 1997.
23. *Guardian*, 28 October 1996.
24. *Independent*, 28 October 1996.
25. *The Times*, 19 January 1988.
26. Confidential source.
27. Ibid.
28. *The Times*, 19 January 1988.

29. *Scotland on Sunday*, 27 October 1996.

30. *Daily Express*, 29 October 1996.

31. *Guardian*, 28 October 1996.

32. *Daily Telegraph*, 19 May 1998.

33. MORI Poll, reported *Guardian*, 23 June 2000.

34. 'Such a patronising word; it's like patting someone on the head.' Margaret Thatcher, quoted by Archbishop Derek Worlock in his Pope Paul VI Memorial Lecture, 1995. See Clifford Longley, *The Worlock Archive*, Geoffrey Chapman, 2000, p. 332.

35. Conversation with the author.

36. *Associated Press*, 14 May 1983.

37. Apostolic Exhortation, *Reconciliatio et Paenitentia*, 2 December 1984.

38. Alice Miles, *The Times*, 28 June 2000.

39. *Guardian*, 2 November 1995.

Chapter 8

1. Sermon, Westminster Cathedral, Midnight Mass, Christmas 1999.

2. Quoted by Gregory Wolfe in his foreword to Malcolm Muggeridge, *Conversion*, Hodder & Stoughton, 1996, p. xiii.

3. *Time*, 13 December 1982.

4. *Spectator*, 4 December 1982.

5. Ibid.

6. Malcolm Muggeridge, *Confessions of a Twentieth-Century Pilgrim*, Harper & Row, 1988, pp. 140–141.

7. Malcolm Muggeridge, *Conversion*, op. cit., p. 6.

8. William F. Buckley, Jr., *Nearer My God*, Doubleday, 1997, p. 211.

9. William F. Buckley, Jr., op. cit., p. 215.

10. Conversation with the author.

11. Source: Paul Johnson.

12. Alan Watkins, *Brief Lives*, Hamish Hamilton, 1982, p. 81.

13. *Observer*, 17 May 1998.

14. Ibid.

15. Alan Watkins, op. cit., p. 81.

16. Quoted in *Guardian*, 29 April 1998.

17. Paul Johnson, *Wake Up Britain!: a Latter-day Pamphlet*, Weidenfeld & Nicolson, 1994 quoted in *Guardian*, 4 May 1994.

18. *Daily Mail*, 8 June 1995 and 16 June 1995.

19. *Daily Mail*, 27 October 1997.

20. *Daily Mail*, 6 January 1994.

21. Conversation with the author.

22. *The Times*, 29 January 1994. (N.B. Owing to a subsequent libel action this article has been withdrawn from libraries and cuttings services. I have relied on reports of court proceedings to describe its contents. See *Daily Telegraph*, 8 June 1994, for details of retraction and apology.)

23. Paul Johnson, *The Quest for God – A Personal Pilgrimage*, Phoenix, 1997, p. 199–200.

24. *Spectator*, 23 November 1996.

25. Paul Johnson, *Quest*, op. cit., p. 65.

26. *Daily Express*, 12 May 1998.

27. *Evening Standard*, 12 May 1998.

28. Paul Johnson, *Quest*, op. cit., p. 112.

29. William Rees-Mogg, *An Humbler Heaven*, Hamish Hamilton, 1977, p. 96.

30. Interview with Megan Tressider, *Daily Telegraph*, 7 June 1993.

31. William Rees-Mogg, op. cit., pp. 97–8.

32. Ibid.

33. Bruce Kent, *Undiscovered Ends: An Autobiography*, Fount, 1994, p. 50.

34. *Sunday Telegraph*, 25 May 1997.

35. *The Times*, 13 May 1993.

36. *The Times*, 10 May 1993.

37. *Daily Telegraph*, 7 June 1993.

38. *The Times*, 31 October 1996.

39. *The Times*, 23 October 1996.

40. Letter to *The Times*, 31 October 1996.

41. Letter to *The Times*, 26 October 1996.

42. Quoted in *The Times*, 8 October 1993.

43. *Sunday Telegraph*, 14 April 1996.

44. Ibid.
45. Kate Saunders and Peter Stanford, *Catholics and Sex*, Heinemann, 1992, p. 1.
46. Quoted in *Guardian*, 21 September 1992.
47. *Sunday Telegraph*, 20 June 1999.
48. Remark recalled by Auberon Waugh, who vouched for its accuracy.
49. Conversation with the author.
50. Conversation with the author.
51. Conversation with the author.
52. Conversation with the author.
53. Pope John Paul II, address to the Jubilee of Journalists, Rome, 4 June 2000.
54. G. K. Chesterton, 'Back to Fleet Street', *The Collected Poems of G. K. Chesterton*, Methuen, 1937, p. 185.
55. *Daily Telegraph*, 15 June 1993; see also Noel Whitcomb, *A Particular Kind of Fool*, Quartet, 1990.

Chapter 9

1. Interview, *Manchester Guardian Weekly*, 18 September 1983.
2. Paul Claudel, 'La Catastrophe d'Igitur', *Nouvelle Revue Francaise*, Paris, 1 November 1926; see also George Schuster, *The Catholic Church and Current Literature*, Burns, Oates and Washbourne, 1930, p. 22.
3. Andrew Greeley, *Catholics and the Fine Arts: an Investigation of the Liturgical Imagination*; privately published; see *www.agreeley.com*.
4. David Tracy, *Analogical Imagination: Christian Theology and the Culture of Pluralism*, Crossroad, 1981.
5. Andrew Greeley, op. cit.
6. Quoted in Ronald Weber, 'A Good Writer is Hard to Find', *Catholic Dossier* 5, no. 4 (July–August 1999):30–32.
7. Ibid.
8. Quoted in Patrick McCormick, *US Catholic*, September 1999.
9. Graham Greene, *A Sort of Life*, Penguin, 1974, quoted in *Irish Times*, 15 January 2000.

10. Evelyn Waugh, quoted in A. N. Wilson, *Evening Standard*, 14 February 2000.

11. Sean MacReamoinn, *Laylines: Partial Views of Church and Society*, Dominican Publications, 1997, p. 127.

12. See Piers Paul Read, 'The Decline and Fall of the Catholic Novel', *The Times*, 29 March 1997.

13. *The Times Higher Education Supplement*, 7 April 1995.

14. *America*, 11 November 2000.

15. Ibid.

16. Timothy Radcliffe OP, *I Call You Friends*, Continuum, 2001, p. 140.

17. Ibid., p. 51.

Index